I0818988

EL PASO

EL PASO

Five Families and One Hundred Years of Blood, Migration, Race, and Memory

JAZMINE ULLOA

An imprint of Penguin Random House LLC
1745 Broadway, New York, NY 10019
penguinrandomhouse.com

Map by David Lindroth Inc.

Image on page iii, 9, 115, and 213 by *The Boston Globe* via Getty Images.
Image on page i and ix by Paul Reyes.

Book design by Katy Riegel

LIBRARY OF CONGRESS CATALOGING-IN-PUBLICATION DATA

Names: Ulloa, Jazmine, author.
Title: El Paso: one hundred years of blood, race, and memory / Jazmine Ulloa.
Description: New York: Dutton, an imprint of Penguin Random House LLC, [2026] |
Includes bibliographical references and index. |
Identifiers: LCCN 2025035854 (print) | LCCN 2025035855 (ebook) |
ISBN 9780593471869 (hardcover) | ISBN 9780593471883 (ebook)
Subjects: LCSH: Mexican Americans. | Hispanic Americans. |
El Paso (Tex.)—History. | Mexican-American Border Region—History.
Classification: LCC F394.E4 U55 2026 (print) |
LCC F394.E4 (ebook) | DDC 976.496—dc23/eng/20250814
LC record available at https://lccn.loc.gov/2025035854
LC ebook record available at https://lccn.loc.gov/2025035855

Printed in the United States of America
1st Printing

The authorized representative in the EU for product safety and compliance is Penguin Random House Ireland, Morrison Chambers, 32 Nassau Street, Dublin D02 YH68, Ireland, https://eu-contact.penguin.ie.

For Zack

CONTENTS

PART THREE

Borders and Bridges

EL PASO

PROLOGUE

From the Halls of Montezuma

YOU MUST KNOW about the boys. There were six, clean-cut and baby-faced. At least, that is how I always envisioned them when my mother told their story. Juan de la Barrera, Juan Escutia, and Francisco Márquez. Agustín Melgar, Fernando Montes de Oca, and Vicente Suárez. They were Mexican military cadets, ages thirteen to nineteen, in polished black boots and uniforms of deep blue, when the United States under President James K. Polk invaded Mexico, part of a two-year war to alter its borders. Polk called it Manifest Destiny. Others saw it for what it was: a land grab.

On a cold, hazy morning in September 1847, before the sun had risen on the rural western edges of Mexico City, the boys rushed to arms. About 7,000 American Army soldiers and marines were descending on Chapultepec, the run-down castle that served as the Mexican military academy. The Americans fought back lines of Mexican defenses. Their mortars thumped and cannons blasted. Their bayonets cut through thick swirls of smoke. El Castillo de Chapultepec sat on an inactive volcano that the Aztecs had once held sacred. The Americans climbed the rocky hill, past cypresses and laurels, past the spring where the Aztec leader Montezuma was believed to have once sipped from crystal waters. At the top, with shells flying overhead, against soaring views, they used ladders to scale the castle's stone walls and flooded the corridors, spilling blood on ramps and stairwells.

Inside, they expected to face down more Mexican soldiers. They found some 140 military cadets instead. A garrison commander gave the youngest combatants, dozens of teenagers, orders to fall back. But as the Mexican lore goes, six of the young men, los Niños Héroes, did not retreat. They disobeyed and fought for their country to the death. What would come next would change everything for Mexico, for the United States, for the place that would become a gateway at their dividing line.

The Battle of Chapultepec led to the capture of Mexico City, which essentially ended the war. Five months later, on February 2, 1848, Mexico and the United States signed the Treaty of Guadalupe Hidalgo. The peace deal carved a jagged new border between the two nations, spanning almost 2,000 miles from the Gulf Coast to the Pacific Ocean. Along the Rio Grande, in the West Texas borderlands, where I am from, it split a place deep in the heart of Mexican territory into two: what would, in time, become El Paso to the north and Ciudad Juárez to the south. The mountain valley, long a trade outpost for Indigenous Mexicans and Spanish colonizers, would become a portal to the American Southwest as Mexico was forced to relinquish all of its claims to Texas and cede 55 percent of its territory to the United States—including what is now California, Nevada, New Mexico, and Utah, most of Arizona and Colorado, as well as parts of Kansas, Oklahoma, and Wyoming.

Historians and scholars all identify their own centers of gravity for when the modern-day concept of the southern border emerged and the fear of the Mexican took hold. But one point of origin is here in El Paso and the Splitting, in the severing of a large Native American and Mexican and Spanish region into a thin strip of land onto which Americans would project their basest fears of the outsider. The invaders now wary of invasion.

THIS BOOK IS a narrative history of El Paso as told through the stories of those who have crossed it. It traces the lives of five families—the Chews, the

Martinezes, the Holguins, the Rubios, and the Mura'ls—whose members have passed through the Pass or made it their home, as well as some of the legendary figures who have shaped the city and, in so doing, shaped America, too. Part One centers on Herlinda and Antonio Chew and Victoria and Miguel Martinez, Chinos Mexicanos and Mexicanos, respectively, navigating changing physical and personal borders through the foundational period of the U.S. immigration system. Part Two follows the Rubio sisters and the Holguin brothers—Mexicans soon to be Americans—as they grow up and rise as politicians and entrepreneurs during wars against drugs and terror that help expand that system into a detention and deportation machine. Part Three then captures the journey of Kaxh Mura'l, a Maya Ixil activist, who flees Guatemala as one hundred years of fights over race, labor, and immigration have escalated into an all-out assault on migrants and the fabric of the United States itself. Each family is emblematic of a critical turn in the history of the U.S.-Mexico border and its enforcement. I have thought a lot about this history as I have covered the immigration debates that have been central to recent American elections, the battles over democracy, and the aftermath of a rampage instigated by a self-proclaimed white supremacist who drove into the city to shoot down Mexicans, decrying the "Hispanic invasion of Texas." The more I traveled across the country interviewing Americans, the more I realized that El Paso, my hometown, had not been given its due place in the founding mythos of our country.

It might be Ellis Island that we see and remember as integral to our American story, the bustling ocean port of entry where the nation first sorted immigrants, in what historians like Vincent J. Cannato have described as a timeless tension between its ideals and nativist fears. Ellis Island was an American place where others arrived. But El Paso, fronterizo historians David Dorado Romo and Yolanda Chávez Leyva remind us, was a crucial mountain pass into the land that would become the United States long before the first impoverished European ever set foot in New York. And it has been in El Paso, the gateway to the American Southwest, that the United States has since incubated some of its harshest tactics to inspect, surveil, and criminalize the immigrants—once Chinese, Jewish, and Slavic, more recently

Venezuelan, Guatemalan, Congolese, and Haitian, always Mexican—it relies on for labor to this day.

This book is an attempt to restore El Paso to its rightful position: at the center, rather than at the margins of our American story. Only in studying this lasting gateway in the desert—and the treatment of the people who cross it—can we begin to understand the tenuous relationship that Mexican Americans, and Latinos more generally, have had with the United States. It is in its memory that we also see, as historians such as Julian Lim have found, that our southern borderland has long been a rich multiracial, multiethnic stomping ground where Native, Black, Asian, Anglo, and Hispanic identities have been drawn and redrawn, where connections have been forged despite violent divides, where Americans have fought and negotiated over race, power, and privilege for generations. Without knowing El Paso, we do not know our nation. We do not understand that there is no invasion of Texas or of the United States by Mexicans, Hispanics, or "others": Mexican and Mexican American culture and history have always been a part of who we are as Americans because the United States was formed on land that was Native before it was Spanish, and Spanish before it was Mexican, and Mexican before it was American.

Before the United States and Mexico went to war, before there ever was a Mexico or a United States, El Paso and Ciudad Juárez were not two cities on either side of an international border but one lush, green valley in the chasm of two great mountain ranges. They were an oasis in a place of extreme temperatures and stark desert terrain, with a river that poured into a lake and followed its own whims, mostly flowing gently, at times drying up, raging, or changing course, invariably giving life.

The earliest peoples to cross El Paso knew it as the "pass through the mountains." Most were nomads. Some lived in rancherías, small villages of one hundred people or so, spread out across the Chihuahuan Desert. They traded turquoise, furs, and shells with pueblos as far as what are now the states of New Mexico and Arizona to the north and Sonora and Chihuahua to the south. We call some of these Indigenous tribes the Suma, Manso, and

Jumano, though their real names we will never truly know, as these are the ones given to them by outsiders: Spanish, English, and French explorers, priests, and colonizers, whom Natives would try to stave off as they sought to defend their ways of hunting and careful farming.

The Spaniards who first passed through the Pass in the early 1500s were lured by a mythic empire awash with gold, sapphires, and rubies, but an expedition gone awry deterred the Spanish crown's interest in the deserts north of Mexico City for almost half a century. The Europeans did not return to the El Paso region until 1581, when three Franciscan friars, Agustín Rodríguez, Francisco López, and Juan de Santa María, followed the Indigenous paths of commerce in a quest for missionary work. They ambled across the mountains, opening the way for the Spanish to enter New Mexico and the rest of the Southwest. Don Juan de Oñate, the Spanish conquistador and explorer, named the gateway Paso del Norte in 1598 when he took formal possession of the land for a Spanish king in a ceremony known as la Toma: the Taking. The Spanish would set up missions along the river, and El Paso and Juárez would become a thriving trade outpost then on the historic Camino Real, or Royal Highway, running from Ciudad Chihuahua to Santa Fe. In 1680, they would serve as a refuge for Spaniards and Tigua people escaping the Pueblo Revolt against Spanish colonizers to the north.

After the United States and Mexico each fought for their independence and won, and the Spanish were gone, Anglo settlers pushed into the land that would become Texas from the east, driving out Native Americans and Mexicanos in a push for white dominance and American democracy and capitalism known as Manifest Destiny. Native Americans escaping the brutality of the Anglos in the plains moved in from the north, often holding on to the prejudicial and racist views of their oppressors and looking down on the enslaved Black people coming in from the Deep South. All the while, Mexican mestizo colonists marched in northward, wiping out Mexico's Indigenous peoples.

El Paso lay too far west to be included in the initial bounds of Texas, which Anglo Texan settlers first drew in 1836 as they revolted from Mexico in the name of "liberty" and fought to sanction slavery. But Paso del Norte became a prime target in the American pursuit of Manifest Destiny during the war between Mexico and the United States. Colonel Alexander Doniphan and his soldiers occupied its valley, flourishing with tall cottonwoods and vineyards of grapes, figs, and ripe peaches, the year before American troops stormed the military academy at the Castle of Chapultepec.

After the Treaty of Guadalupe Hidalgo was signed, days after gold was discovered in California, the settlements to the south remained Paso del Norte. And those to the north became known as Magoffin or Franklin, after the wealthy Anglo businessmen who helped develop them, as more Americans rushed through on wagon trains and buggies in hopes of striking it rich out west. In time, Franklin was renamed El Paso and Paso del Norte became Ciudad Juárez.

Some historians see the Splitting, essentially, as a real estate transaction: The United States paid $15 million and gained a bounty of land, plus all of California's gold and Texas's oil. But Gloria Anzaldúa, a writer from South Texas, saw the treaty of 1848 as an instrument that cut an open wound in the land—"una herida abierta," she wrote—one that has never fully healed. I used to imagine the break as cracks in the desert, a rumbling, the underground shifting of hot tectonic plates, such as those that had formed the volcano under Chapultepec. The reality was far less dramatic, though no less seismic: A troupe of American men with notebooks in hand traversed rugged country and, with sticks and stones, demarcated the new border that would separate El Paso from its Mexican sister. America's new landholdings would transform the slavery debate there, with white Southern enslavers pushing to expand the trade across the country's new territories and abolitionists resisting it, a fight that would culminate in the Civil War. And even here, historian Laura E. Gómez has written, the influence of the war between Mexico and the United States would persist as U.S.-Mexico war veterans rose to become its top generals and commanders, including both General Ulysses Grant and General Robert Lee.

WITH TIME, EL Paso would become a place that, like the rest of the United States, would be caught in a perpetual battle over its story, forever asking if it will be defined by its borders or its bridges. The vigilantes and minutemen, the walls of steel, of officers, of cameras and razor wire and shipping containers, the political stunts and fierce debates over immigrants, asylum seekers, and refugees, would all follow. Through this gateway, families like the Chews, the Martinezes, the Holguins, the Rubios, and the Mura'ls would cross the dividing line, from the past to the future, from hardship to opportunity, always calling on the other side, no matter how elusive it sometimes turned out to be in the end.

PART ONE

Rebellion and Resistance

Factory is both fact
And act, and mere letters away from face
And story.

—Rosa Alcalá

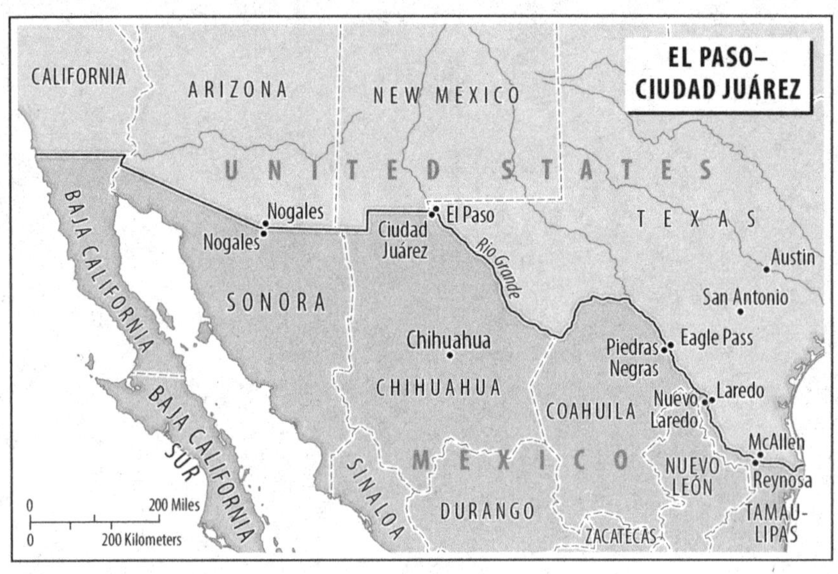
EL PASO–
CIUDAD JUÁREZ
CALIFORNIA
ARIZONA
NEW MEXICO
UNITED STATES
TEXAS
BAJA CALIFORNIA
BAJA CALIFORNIA SUR
SONORA
CHIHUAHUA
COAHUILA
NUEVO LEÓN
TAMAULIPAS
SINALOA
DURANGO
ZACATECAS
MEXICO
Nogales
Nogales
Ciudad Juárez
El Paso
Rio Grande
Chihuahua
Austin
San Antonio
Piedras Negras
Eagle Pass
Nuevo Laredo
Laredo
McAllen
Reynosa
0
200 Miles
0
200 Kilometers

1

Amazing Grace

El Paso and Ciudad Juárez sit at the foot of the mountains. The two cities remain so bound together by land and fate that they almost seem to blend, all rust and amber hues, stretching on either side of a narrow, shallow river that Juarenses call the Rio Bravo, and El Pasoans the Rio Grande. International bridges connect them like arteries. People ebb and flow through them like blood.

On the Mexican side, a giant Mexican flag and a red sculpture in the form of an X, a symbol of country pride and identity, tower over a highway and the thirty-foot-tall steel bars of the border wall. On the American end, a small cluster of downtown skyscrapers rise far above the urban sprawl, flat redbrick offices and old churches, strip malls and restaurants and spaghetti soups of roadways, grids and grids of terra-cotta, Prairie-style, and stucco homes set against the creosote and the yucca.

Interstate 10 cuts through on its way to more exciting destinations like Los Angeles, from metro areas that Americans tend to associate more with Texas like San Antonio, Houston, and Austin. But it is El Paso that is the gateway to the American Southwest—a place of rugged beauty, where from up above as you fly in, the sun reflects off glistening pools and rivulets, where after the blistering heat breaks, before the city lights glimmer, the brownness of the desert is cloaked in gold. A place in between two nations, fixed, depending on your perspective, at their center or at their margins. A place that, no matter where else I've lived or how long I've been gone, I call home.

ON AUGUST 3, 2019, I was nearly 2,000 miles away, in Washington, D.C., where I worked as a national political reporter in the bureau of *The Boston Globe*. It was a Saturday, and I was in a movie theater when my phone lit up with calls and messages. Friends and family in El Paso were checking in on each other and letting me know they were safe: There had been a mass shooting at a Walmart near the most popular shopping mall in town. Photos and videos from the scene showed bloody victims wheeled out in shopping carts, customers murmuring prayers through the gun blasts.

The nation had scarcely processed what had unfolded when another mass shooting wracked Dayton, Ohio, thirteen hours later. We jumped into covering the twin tragedies from afar, another deadly day in a politically divided nation replete with guns. But I could not help but feel we were missing the story in the place where I was from. Unlike the killings in Ohio, where authorities had found no political or racial motive, federal enforcement officials were calling the El Paso rampage an act of homegrown terrorism and one of the deadliest attacks on Latinos in the United States. The massacre, as one federal prosecutor would later say, had "spared no one—no one, not the old, not the young, not men, not women, not white, not black, and certainly not brown." Yet a police detective who filed a report from the scene on that day said the shooter had stated his target as simply "Mexicans."

So on Monday morning, with our breaking news deadlines met, I got on a plane to El Paso. When I landed that afternoon, word was still spreading of lost loved ones and close calls. Nearly every passenger around me was scrolling through news stories or murmuring, in shock and in grief, about what they had heard or thought they knew. One of my closest childhood friends, Andrea, had texted a group of us to let us know her father was safe, though I did not know yet just how close he had been to the gunfire.

I grabbed my bags and made my way through the terminal, a sense of comfort swelling inside of me at the sight of the old carpet with Southwestern motifs and the mountains beyond the glass windows. It was a familiar routine, the coming and the going. I had been doing it since I had left for college at seventeen. Outside, the desert heat warmed my cold, bare arms. My eyes adjusted to the glare of the brightness. I spotted my uncle Fernando waiting for me in his car by the curb, and I hopped in. We drove west through winding highways as we chatted in Spanish about my life in D.C. and where each of us had been when we learned of the shooting. EL PASO STRONG signs already decked billboards and businesses. There was a sadness in the air. The city felt apagada—dim and in mourning.

We stopped at the adobe bungalow where Fernando and my aunt Bertha, public-school principals, lived on a hilly street named after a dead president. I said a quick goodbye and moved my luggage into a worn black SUV that they loaned me for reporting. As I pulled out of their driveway, I debated whether to head straight to the crime scene or make one more quick stop to see the rest of my family. We're Mexican American, tight-knit and proud and complicated, and I was sure to answer for it later if I did not. But before I knew it, I found myself taking a detour through the scenic road that curves around the edge of the Franklin Mountains. High above the city, I stopped at the main overlook and sat on one of the stone walls.

POLICE SAY THE shooter left his home north of Dallas on a warm summer night. He was twenty-one. I picture him as he appeared in his mug shot: pale and disheveled, with dark, matted hair and dull brown eyes. The court records I have read say he could not sleep, that his mind was racing with violent thoughts when he climbed into his car and started driving. On his way out, he passed manicured lawns and shady oak groves, running paths, tennis courts, and affluent homes with tall, pitched roofs and walls of stone veneer—quiet blocks, each one nearly identical to the next, carrying the faraway sounds of grackles and the faint scent of freshly mowed Bermuda grass.

He traveled for at least ten hours. Ten hours to reconsider. To stop. To turn around. But he did not. Suburban roads gave way to open Texas highways, to farms and ranchland where other men had waged other wars. The place he had left behind was one of the many across the United States that had become so diverse in recent years that it reflected what demographers describe as the changing face of America. The place where he arrived the next morning had always been that kind of place, the borderland between Mexico and the United States, where life and culture can be fluid and identities often bend, meld, and collapse into one another.

The temperatures in El Paso that Saturday had been hot and quickly getting hotter. Prosecutors say he drove around aimlessly for a while. Delusions in his broken brain. Hate in his heart. It was in those wayward moments when he posted an angry screed to a website known to attract white supremacists and extremists. It ran some 2,300 words and issued a warning against the "Hispanic invasion of Texas." Its ideas embodied a racist doctrine known as the "Great Replacement," which has long circulated in the far-right corners of the internet and holds that Western elites, sometimes led by Jews, want to diminish the power of white Americans by encouraging the immigration of Black and brown people. He and his way of life were under attack, the shooter wrote, by foreigners and immigrants, by people who did not look or act or sound like him, and who he believed were supplanting white people. "If we can get rid of enough people," he said, meaning Mexicans and Hispanics, "then our way of life can be more sustainable."

Seventeen minutes later, court records say, he arrived at a Walmart lot in a commercial center, encompassing big-box stores, a cinema, and a shopping mall frequented by residents on both sides of the border. He had in his trunk a loaded semiautomatic rifle in the mold of an AK-47 and 1,000 rounds of hollow-point bullets that he had bought online. He pulled out the weapon, slung it up against his shoulder, and opened fire. The grounds descended into chaos. Workers and customers, some hurt and bleeding and carrying others, ran for the exits or fell to the ground. Hundreds of people scrambled to their cars, ducked under tables, or fled into movie theaters and storage rooms. First responders and SWAT teams and helicopters rushed to the scene, encircling the area and blocking off roads. People who were there that day have told me what they remember. Billowing smoke. Blood on the pavement. Surveillance footage captured the man moving through the Walmart's clear sliding doors and stalking the aisles, a cold and unfeeling figure dressed in a black T-shirt, khaki cargo pants, safety goggles, and protective earmuffs that drowned out the screams.

Police said that they caught up to him at a nearby traffic light after he fled, and that, with his hands raised in the air, he exited his car and declared himself the shooter. He was arrested near a park, a stone's throw away from where I went to high school. With those hours of terror in August, El Paso became one more battleground over the nation's identity—a place, much like the rest of the United States, caught between two visions of itself, one rooted in division, another in connection.

FROM MY PERCH on top of the mountain, I thought about how, when I was in high school, my friends and I would come up to this same spot in the evenings. The stone steps and ledges would be packed with people: Teenagers kissing. Children and their parents straddling the tower viewers. Young women wandering about in sparkly quinceañera dresses, their royal courts, families, and photographers in tow. My mind then was often on the future and where I would go next. On that afternoon, however, the overlook was nearly empty. There was a warm breeze blowing, and I wanted to take in the city one last time the way I remembered it, before the violence.

I knew the next few days would be like entering the darkest depths of a pit. I knew this because some of my earliest years as a young reporter had been on the night cops' beat. With heavy police scanners strapped to my belt, I had become well acquainted with the circling highways of San Antonio by homicide. The codes and chatter from the radios led me from scene to scene. I learned to arrive quickly, to gather my bearings, and to withdraw somewhere deep inside of myself in the face of fierce, raw emotions—to become someone on the outside looking in—as I knocked on doors or tracked down officers and firefighters, witnesses and survivors, people who were living through what could well be one of the worst days of their lives. It was a grisly assignment and a lowly one. Veteran journalists who had been around when newsrooms had larger staffs and people read the morning print paper often told me that if I could do this job, I'd be able to do any in the business.

I had expected covering American politics to be different. But as Donald J. Trump rose to power in 2016, he demonized Mexicans and immigrants as gang members, murderers, and terrorists. He promised to build a wall along the nation's southern border and to have Mexico pay for it. He called for restrictions on trade and warned of threats from abroad. Once in the White House, he embarked on an isolationist "America First" agenda and a harsh immigration crackdown. The moves energized many everyday Americans—largely white and Christian—who felt their values under attack by foreigners and had for years watched manufacturers shutter plants and ship jobs overseas. They also emboldened the Patriot militias, border vigilantes, and white power activists who had operated in the shadows of our national political system for decades. All through Trump's first term, we reported on the anti-Trump protests and counterprotests flaring up across the nation. Clashes between neo-Nazis and anti–white supremacists erupted on college campuses and on the grounds of the California state capitol.

In Trump's telling, immigration was at the root of all of the nation's problems. By the summer of 2019, with another presidential election cycle beginning to heat up, the border—and El Paso specifically—had become a powerful backdrop: a symbol of the fear of the other and the outsider, of the invaders and the invaded, of the potential loss of white cultural status and power in a quickly changing nation. In the weeks and months before the shooting, the images circulating online and on television from my hometown had been jarring. Migrants penned up and waiting to plead asylum at an international bridge. Brown children marching out of nearby tent camps. Families separated at the border.

We were only starting to understand it then. We were not covering everyday political contests and disputes. We were at the front lines of a grave and fundamental fight over who we were—over who should belong in the United States and who should not, over whether we believed in, would live up to, and could uphold a multiracial, multiethnic democracy or craved a strongman's control and promises of a return to a white Christian nation—in a world where companies and industries were getting too big, moving too fast, breaking too many things, and leaving too many people behind. Those tensions had drawn a white supremacist to the border, and now they had also brought me home.

After lingering for a few moments more, I decided to go see my grandmother Alicia and another one of my aunts, also Alicia, in the Lower Valley. I drove all the way south to the Border Highway, which runs along the Rio Grande. When I was young, the road had been flanked by chain-link fences, but pushes to increase immigration enforcement under both Republican and Democratic administrations over the decades had brought more border patrol vans, federal officers, and rusty, corrugated metal bars that reached high into the air. I went east, all the way to a quiet neighborhood near the border wall, where mesquite trees and wide, open yards are set against irrigation canals. The Alicias live there five houses apart on the same stretch of a curving street. My aunt and I embraced and spoke in low voices, like the passengers on the plane.

El Paso has long been a big city with a small-town feel, and the degrees of separation from the shooting were closing in again. My aunt told me that a friend of hers had worked as a house cleaner for one of the fathers shot and killed. We spoke about how shaken people were, but I could not stay long. I dropped off my things and headed back up into the heart of the city, where a makeshift memorial had sprung up on a tall hill overlooking the parking lot of the store that the shooter had stormed.

THE SUN WAS setting by the time I arrived. Dozens of white TV news vans were stationed around the streets near a metal road barricade where white crosses now stood, bearing the names of the dead. American and Mexican flags waved in the breeze. The site offered sweeping views of the borderland. Down below, cars and semis barreled down Interstate 10 past downtown buildings and into haunting mountain folds. El Paso homes, small businesses, and restaurants faded into Juárez in the distance. A sea of city lights was beginning to glitter under purple and pink skies.

Crowds flooded in and out around me, leaving behind photographs, handwritten notes, large banners and signs, rosaries, and bouquets of real and artificial flowers. Volunteers passed out water bottles and powdered sugar candy sticks. Incense and veladoras burned next to stuffed animals and balloons shaped into red hearts and white stars. A group sung "Amazing Grace" and let the white balloons fly. I wandered among my people united in our grief. Murmurs of prayers and sobbing, the chords of corridos, and snippets of television interviews merged in the darkness.

"I do blame our president. He doesn't know us. He doesn't know our culture."

"I don't know anyone who was killed or injured personally, but I feel the pain for our city."

"El Paso es una ciudad que tiene mucho amor por su gente." ("El Paso is a city that has a lot of love for its people.")

Out there that evening, I could not shake the notion that one of the most lethal killers in modern American history had come not from south of our border but from the north and was born not outside of our country but within. The final death toll would be twenty-three people. Nearly two dozen others were injured, including a baby boy who somehow survived, even as his parents did not.

For my generation of fronterizos, the drug war in Mexico, fueled by U.S. guns and demand, had until then been the most dire threat to our shared sense of identity. The shootouts and kidnappings crept into Juárez from the outskirts as my friends and I moved on from quinceañeras to hanging out at nightclubs and bars along busy strips cutting into the Mexican city. The crosses we grew up with were pink and lined the Chihuahuan desert. They were in memory of women and girls who looked like me, born on the other side of the border, snatched and killed by cartels and copycats. Now the massacre was another reminder that El Paso had long played an incredible role in the American fixation with that dividing line below, and the violence it wreaked—one that continued to shape the perceptions of us and of ourselves as Mexican Americans and Latinos in the United States.

The attack should have also served as a wake-up call to all Americans. Years later, in July 2023, a federal prosecutor would put it best. In a hearing in El Paso, in which the shooter was handed ninety consecutive life sentences, his defense lawyers argued that their client had been in the midst of a schizophrenic break. But the prosecutor countered that the attack—a strike on the very essence of what made El Paso and the borderland so exceptional: its people—was cold and premeditated, its details crafted over at least two weeks and described in the manifesto he had posted online. That dogma, the attorney said, was precisely what had made the killer even more dangerous: Through it, the man had served as a vessel for the Great Replacement theory, he said, "an insidious lie, a lie borne of fear, fueled by ignorance, a lie spread to try to convince people that this country belongs to only a select few." That "malevolent fiction," the lawyer went on, had turned the man against himself, against El Paso, and against a core founding principle of the United States. "That we as a nation, all of us together, are so much more than the sum of our individual parts," he said. "That out of many, we are made one."

THE NEXT DAYS in El Paso following the shooting were heavy, a scramble of emotional interviews and tight deadlines, the thick protective shield I had forged over my years of crime reporting often punctured. A local freelance photographer, Christ Chavez, and I became fast friends as we drove all around the city. We met with survivors, witnesses, and community leaders. We watched a graffiti artist paint through his sorrow with a mural. Often, we struggled not to cry as we ran into people we knew who were also torn up and hurting. One retired news photographer, the kind of grizzled guy who used to tell younger reporters not to get too involved with a story, sobbed at the site of the memorial, telling us, "I had to come down. I knew I would regret it if I didn't."

The tears could come in a rush and at any moment, in the middle of conversations, as we drove under the harsh brightness past the mountains, in the arms of friends and family whom we felt grateful and guilty to still be able to hold close. I sorted through the pain and people's memories at my aunt Alicia's house, her houseplants, cat trinkets, and elegant glass Catrinas keeping watch as I wrote. She suffers from arthritis, and cold air hurts her bones. So I wrote in the heat, with a little sweat on my brow. I would know it was midnight when I could hear the Mexican national anthem cut into her Spanish-language programming, as it does every night on Mexican radio stations and TV channels streamed across the borderland.

All week the city debated, in English and in Spanish, President Trump's complicity in the massacre, with many tracing a direct line from his hostile language against immigrants to the shooter's racial and ethnic hatred. The afternoon that the president arrived at a Fort Bliss hangar, so that he and his wife, Melania, could visit with some of the victims, hundreds of people, including some of the city's top Democratic leaders, gathered in protest at a rally in a central park. At the memorial later, a skinny, brown-skinned Hispanic man in a red MAKE AMERICA GREAT AGAIN hat dropped off a single red rose, irritating mourners who accused him of trolling. Just a few feet away, a far-right-wing border blogger recorded.

In between interviews and vigils, I kept returning to that overlook marking the massacre, where people stopped by the thousands—after work, during lunch breaks, often in scorching desert heat—to march and pray and drop off flowers, stuffed animals, and balloons. It was over one of those days, through texts, that I had learned more about my friend Andrea's father.

She told us he had been in the parking lot down below when the shooter opened fire. He escaped by running and climbing over one of the stone walls. He did not stop running until he reached his house near our high school, the same family home where we had spent so many days as teenagers hanging out. I kept hoping Andrea would call me. I wanted to know how she and her dad were doing. I wanted to come over like in the old days, when we would drive around with nowhere to go.

But on my final afternoon in El Paso that summer, she understandably did not want to see me—or anyone. I waited at the memorial a while longer in case she changed her mind, attempting to finish my last dispatch on my laptop from the front seat of the SUV, then giving up and wandering again. I watched people drop off more plastic roses and rosaries until the desert skies grew dark. There was something knotted inside, a frustration I could not shake. There was something about all the camera crews and white television trucks, the way national reporters—a group that now included me—had rushed in to tell this story and would then be gone.

As I stood in front of the white crosses, one sound remained familiar and comforting: the faraway drone of the freeway. I used to listen to that sound out of my bedroom window when all I wished was to get out of my hometown. Years ago, it seemed the rest of Texas would forget El Paso existed because it sits at its most western tip, a place as much American as it is Mexican and New Mexican and Tejano and so fiercely its own. Once I left, I realized it wasn't just Texas that forgot or misunderstood us; it was the rest of the country, too.

Now it was dawning on me that El Paso had been at the center of the nation's battles over borders and identity since the beginning and that we were once again here because we had never truly afforded the city its rightful place in our American telling. I vowed, then and there, to return—to learn what I did not know and to relearn what I had forgotten—to remind us of its true story, its full story, and where it belongs.

2

The Most Dangerous Girl in Mexico

Guadalajara, Jalisco, Mexico
1890s

Herlinda Wong Chew was born in the embers that would set the north ablaze. The year was approximately 1895, and the Mexican countryside that rambled into the United States had long burned with drought—and then with unrest. It had either rained too little or it had rained too much. Cattle had died, fields of grain had been lost, and mining had shut down in the sierra. The conditions were making rebels and immigrants out of campesinos. As some set villages on fire, the dictatorship that had ruled her country for nearly twenty years was baring its earliest hot cracks. It would all end in a smoldering ruin, though Mexicanos like the Wongs did not know it yet.

Herlinda and her family lived much farther south, in Guadalajara, the capital city of the Mexican state of Jalisco, bordering the Pacific coast. Her childhood would unfold under the grip of el Porfiriato. But her youth, as that of El Paso, would ultimately be shaped by the embers in the air in which she took her first breaths, by the whispers of rebellion and of a young woman, known as la Santa de Cabora, who would cross through the far West Texas city at the base of the mountains that Herlinda would one day call home.

Not much is known about Herlinda's mother, Francisca Vazquez, whom she lost as a child, but her father, Carlos Wong, was a respected Chinese hotelier. He was a bit of a maverick, the kind of wheeler and dealer, his granddaughters would later recall, with a taste for fine things, an enterprising mind, and a tendency to eschew Chinese dress and traditions for Western ones. At the opera house in Guadalajara, he was known to don a top hat and tails. Yet there was one tradition he did not abandon: He gave his daughter a Chinese birth name, Sun Far Wong.

Carlos hailed from a wealthy family in Guangzhou—or Canton, as it was then known—just northwest of Hong Kong, in Guangdong (also formerly Canton) Province, in southern China. As a young man in search of an exciting life, he followed the same trade lines that had once connected Spanish galleons carrying silk, porcelain, and ivory from Manila to Mexico, Panama, and Peru, eventually bringing some of the earliest Asians to the New World. He landed first in Peru, where he married an Indigenous woman and launched a business contracting Chinese laborers across the American West and Latin America.

Through the nineteenth century, as European countries dismantled the Atlantic slave trade, the Spanish and British had expanded the galleon routes into a global system to hire indentured laborers, or "coolies," mostly from China or India, on plantations in the Caribbean and Latin America. As early as the 1860s, American planters and capitalists, sensing the end of slavery in the United States, brought some of these immigrants to plantations in the Deep South, mostly in Louisiana and Arkansas. Many toiled alongside Black enslaved people for exploitative numbers of hours, under dangerous and even deadly conditions.

But by the time Carlos was in business, more Asian immigrants had found new and better ways to work in the United States, lured by the possibility of striking it rich in the mines, railroads, and booming economy of California, the state the Chinese knew as the "Gold Mountain." Carlos's granddaughters believed he helped bring over some of the same Chinese men who braved dynamite blasts and sweltering heat to help build the second transcontinental railroad, which in 1881 linked the American Southwest to the rest of the country. He would have had an ample workforce. Many, like himself, came from Guangzhou, which through those years was sending the vast majority of Chinese immigrants to the United States and around the world.

Carlos went on to Mexico once the railroad was completed. His first wife had died, and the racial hatred against the Chinese had intensified so much in the United States that the phrase "coolie" had become a catchall slur. Starting with the Chinese Exclusion Act in 1882, Congress was making it harder for Chinese people like Carlos to migrate to the country and had banned Chinese laborers altogether—the nation's first immigration measures explicitly based on race. White American politicians and union leaders argued that Asian migrants were taking American jobs, did not assimilate, and constituted an "invasion."

Mexico, on the other hand, was becoming a viable alternative for the Chinese, even if there, too, many would have much preferred the migrations of light-skinned Europeans. Mexican president Porfirio Díaz, seeking to fortify trade with China and Japan, had all but encouraged Chinese migration as he ushered in a major push to modernize and democratize the nation with an iron fist—the Pax Porfiriana. American and European imperialists, tycoons, and businessmen were sweeping into Mexico. They were expanding cattle ranches, sugar plantations, mines, and farms of cotton and guayule. They were bringing in railroads, making it possible to ship larger lots of goods, which were processed and converted in the faraway factories they owned.

Through the first part of el Porfiriato, historian Evelyn Hu-DeHart has found, Chinese immigrants tended to fall into the bottom rungs of this rising social and economic order. But as the Chinese leveraged their managerial skills and connections in their home country to cater to the new working classes, Hu-DeHart writes, they came to form the dominant part of the new petit bourgeois class. They opened businesses in local trade and commerce, as zapateros, or shoemakers, tailors, cooks, launderers, and small grocers, and they prospered.

In Guadalajara, Carlos established a European-style hotel among the city's colonial plazas and near the aging cathedral. Soon he had a chain of hotels up and down the railroad lines that were now stretching into Mexico. European and American guests came and went. He married Herlinda's mother, an Indigenous Mexicana, and after her death he married again. Herlinda's stepmother was a vivacious Spanish dancer with whom he may have had an affair—Herlinda would later tell her daughters that her mother died of a broken heart—but she would take care of Herlinda well. The Wongs made many friends as they traveled widely across Mexico and along the borderland, to El Paso, for business and pleasure.

As Carlos came and went from the north, there were signs that el Porfiriato could not hold. Competition for land and water in Mexico was turning fiercer. As Mexico's federal and state governments continued to confiscate more communal land, or ejidos, for foreigners' ventures, more Mexicano natives and campesinos, long in conflict with the government and with each other, were being displaced. And still the wheels of industry churned, in Mexico and in the United States, across Asia and Latin America, and wherever Western powers crawled. All those opposed to its progress—technological, scientific, and material efficiency, capitalism, and profits regardless of the social costs—were seen as primitives, Natives, and enemies of the state. In Mexico, there was one pejorative term to define them all: "Indios."

The year his daughter was born, Carlos would not have been able to escape the whispers of la Santa in El Paso and the borderland. Many Mexicanos, fed up with the bad harvests, harsh rule, and loss of their property, had begun to head north in search of work. Others had been taking up arms in short, disparate uprisings throughout the northern Mexican border states of Sonora, Chihuahua, and Tamaulipas. Some chanted la Santa's name in prayers and battle cries. The winds carried it over rolling grasses and chaparral, past the line that divided Mexico and the United States, to deserts that had once been Mexican before they were American, and Native before they were Mexican.

Cabora, Sonora, Mexico
1890s

Far in the plunging canyons and flat-topped mountains of Sonora, the Mexican state across the border from Arizona, lived the girl known as la Santa de Cabora. Yaqui and Mayo Natives trekked for miles to see her.

Campesinos collected jars of the soil where she might have stepped. Circles of middle- and upper-class liberals, who followed the teachings of a French occultist and called themselves spiritists, saw her as a conduit for the souls of the dead. A living saint.

The young woman was, in fact, flesh and blood. She was no more than seventeen, tall and slim, with arresting brown eyes and thick, dark hair that fell to her waist and that she often pinned up in a bun, a bushel of curly bangs sweeping over her forehead. Her given name was Niña García Nona María Rebeca Chávez. But by the time the masses had come to know her, beckoning at her door or thronging her in the streets in hopes of catching a gaze or a blessing, she was known simply as Teresa Urrea.

From the hacienda where she lived with her wealthy father, Urrea delivered babies and nursed women through the pains of labor. She cared for the sick, mending bones and rubbing aching limbs, dispensing droplets in their eyes. Her fingers moved nimbly as she prepared tonics or mashed herbs, perhaps hierba del soldado for scorpion bites and rattlesnake root for the common cold, whispering prayers from her lips, a rebozo slipping off her shoulders.

Her mother, one of the many Tehueco Indigenous women who had worked for her father, and with whom he was said to have extramarital affairs, had died or disappeared when Urrea was fifteen. Villagers believed the young woman had acquired her powers when, just days after her sixteenth birthday, she suddenly shook with convulsions. Some historians believe she lingered in and out of a trance, others that she fell into a coma, the likely result of a seizure, perhaps stemming from the trauma of a sexual assault or some undiagnosed illness. What is widely agreed on is that the girl opened her eyes as she lay in her coffin, stunning loved ones gathered for her wake. She predicted that Huila, the Yaqui curandera who had taught her the ways of Indigenous folk healing, would die within days. And Huila did.

Word spread of la Santa's miracles and of her counsel. Her following grew across Mexico and Puerto Rico, then in Europe and South America and around the world. It was said the young woman could foretell deaths, births, and accidents; that she cured a man of leprosy and helped another walk again. It was said that when she sweat as she worked or wet the dirt with her saliva for one remedy or another, the smell of roses would fill the room. Some reported that when she slept, her spirit left her body, and that she wandered through pitch-black nights on the glow of a phosphorescent white horse, inciting rebellion across the Mexican countryside.

WITHIN THE STONE walls of el Castillo de Chapultepec, in Mexico City, Díaz watched the religious fervor around la Santa rise with concern and suspicion. Díaz knew what power lay in the embers better than most. He had made his name as a soldier in a young Mexico enveloped in flames—in battles and bitter feuds, between the Church and the Republic, between a nascent Mexican state and a variety of imperial powers, between Mexicans and the Comanche and the Yaqui and Apache peoples.

The son of a poor Spanish innkeeper and a woman of Mixtec heritage, he had been a die-hard liberal who had risen on the wings of his mentor, Benito Juárez, the first Indigenous president of Mexico and its most beloved. The two men had devoted themselves to the cause that liberal Mexicanos had been fighting for since Mexico had won its independence from Spain in 1821: delivering their country from the vestiges of Spanish rule, feudal-like systems of realm, religion, labor, and caste that favored the Spanish-blooded upper crust and light-skinned criollos. Díaz had promised to transform Mexico into a democracy, driven by capitalism and economic development, where a strong rule of law and constitution would treat all Mexicanos—criollo, Black, Indigenous, and mixed, or mestizo—as equals. And yet, after he had finally assumed power in 1876, he had not let go.

La Pax Porfiriana had bestowed Mexico with education for its wider masses; a middle class; better public health and transportation; electric lights, telegraphs, and streetcars; and economic growth and stability like it had never before seen in its young history. But old Porfirio wielded power with paramilitary forces, known as los rurales, who enforced his will with cavalry swords and Remington rifles. His constellation of political loyalists helped him fix elections, squelch protest, and muzzle the press. His circle of advisers, or los Científicos, strictly adhered to the global "scientific" principles that dominated the era: racist and since-debunked European ideas and philosophies, like social Darwinism and Victorian anthropology, essentially holding that scientific methods could be practically applied to finance, industrialization, education, and biology, making some races—white Anglo-Saxon races—inherently superior to others.

As adoration for la Santa grew, Díaz still cut an imposing figure in military black, all straight angles and gleaming medals, a man with a thick white handlebar mustache, a stocky neck, and barrel-chested frame. He had acquired a taste for lavish French decor, validation from the U.S. liberal intelligentsia—which heaped it on him—and reportedly skin-lightening creams. All through their climb, says historian Paul J. Vanderwood, Díaz and Juárez had compelled Mexicanos to weigh the balance of Church and state, God and government. Now, as Porfirian "progress" left many behind, trust in the country's institutions had fallen and a rift was widening between Mexicanos who still believed in the rule of law and those who, like Urrea, believed in the rule of God but not that of the Catholic Church and its clergy, and most certainly not Porfirio's state. Urrea spoke out against money and greed. She attributed her powers to God and relied on Christ's teachings to offer solace, but she did not recognize the authority of the Church. Her detractors, Vanderwood writes, called her a heretic—and Díaz considered her a threat to his rule, "the most dangerous girl in Mexico."

To help explain la Santa's miracles, what she stirred in people, campesinos pointed to God and la Virgencita, the brown-skinned virgin who appeared to el Indio Juan Diego on the sliver of a moon, wearing a mantle full of stars. Spiritists turned to grand, complex theories about the cosmos and electromagnetic fields. Yet, in the stories of her friends and patients, it is possible to see another root to her power.

In this age of men with deep pockets and blind ambitions, Mexico's Indigenous tribes, its villagers and small farmers, were in the midst of being converted themselves. Once campesinos who worked the soil and picked the crops and shared the fruits of their labor, they were becoming a nameless, faceless class, a working class—la clase obrera. Urrea was mesmerizing because she looked into the eyes of those who no longer felt seen, touched each hurting part of those who no longer felt human—body, blood, and bones, hope and dreams—but machine. Her informal ministering, words of care and love for thy neighbor, moved souls because it laid bare their very absence under the iron rule of el Porfiriato. The more people listened, the more people, inspired and empowered, began to dissent.

The Teresita Rebellion, historians say, began in the summer of 1890, when murmurs of la Santa passed through the lips of Mayo natives assembled on a hill just outside of Cabora. A Mexican military officer dispatched to investigate reports of a large gathering there found more than 1,000 people waiting for a flood they believed would wash away the wicked, including the Mexicano settlers who had taken their land. Damián Quijano, a sixteen-year-old Mayo, claimed he had heard the prophecy from la Santa herself in a dream. Dozens were arrested, but the sightings of Urrea did not stop.

In May 1892, about two hundred Mayo Natives sacked the nearby Sonoran town of Navojoa, shooting down public officials and crying, "¡Viva la Santa de Cabora!" A few days later, one of Porfirio Díaz's generals and a phalanx of troops surrounded the home of the Urreas. Teresa and her father, Don Tomás, were arrested for the attack. They were taken through Yaqui country to Guaymas, a historic little port off the Pacific Ocean, and then forced to leave Mexico or else face time in prison. Early the next month, they boarded a train on a new rail line running north and crossed into the Arizona border city of Nogales. Their friend Lauro Aguirre, a spiritist and engineer who had his own disputes with el Porfiriato, soon followed them.

Tensions continued to build that fall, this time in Tomóchic, the largest pueblo run by mestizos in the lower sierra of neighboring Chihuahua. Land in the region had surged in value with the expansion of nearby mines, in towns like Santa Eulalia and Parral, and a petty feud between a powerful local politico and federal officials over the practice of religion had devolved. It fed into the wider Teresita Rebellion gripping the north and the borderland.

The final battle for Tomóchic began on October 20, 1892, when 1,200 of Díaz's troops descended on the village before being repelled by Tomochiteco defenders. Díaz's forces then put the rebels under siege. Days later, their ammunition and food supplies depleted, Tomochiteco families and roughly a dozen fighters were forced to take refuge in a small church on an isolated plateau near a stream. That afternoon, Díaz's soldiers lit its front door on fire with petroleum, dried cornstalks, and light tinder. People struggled to escape as flames and smoke quickly engulfed the building. Screaming women grabbed children in their arms. Those who managed to flee were shot by snipers keeping watch in a nearby cave or by soldiers waiting outside. A few women and children found safety with the last rebels keeping up the fight, but more than sixty people were killed. Others who were injured died of cold and starvation. Before their struggle culminated in slaughter, shouts and hosannas in honor of la Santa had merged in the winds.

The governor of Chihuahua tried to downplay the brutality and significance of the attack. He labeled the Tomochitecos religious fanatics. He called them criminals, bandidos, and enemies of progress. He called them Indios.

El Paso, Texas, United States
1890s

Along the borderland, when Herlinda was only months old, the embers of northern uprisings were still glowing amber. Reports of la Santa and the Tomóchic uprising would have yet been splattered across Spanish-language newspapers. The horrors of Tomóchic had touched off a liberal student movement against Díaz in Mexico City in the spring of 1893, and in El Paso they sparked a surge of revolutionary activity. La Santa was a modern-day reality star if modern-day reality stars inspired rebellion.

El Paso stood then as it stands now: a city after its namesake, a passageway between two uneasy nations divided by a border and tied by blood, trade, and industry, a crossroads at a crossroads, wheeling people in all four cardinal directions across time. In capitalism's game of winners and losers, the city had come out on top, prospering from the rush of American westward expansion and Asian and Latin American migration—so big, so booming, and so far west that one journalist from San Antonio had once proclaimed it the "Future Immense."

The El Paso skyline did not have a single skyscraper yet, but flat redbrick factories and shops and hotels in terra-cotta buildings were already rising against the mountains under the desert sun. The industrial development of the city, which transformed it into the one we know today, had been set in motion when four major railroad companies barreled toward it in a race to build the second transcontinental line through the United States. The Southern Pacific company won the contest on May 13, 1881, when about 3,000 Chinese workers—perhaps even some of the same men contracted by Herlinda's father—pounded the final steel spikes in the ground with sledge-hammers. Engine Number One, a small black-and-silver 4-4-0 locomotive, rumbled through the city a week later to salutes, speeches, a banquet, and a grand ball.

The railroad race doubled the El Paso population of some eight hundred residents, then tripled it within months. Humble homes of brick and wood went up alongside Victorian mansions and Western-style stores and saloons. Over the span of a year, Baptists, Catholics, Episcopalians, Methodists, and Presbyterians had all built new churches. By 1883, the city had established a local government, a couple of banks, and several newspapers. The first public school and the first African American church in El Paso, Second Baptist, were founded a year later, and the African Methodist Episcopal Church a year after that. Then came mining and agricultural businesses, packing-houses, shoe factories, and cigar manufacturing companies, along with dance halls, gambling establishments, theaters, and opera houses.

Hundreds of the Chinese railroad workers who won the race to El Paso stayed in the city even as the Southern Pacific Railroad immediately fired more than 1,000 of the tracklayers after the contest was over and the Chinese Exclusion Act came down roughly a year later. Others eventually drifted back. Many of the newly arrived immigrants, largely young men, wore thick-soled slip-on shoes, their hair long and braided in queues in the tradition of the Qing dynasty, imposed on Chinese men after the Manchurian invasion. They settled in an old adobe boardinghouse near the Southern Pacific train depot and a municipal dump that was cleaned up and transformed into San Jacinto Plaza.

Almost immediately, some of the men established a large grocery store on the same block, supplying Chinese residents in the entire region. Soon a cluster of downtown Chinese laundries, stores, and chophouses had emerged alongside the city's red-light district. More men moved into the surrounding homes—mostly humble one-story dwellings of wood and adobe—resulting in more Chinese storefronts around the city and the rise of a small professional class of traditional Chinese merchants, doctors, physicians, and surgeons.

By 1896, El Paso had become home to roughly 15,500 people, the most populous place between San Antonio and Los Angeles. Herlinda's father continued to pass through the city on business, and the Spanish-language press had not forgotten Tomóchic. Lauro Aguirre, who followed the Urreas into exile, moved to the city that year, presumably because he was being closely tracked by law enforcement officials in both Mexico and the United States. He had left engineering to become a journalist back in Nogales and had founded *El Independiente*, an influential anti-Porfirian rag.

The battles of Tomóchic, historian David Dorado Romo writes, had radicalized Aguirre. At the Nogales home of the Urreas in 1893, Arizona agents believed, he and others had drafted "El Plan de Tomóchic," a revolutionary manifesto that denounced the slaughter in the small village in Chihuahua and the Mexican government's extermination rampage against the Yaqui people. It also called on Mexico to restore the liberal constitution of 1857, which Díaz's mentor, former Mexican president Benito Juárez, had drafted when the two were still fighting the nation's liberal battles.

Soon after settling in El Paso, Aguirre persuaded the Urreas to join him in the city and help him out in the news business. Their arrival was thwarted at first. That spring, Aguirre and his news partner, Manuel Flores Chapa, were arrested and charged, at the request of the Mexican government, for neutrality violations and fomenting revolution. Mexican officials had taken issue with their coverage of the trial of the city's first revolucionario, Víctor Ochoa, who had been arrested for "employing and equipping insurgents." Ochoa, too, had used the Tomóchic uprising as his banner cry, even embellishing details to serve his cause. (He once claimed that his own family had been slain in the struggle. They had not.) Aguirre and Chapa were released sixteen days later after no clear evidence was found against them.

Teresa Urrea and her father, Don Tomás, finally stepped off the train in downtown El Paso on June 13, 1896. Many traveled by foot, wagon, and train to greet the woman, now twenty-two, whom they knew as la Santa. Some 3,000 people waited for the Urreas at their new home in El Segundo Barrio, a bustling working-class ward at the city's southern edge where Black Americans and Mexican, Chinese, and European immigrants clustered together in rows of brick tenements and humble one-story adobe homes. The Urreas moved into an apartment building at the corner of Overland and Campbell Streets, near a redbrick Catholic church named Sacred Heart, which served as a community anchor.

Contempt for Díaz ran deep in El Segundo. The ward had been built on a strip of land that had once been a marsh along the Rio Grande and had often shifted sides between Mexico and the United States, its boundaries following the changing course of the river. So many Mexicanos, allegedly from Chihuahua, lived within a few of its blocks that some called that part of the district "Chihuahuita," or "Little Chihuahua."

Over time, Teresa would live in different homes in the neighborhood and South El Paso, administering her services to both affluent and impoverished paisanos and, depending on your read on history, inciting revolution. Aguirre went on to publish a series of articles bylined by him and Urrea and even wrote his own book in El Paso on the Tomóchic uprising. Urrea herself never did call for violence or revolt, and historians and feminist writers have ardently debated whether it was men like Aguirre and Tomochiteco politicos who were behind her rebellion or whether such theories rob la Santa of her agency. If the former was true, Romo has pointed out, her relationship with Aguirre never soured. She even named one of her children Laura in his honor. Whatever the case, there was no denying that Urrea infused the city with liberalism—and that Díaz feared her power.

Almost two months after Urrea arrived in El Paso, forty rebels, most of them Yaqui, seized the customhouse in the Sonoran border city across from Nogales, also named Nogales. They killed two federal officers and prompted roughly 150 Arizona militiamen and a band of Díaz's rurales to exchange fire with the guerrilleros until they fled into the mountains. Officers searched the bodies of the men killed, laying out seven of them in front of the building as a warning to other revolucionarios. They found scapulars, copies of articles in *El Independiente,* and a letter signed by Urrea and "John the Baptist," which might have been Aguirre's code name. One Yaqui rebel had a lock of Urrea's hair. Another was carrying a photograph of her with an inscription. It read: "Mexican Joan of Arc."

3

Revolt in the Borderland

El Paso, Texas
1900s

Lauro Aguirre had eyes following him everywhere. He had not stopped writing the seeds of the revolution, or getting into trouble for it. The Urreas had long returned to Arizona, and the uprisings in northern Mexico had appeared to burn out. Yet Aguirre had stayed behind, kindling the embers.

El Paso had become a refuge of liberal thought. A stream of political exiles from el Porfiriato—writers, thinkers, activists, and workers—kept settling in or passing through, riding in on the Mexican Central rail line that Díaz himself had chartered from Mexico City. All along the borderland, in broadsides and newspapers that circulated from Nogales to Laredo, in secret and not-so-secret clubs, unions, and political groups, Mexicanos and México Americanos debated the expansion of capitalism and its systems of racial, ethnic, and class order. They opposed the concentration of land and wealth among a handful of tycoons and elites. They denounced the lynchings of Black people, Mexicanos, and Indios. They called for the protection and empowerment of the worker. But mostly they watched and they waited for the ouster of old Porfirio. In the dimly lit bars and hotels of El Paso, those tired of waiting plotted it, and in the recesses, Mexican and American spies, federal officials, and secret agents—eager to track down subversives, socialists, and anarchists—listened to the whispers.

Aguirre held a disdain for the dictator that ran so deep, he had been prone to openly discuss it at the séances he had hosted for high society spiritists back in Sonora. He was a thin man with serious eyes and spiky, tousled hair, a bit of a crank, as historian David Dorado Romo puts it, but incorruptible and relentless. And he was now running one of the most influential publications in the region, *La Reforma Social.* Tagline: "Diario Libre-Pensador." A freethinking journal. Mission statement: "Por medios, la Verdad y lo racional; por Guía, la Justicia; y por fin, el Progreso y el Bien" ("The means, the Truth and the rational; the Guide, Justice; and the ends, Progress and the Common Good").

Aguirre operated his printing presses at 403 South Campbell Street, at the northern limits of El Segundo, in South El Paso. The Texas border city he had adopted was at the edge of a modern American future, growing faster and faster. Cars and black horse-drawn buggies rumbled down wide caliche roads, and brick storefronts and factories lined its main thoroughfare, El Paso Street. Black cowboys and families, fleeing Jim Crow segregation in the Deep South, passed through on their way west. East Coast and white Midwestern transplants arrived in search of warmer climates and relief from health ailments. Chinese and Mexican workers and businessmen like Herlinda's father continued to use it as the door to the American Southwest.

Near Aguirre's print shop, two large dance halls, the Monte Carlo and the Red Light, spewed drunken people onto the streets day and night. They sat alongside flourishing downtown Chinese businesses and upscale theaters and opera houses. Immigrant families leading quiet lives commingled with outlaws and hustlers, a rough crowd that, in 1902, according to one *El Paso Times* news editor, encompassed some six hundred professional gamblers. They earned the city nicknames like "Hell Paso," the "Six-Shooter Capital of the Southwest," and the "Monte Carlo of America." But in the eyes of both the Mexican and American governments, far more dangerous than the drunkards or gunslingers on South Oregon were the liberal ideas ebbing and flowing across the U.S.-Mexico dividing line—la conciencia colectiva—

shaping a countercurrent to the no-holds-barred capitalism, industrialism, and white supremacy of the era.

Among the most active Mexicanos in El Paso were members of el Partido Liberal Mexicano, or the PLM, cofounded by the brothers Ricardo and Enrique Flores Magón. Aguirre had been a key ally of the Magón brothers since they had fled Mexico in 1904, after their newsrooms had been raided and their popular anti-Porfirian newspaper, *Regeneración*, shut down multiple times. It is likely the three bonded over the Tomóchic uprising. The Magón brothers had been at the center of the Mexico City student movement it fueled. Like Aguirre, Ricardo Magón, a law school dropout and self-made intellectual, had privately become convinced that Díaz could only be ousted through armed revolt. As they made their lives on the lam from Porfirian authorities, the Magón brothers and their followers eventually split with the moderate flank of the liberal movement. They set up the PLM in 1905, from St. Louis, Missouri. Aguirre became the president of their liberal club in El Paso.

Over the next year, Aguirre began serving as their spokesman and print distributor of sorts, cranking out copies of *Regeneración* from his presses and smuggling them to Juárez railroad workers, who then disseminated the issues throughout Mexico even though Díaz had banned them. The far-left group was also forging ties with white labor unions in the American heartland as it advocated for democratic reforms, free speech, labor rights, and social justice. Their demands included presidential term limits, eight-hour workdays, higher wages, and a breakup of the largest land estates in Mexico. Their campaign was not without its flaws. Even as their Mexican and American members blasted the fear and racism against the Mexican in the United States, some reserved their own fear and racism for the Chinese.

Magonistas slipped in and out of El Paso, working out of the same brick tenements in El Segundo where Urrea had cared for the ailing. They used pseudonyms and wrote in codes as they secretly rallied caudillos, or leaders, to the revolutionary cause. Most of their potential recruits were workers on Mexican mining camps, railroad sites, and plantations, where the literate few read *Regeneración* articles aloud to the many others who could not read and groups could spend days debating the ideas in its pages. Though many had little or no fighting experience, some were organized, particularly in mining camps, where American labor unions were also active in helping workers push for higher wages in strikes that sometimes ended in violence.

By 1906, the PLM had established a string of focos, or satellite groups, just across the border from Texas and Arizona, and the magonistas were ready for revolt. Based on what he had learned watching the Tomóchic protests, Ricardo Magón believed his group's revolucionarios were the boldest because they were workers, and no one—no journalist, intellectual, politician, or student—was bolder than a worker with little to lose and a fierce desire to defend their rights.

On a cool desert night early that September, Aguirre made his way to a flat-roofed redbrick rooming house in El Segundo Barrio—número 7, en la calle 3—where he met more than half a dozen rebels amid the smoke of cigars. Present was the bigwig himself, Ricardo Magón, a burly man with a shock of black hair and a black handlebar mustache. He had taken the train in from his lair in Montreal, Quebec. Present were also other high-level PLM members and veterans of past northern uprisings, including the Teresita Rebellion. It is unclear if Aguirre was there solely to report or to contribute, but, as Romo notes, he was not beholden to modern notions of objectivity.

The meeting lasted two hours and produced the "Acuerdos de la Junta Revolucionaria Establecida en El Paso, Texas." The accords stipulated that two hundred men—"resueltos y armados," determined and armed—would be redirected to El Paso. They were to march into Ciudad Juárez to blow up the federal military barracks, the police station, and city hall. Other attacks were planned farther south, in Ciudad Chihuahua and Santa Eulalia, but the men believed the assault on Juárez, the largest and most important Mexican border city, would be the match to light the spark of rebellion across Chihuahua and beyond.

HERLINDA WONG CHEW, a thin girl with long black hair, would have been eleven by then, old enough to read Aguirre's screeds, as she accompanied her father and stepmother on their trips to El Paso, where Carlos Wong was close friends with some of the major empresarios enabling the city's boom. Her business education would start at a young age as she mingled with her father's prominent milieu—though, formally, she would only attend a Methodist Episcopal school to the sixth grade, and her academics would mainly encompass home skills, such as sewing and embroidery, at a time when Mexican, Chinese, and American customs all dictated that women should not learn too much.

She had a curious nature and a natural aptitude for languages, picking up words and phrases in French and English from her father's most loyal hotel guests. She would often read late into the darkness, she would later tell an El Paso columnist, hiding under her bed with a book and the glow of candlelight.

If the Wongs had dropped into El Paso that fall of 1906, word of la Junta's plan would have been spreading among the spies in their midst. As Mexican Independence Day neared, Díaz's rurales, the Arizona Rangers, the U.S. marshals, and detectives with the private Pinkerton security company fanned out across the desert brush and staked out locales as far as St. Louis.

In early October, Enrique Creel, the governor of Chihuahua, fired off missives to Díaz's vice president, warning that Ricardo Magón had chosen El Paso as "his base of operations," as he traversed la frontera to incite revoltosos. Aguirre, he added, was holding nightly meetings with magonistas, taking in auxiliary members from Coahuila, and using the press to agitate and instigate, to "libel" and distribute "negative propaganda." Aguirre had even complained to El Paso police that the Mexican government wanted him detained, Creel said, prompting the police chief to order the department to protect him and to watch his house. "It is a fact that in El Paso, Texas, there is a center of revolutionary activity," Creel warned Corral, "and I think we should organize our elements to destroy it, proving to the American Government what the true criminal and revolutionary character is of those men."

The men were not deterred. On October 15, 1906, from Aguirre's printing presses on South Campbell Street, Ricardo Magón published a set of "general instructions" to the members of his party in Aguirre's *La Reforma Social*. For the PLM to triumph through nonviolent means, his open letter went, Mexicanos would have to be free to gather in clubs, exchange ideas, and elect the officials they desired. Instead, in Mexico, Magón said, people who tried those actions were jailed, murdered, or suppressed in a thousand other ways. He concluded: "The people have only one supreme and terrible resource left: Rebellion! Rebellion, holy right of the oppressed!"

And yet the magonista revolt would be all over before it ever began, four days later. In their company at that junta meeting in El Segundo, there had been a Mexican undercover agent disguised as a disgruntled paisano. He heard their whole plan. A Porfirian official later dispatched two soldiers to infiltrate their ranks. One of those men, a lieutenant, feigned defection from the military and betrayed a childhood friend, a top PLM leader, as he led a group of their men into an ambush at a Juárez jail. Over the next twenty-four hours, police on both sides of the border arrested more than twenty people and confiscated two hundred bombs, rifles, a large roll of fuse, and a cartridge belt in a one-room adobe hut in El Segundo. Once again, Aguirre was arrested and soon released. The Chihuahua governor provided American authorities with forged documents claiming that Aguirre had committed murder, charges that remain in the Justice Department files in Washington. But Aguirre was tried and released that December after a judge rejected the false evidence. As he went back to publishing *La Reforma Social,* the magonistas were already plotting their second attempt to take Juárez.

Ciudad Juárez, Chihuahua, Mexico
1908

The man whom Herlinda would one day call her husband settled in Ciudad Juárez in 1905 sometime after he had made the journey east from Guangzhou, like her father. Antonio Chew, born Yee Wing Chew, landed off the Pacific coast of Mexico with the hope of reaching the gold and silver mountains of California. He made it only as far north as Juárez with $100 in his pocket, which, according to the family lore, he used to open his first grocery store, La Garantía, two years later. It sat in the city's main plaza, near an old mission that the Spanish had founded in 1659, making Juárez the oldest colonial settlement along the U.S.-Mexico border.

The Mexican city, formerly Paso del Norte, had been renamed in 1888 in honor of Mexican president Benito Juárez, who had made it the capital of the entire Republic of Mexico for several months when he took refuge there in 1865. At the time, Juárez had been ruling his country by coach—chased into the Mexican state of Chihuahua in a bullet-ridden black carriage—as he and Díaz fought off an invasion by the French. When the railroads arrived, Ciudad Juárez had been a villa of at least 10,000 people, far larger and more prominent than El Paso, with a modest business district and squat adobe homes nestled among empty lots and vineyards. But the rumble of progress that transformed its northern American sister, historian Oscar J. Martínez has chronicled, initially devastated Juárez because it had less capital and less rail, making it ever more reliant on El Paso for trade with the eastern United States.

Juárez finally saw its own burst of growth when Díaz extended free trade restrictions along the entire Mexican side of the border. That allowed major American, European, and Asian stores to flood in, bringing fine goods and merchandise, including silk and wool. But the short-lived free trade zone era ended in 1891 when Díaz caved to pressure from Texas businessmen and Washington politicians angered that Americans were losing out on commerce. Businesses moved to El Paso, and many Juarenses joined the first major migrations of Mexicanos into the United States. And so it would be: two cities caught in a game of industry and capitalist ambitions, one often fated to rise at the expense of the other.

As Antonio stocked shelves and rang up customers in the spring of 1908, debate would have been simmering in Juárez, as it was across Mexico, over whether Díaz, now pushing eighty, would indeed run in the next presidential election in June 1910. The speculation would reignite the recruitment of the magonistas in a city now replete with working-class men and women from the region and from their country's deep interior as more campesinos lost land and went north.

Over the summer, the group began stockpiling homemade bombs, weapons, and ammunition for their next attempt to attack the city. Ricardo Magón had been captured and was locked up in a Los Angeles jail, but Aguirre and the other rebels in El Paso continued to fuel his rebellion. Magón's screeds were still being published in *Regeneración*, written in black ink inside the waistband of his pants and smuggled out by others.

Antonio's La Garantía would have benefited from the revolutionary commotion and the foot traffic along the nearby Avenida Juárez, which stretched from the main plaza to the rickety wooden planks that were then the Santa Fe International Bridge. Federal soldiers, at Díaz's behest, were filling a nearby garrison to enforce martial law in Chihuahua and the rest of the north. Workers, union activists, and revoltosos streamed in and out of the city, along with tourists and fronterizos, who came in for bullfights and sports games as Juárez found its financial footing in tourism and entertainment. At the Santa Fe, early in the mornings, Chinese truck farmers waited for customs inspections in lightweight horse-drawn wagons hauling fruits and vegetables from their farms in the Juárez Valley to sell to housewives on the other side.

If Mexicano liberals saw El Paso as a refuge of ideas, Chinese and Asian immigrants called it a "beacon of hope," says historian Irwin A. Tang. The city's Chinese community had become a popular stop in a circuitous route—aided by an underground network of Asian organizations, fixers, and smugglers—that helped Asian immigrants move across the United States in evasion of the immigration laws that designated Chinese laborers as an illegal "alien" class. After landing in San Francisco, historians say, many Chinese men sailed south on steamships to Mexican cities along the Pacific coast and then rode rail lines back up north to the border. Some paid smugglers to take them across for a fee. Others cut their queues, traded their blue jeans for trousers and serapes, and fooled inspection officers with a few crucial words in Spanish: "Yo soy Mexicano."

Once in El Paso, Tang and other scholars say, most picked up fake documents, spent the night with a friend or in a safe house, and boarded a boxcar on to New York, Chicago, or San Francisco. With time, Japanese, Korean, and Indian immigrants began tracing their steps. But, in 1908, Antonio would have seen the Chinese community in Juárez mushrooming around him as the United States continued to harden its measures to expel and deny Asian workers and more decided to stay. Chinese "line riders," the first version of the U.S. border patrol, now surveyed the region, and the nation's first federal immigration bureau had been set up, with spies who counted and traced Chinese immigrants. Agents took pictures of all the Chinese people deported to match them with the faces of those attempting to enter the United States.

As the whispers spread that the magonistas were on the verge of another attempt to seize the city, El Paso courts revolved with the cases of Mexican rebels and Chinese immigrants, "bad men," "criminals," and "aliens"—workers threatening the social order with their presence and their big ideas. Díaz's federal soldiers and other law enforcement officials again flooded the zone. Tensions in the borderlands rose once more, and in Juárez and across Chihuahua the embers stayed hot even after the PLM was again thwarted.

In late June 1908, responding to a tip from a suspicious neighbor, El Paso police raided the home of a Teresita Rebellion veteran coordinating between PLM leadership and its rank and file. They found guns hidden under mattresses, 3,000 rounds of ammunition, and a crucial stash of records, written in code, in a trunk. The cache included a letter naming all the PLM groups ready to attack. El Paso police again picked up Aguirre and again let him go.

The seizures and arrests led to more seizures and arrests, helping Díaz weaken the PLM and dampen the few uprisings that nevertheless flared up across the Chihuahuan countryside. But it was too late: By then dissatisfaction with el Porfiriato was cutting across race and class, and the liberal ideas of los magonistas, of Aguirre and Urrea—of Mexicano and Mexicana journalists, activists, poets, thinkers, and healers—had taken hold. Mexicanos were done with the dictatorship and a relentless "progress" without attention to its costs. The revolution was brewing, and Herlinda and Antonio would meet in its dead heat.

El Paso–Ciudad Juárez

1909 to 1911

Herlinda moved to Ciudad Juárez with her father and stepmother sometime in 1909. That October, old Porfirio Díaz, clad in a military tunic laced with medals and gold epaulettes, was welcomed in El Paso with the thunder of a twenty-one-gun salute as he arrived at the Santa Fe International Bridge. It was the first time a sitting Mexican president had stepped foot on American soil since Mexico had become a republic, and it would be the first time an American president, William Howard Taft, would return the honor. Díaz, historians say, was hoping to quell the revolt at his heels. And Taft . . . Taft was mostly interested in making sure American businesses in Mexico were safe.

The federal brick buildings in downtown El Paso were decked in patriotic bunting and wall-sized American flags. Men in silk top hats and Prince Albert coats waited to catch a glimpse of the presidents in the streets and in San Jacinto Plaza. Schoolchildren sang the Mexican anthem and waved Mexican and American flags. A parade in honor of the presidential pair later that day featured a long, winding dragon of papier-mâché that Chinese residents brought out every Chinese New Year, and the Chews could have even been in attendance that day.

The two presidents spoke at the chamber of commerce and were then shuttled in carriages, along with their military escorts, to Juárez for a lavish evening banquet at a customhouse. Only 150 distinguished guests were invited. The hall was transformed into a replica of the famous Versailles salon of King Louis XVI, with decorations valued at tens of millions of dollars in today's currency. There were red velvet draperies, cut glass from Chapultepec, and three train cars of flowers brought in from Herlinda's Guadalajara. The dinnerware and solid gold cups on the presidents' table were the same as those used by the Austrian archduke Maximilian, whom the French had installed in Mexico as emperor in the 1860s.

But no amount of diplomatic overtures and opulent gifts could stop the Mexican Revolution that would tear the borderlands asunder—putting El Paso at the center of American debates over the flow of people, labor, and ideas for decades to come. In the southern Mexican state of Morelos, as its governor mingled with the Juárez and El Paso aristocracia, Emiliano Zapata, a charismatic rancher, was organizing campesinos and Indigenous farm laborers to take up arms against the sugar plantation owners encroaching on their forests and villages. He was a reader of the Magón brothers' *Regeneración* and rallied his men with a signature phrase of los magonistas: "¡Tierra y libertad!"

In Mexico City, Francisco Madero, the short and squeaky-voiced scion of the wealthiest family in the northern state of Coahuila, had formed the Anti-Reelectionist Party and, at the time of the Taft–Díaz meeting, was mounting a long-shot presidential bid against Díaz. Madero, too, had been a reader of *Regeneración*—until the Magón brothers bent toward violence. Yet as Madero began drawing thundering crowds, including as he passed through El Paso months later, Díaz grew angry and realized he may have underestimated his rival. On the eve of the election, in June 1910, he had Madero arrested and jailed. Madero escaped and fled north to San Antonio, where he wrote a passionate call to action, insisting that there was no way to reinstate democracy other than through direct armed revolt.

He set the first rebellion against el Porfiriato to begin on November 20, 1910, the same date that los magonistas had been planning their third attack on Juárez—an action some historians believe Madero took to co-opt their movement. Initially, Madero's efforts appeared to fail: On November 20 he crossed the Rio Grande into his home state of Coahuila to lead the revolution, expecting, on the promises of an uncle, one hundred men to meet him on its banks. Only seven made it. Madero retreated to New Orleans, Louisiana, in embarrassment and exile. When Madero had all but deserted the cause, a friend and El Paso cattle agent convinced him to move to his Texas border city. Unbeknownst to them then, the uprisings had already broken out, first in Chihuahua and then in Morelos.

Soon the north and the south were in flames.

JOURNALISTS, PHOTOGRAPHERS, AND tourists flocked to El Paso and Juárez, as Romo has written, for a "ringside seat" to the revolution. In the spring of 1911, Madero and his revolucionarios were operating out of their junta's headquarters on the fifth—and at the time highest—floor of the Richard Caples Building in downtown El Paso. In the elegant, Victorian-style Merrick Building across the street, the Shelton-Payne Arms Company supplied arms and ammunition to many of Mexico's rebel factions. Just blocks away sat the Santa Fe Bridge.

From the confines of rooms 507 and 508, Madero and others enlisted the help of more guerrilleros. But as the Maderista rebels sought to keep their momentum, one plot remained unaccomplished: the takeover of Ciudad Juárez. They soon assembled an army at a camp on the western fringes of the Mexican city. The isolated stretch of dry brush was dotted by a few low-slung adobe huts that used to be a pig farm and hugged the border, a desert arroyo, and the towering viaducts of a railroad. On the other side, in El Paso, spread Smeltertown, a village that at one time had been home to more than 2,500 workers, mostly Mexicanos, who lived and labored under the shadows of the mountains and the American Smelting and Refining Company (ASARCO).

In the hut that became known as La Casa de Adobe, Madero holed up with his leadership, plotting and arguing over how and when to start la batalla de Ciudad Juárez. The city was heavily fortified, and many of the men still doubted whether Madero—a rich kid and spiritualist who had studied in Paris and Berkeley—had the military muster to lead them. Some worried he was too much of a moderate. But Madero knew how to curry favor with the public and the press. He also had the backing of much of the liberal political establishment in the United States, which had lost faith in Díaz after a PLM member had published a yearlong investigation into his administration's treatment of Yaqui Natives at work sites. It likened them to death camps.

As the borderlands were once again gripped in suspense, Madero's camp became a spirited meeting ground. He and other rebels, along with photographers and journalists from around the world, crossed into the camp from El Paso nearly every day on foot, using a long, narrow, and tottering rope bridge. Tourists took pictures in front of the huts with—and as—guerrilleros dressed in bandoliers and big sombreros, holding Winchester rifles or sitting on horses. Madero freely gave interviews, organized parties, and brought in bands and orchestras to keep the spirits up.

Herlinda would have been about sixteen. She and her friends, including the sons of some of her father's business associates, would buy food from a wholesale grocer in South El Paso and sell it to Mexican rebel soldiers encamped farther down the river, in a path of cottonwoods called Peace Grove. The meeting, courtship, and date of the marriage between Herlinda and Antonio remain a mystery to this day, but her family believes that it was during this spring that the two first crossed paths.

There is one photograph in particular that has survived, of a young woman with dark, straight, long hair. She is dressed as a soldadera, a female combatant of the war, wearing a black cotton dress that flows to her ankles, an embroidered belt, and a light bandanna around her neck. On her head is a black wide-brimmed hat, and crisscrossed over her shoulders are two ammunition belts, known as cartucheras. She holds binoculars in one hand and a rifle in the other. It is resting on the ground, barrel up, as she poses next to a worn-down adobe building with a wooden door and a large, circular crack in its wall.

Years later, some historical archivists would mistake the woman in the photo for a Yaqui fighter, but she was in fact Herlinda, a China Mexicana now coming of age in the embers that had been burning her whole life, whether she knew it or not. All around her, out of the frame, are Mexicanos and México Americanos engaged in the intellectual project of Western democracy, their debates—over race and class, immigration, land, and labor—playing out in not one nation but two.

On April 30, 1911, all of the leaders who would become the most recognizable figures of the Mexican Revolution—except for Zapata, who was too far south—gathered at Madero's camp at the edge of the El Paso and Ciudad Juárez border. The group of more than a dozen men posed for a photo in crisp shirts, double-breasted jackets, and Panama and bowler hats. They sat on wooden chairs in front of the adobe huts and dirt terrain. Madero is there in the middle, hands clasped, legs elegantly crossed. To his left is Abrahám González, the cattle agent who helped him establish la Junta in El Paso. He looks straight ahead, legs outstretched and crossed at his ankles. (Unlike Víctor Ochoa, El Paso's first revolucionario, he could indeed count relatives among the dead in the battles of Tomóchic.)

To Madero's right, staring into a different camera, is Francisco Vázquez Gómez, Díaz's former personal physician. And next to him is Venustiano Carranza, with his long, shaggy white beard and mustache, long before he broke with Pancho Villa, a former cattle rustler standing awkwardly behind him in a sombrero. And on the far opposite side from him is Pascual Orozco, a guerrillero who would eventually turn on Madero. He is wearing a campaign hat, slouched and manspreading.

There would be more disputes, more wrangling among the men and with Madero over logistics and timing. But on May 10, 1911, Villa and Orozco would take Juárez, two days after the shooting began and did not stop.

4

Pancho Villa's Teen Soldier

MEXICO WAS BURNING. Guerrilleros rose from the north to the south, Villistas, Maderistas, and Magonistas, Zapatistas, Orozquistas, and Reyistas, many of whom kept lairs in El Paso as they went out in search of young and able-bodied recruits to take up arms. They raided haciendas and occupied towns and villages. They set bridges on fire. They laid siege to the remnants of Porfirio Díaz's rurales, hiding out with Yaqui and N'dee tribes in the parched mountain ranges of northern Mexico.

El Paso had been Native before it was Mexican—before it had ever become American, its origins tracing those of our very nation. Now the ideological seeds that had been sowed in its back alleys and barrios had helped flare up the revolution that would from here on out shape the perceptions of our border and all those who cross it—a war that would set the foundations for all that was yet to come. Through this gateway of sand and brush, the Chews and the Martinezes, the Rubios, the Holguins, and the Mura'ls would pass in search of opportunity, refuge, and a better life. With each decade, the southern divide flanking the city would become sharper and more menacing, the journey to reach it deadlier. But El Paso would always remain a portal into the United States, the beacon at the edges—or the center—of its nation building and capitalism, sanctuary and exclusion, liberalism and conservatism, white supremacy and mestizaje.

The land trembled under the feet of fronterizos. The land trembled under the feet of Mexicanos. Only days after the fall of Ciudad Juárez in May 1911, Díaz surrendered and fled to Paris. Francisco Madero was elected the new president of the republic that very month, but just as quickly his supporters became disaffected. First of all, there was the matter of the land. There was always the matter of the land. There had been a time when more than 90 percent of Mexicanos had lived on farms or ranches or in rural villages. But when the revolution broke out, all of that land trembling under Mexicanos' feet had been in the hands of a powerful upper class that made up only 5 percent of the Mexican population. With Madero now in office, some of his far-left revolucionarios did not believe he was moving fast enough to fairly redistribute it. The conservative Porfiristas whom Madero had welcomed into his fold, on the other hand, vehemently disagreed.

To the south, Emiliano Zapata, the hero of Morelos, was the first to break, feeling betrayed that Madero seemed to have abandoned a fundamental principle: "La tierra es de quien la trabaja" ("The land belongs to those who work its soil")—the campesinos. To the north, in San Antonio and along the Texas border, Bernardo Reyes, a general who had once been banished by Díaz, saw a chance to grab power. His efforts fizzled as yet another Madero opponent, Emiliano Vázquez Gómez, attempted to lead yet another disaffected group in yet another capture of Juárez. Madero dispatched his two most trusted and popular fighters, Pascual Orozco and Pancho Villa, to blunt Vázquez's insurgency, only to watch Orozco—resentful he had been passed over for higher posts when so many of Madero's own relatives had been promoted—defect to the Vazquistas. Through the battles that followed, pitting Villa against Orozco, Villa would build his legend, and from the borderlands of Texas and Chihuahua to the agave fields of Jalisco, the people would call his name—"¡Viva Villa!"

To hear his supporters tell it, Pancho Villa was the guerrillero who took from the rich to give to the poor. Todo un Robin Hood, with his big mustache and even bigger belly. He was the Mexicano who gave the Yankees hell, a military mastermind with a persona so larger-than-life that he would come to appear in his own Hollywood films. Todo un movie star. Villa had learned a lesson or two about media image in Madero's camp, and he fashioned his own myth. As he climbed the ranks of Madero's military, he tended to exaggerate the grandness of his exploits, he learned to stand up straighter in his photos, and he leaned into his signature uniform, a wide-brimmed sombrero, cotton frock and trousers, and ammunition belts around his shoulders.

Before the revolution, Villa had been neither one of its intellectual architects nor one of its idealists but a business owner and a reformed thief. His real name was José Doroteo Arango Arámbula, and by his own accounts he had become an outlaw after he had shot a wealthy landowner in the foot when the man had attempted to abduct his teenage sister. Less generous versions of this story say Villa skipped town after he forced the county sheriff who eloped with her to dig his own grave and then shot and killed him.

As a bandit, Villa had taken on his grandfather's name, Francisco Villa, and though he had been born in Durango, just south of Chihuahua, he had come to know the golden hills of Chihuahua's Sierra Madre better than most men know themselves. Like la Santa, he knew which desert herbs could save the life of a man—or take it. These skills, according to historians like Kelly Lytle Hernández, allowed him to establish his own transportation company, moving ore extracted from the mines across the state's most dangerous mountain paths—routes that he had once taken and that were brimming with the kinds of bandidos he had once been. They also propelled his quick rise as an expert in ambushes.

As he took on Orozco, the keen-eyed general he had once called a friend and an ally, Villa roamed the borderland, often commanding his soldiers from the heart of Ciudad Juárez and filtering into and out of El Paso. He kept American journalists and diplomats abreast of Madero's progress and worked to ensure American companies continued to channel weapons and ammunition to Madero's army. Villa's fleet of carrier pigeons, which he was said to keep in a dovecote in Chihuahuita or elsewhere in South El Paso, brought him news from the battlefield, and his guerrilleros infiltrated deep into the country, rallying men to Madero's side even as Villa himself might have already been growing impatient with Madero and his failure to deliver on the revolution's most important cause: the land.

San Juanito de Escobedo, Jalisco, Mexico
1911

Chihuahua was burning, and so was Jalisco. The revolution was sweeping through Mexico when Pancho Villa's soldiers arrived at Miguel Martínez's door. Fifteen and an orphan, Miguel lived with his uncles on a ranch in San Juanito de Escobedo, a small town of farms and Spanish haciendas just west of Guadalajara, where he spent most of his days tending crops and herding cattle. It is impossible to know how Miguel felt about any of it—whether he believed in the war's lofty ambitions or craved Villa's glory, as so many men of his time did. Miguel is dead now, as is his son, Little Miguel. But in his living days, the son once recalled the time his father came to join Villa's army.

The story, as told to a nephew on New Year's Day in 2001, goes like this: The elder Miguel had been sitting at home with a cousin when a captain burst in.

"What are you doing here?" said the captain.
"I live here," Miguel replied.
"Do you have a job?"
"No."
"And you?" the captain said, turning to his cousin.
"No, me neither."
"Do you have a mother?"
"No," they responded.
"Do you have a father?"
"No," once again came the answer.
"Then you should come with us."

Before the troops departed, the boys told their uncle about the captain's proposition. He warned Miguel to do as the officer said. They had to go. The revolution wasn't kind to those who rejected the call to battle:

> "Son, you listen. Better I learn you were killed far away, very far away from me than to find you here one day, hanging from a tree."

Miguel did as he was told and left with the soldiers, though he didn't even know how to ride a horse. All he had were his uncle's parting words: "You'll teach yourself along the way."

Santa Eulalia of Aquiles Serdán, Chihuahua, Mexico,
1911 to 1914

At the first glimpse of Villa and his men riding in, their horses kicking up dust in arid winds, wealthy hacendados in villages across Chihuahua would scramble to stow away their gold and silver in wooden chests and large barrels, in canisters of tin, which they buried deep beneath the earth. The women, fearing rape or abduction, would hide in los hornos, large outdoor ovens of brick and clay that resembled beehives and were used to bake bread.

Santa Eulalia lay just southeast of the capital of Ciudad Chihuahua, a small mining settlement isolated in the sierra of the central part of the state. An eighteenth-century white stone church rose from the cobbled streets of Santa Eulalia's square and sheltered a gilded retablo honoring the village's namesake, Eulalia of Mérida, a teenage girl and martyr burned at the stake in Spain during a period of Christian persecution. Campesinos turned obreros settled in adobe homes along narrow dirt roads that curved around its silver mountains. Americans and foreigners had expanded the region's mines so much that a land price surge had helped spark the deadly 1892 battle between caudillos and Díaz's soldiers in Tomóchic, just to the west.

When Villistas came for Miguel, Victoria de la Rosa, the woman who would later become his wife, would have been three or four. Like Miguel, she is gone, and her relatives say they know little of her childhood in Santa Eulalia except that she was una chaparrita morenita, a plucky little brunette with chubby cheeks who was already exhibiting the independence and self-confidence of a Chihuahuense. They also know Villa killed one of her uncles and that she dreaded the thought of him storming into town so much that she carried an aversion for the guerrillero well into her later years.

Victoria's mother, Tiburcia, was said to have run her home with a stern hand. Her father, Ylario, rose with the sun to blast dynamite and claw silver ore from the depths of the darkness in a town where every day revolved around its silver mountain. Miners like him hauled rocks and crystals on their backs from a peak that rose behind Santa Eulalia and piled them into wooden baskets that they eased down with pulleys and wires into a plaza that stood near its church. At the bottom, workers melted some of the ore and purified the silver inside a hacienda with rustic furnaces. The rest they shipped to larger nearby smelters on the small black-and-silver steam trains that chugged along on private lines and connected the town to other mining villages in the region.

Santa Eulalia had been one of the many places where magonistas had recruited and organized disgruntled workers into rebels. As the Mexican government and foreign enterprise consumed arable land, the mining town was one of many where Mexicanos first stopped before ultimately deciding to keep heading north to the passageway in the mountains where El Paso and Juárez lay. In northern states like Chihuahua, workers could earn three times as much in mines, quarries, and textile factories and on railroads than the daily 25 cents they earned in the central regions of the country.

Victoria had been born near the camp in the fall of 1907. That same year, the mines of Santa Eulalia—and its miners—had helped make Mexico the top producer of silver in the world, but the prices of silver and copper dropped, causing financial panic in the United States. The de La Rosas, like Antonio Chew, who had just opened La Garantía in downtown Juárez, received an early glimpse into the precarious place of Mexicanos in a borderland where their labor could be just as easily dismissed as it was sought. American-owned mines shut down their operations across northern Mexico and laid off Mexican workers in the Southwest. Americans sought to declare a ban on Mexican immigration, and companies gave some 2,000 Mexicanos railway tickets to El Paso, where they crossed into Juárez, increasing the ranks of the unemployed in Chihuahua.

As historian Oscar J. Martínez describes it, the message to Mexicans was clear: "Don't come!" The situation got so bad, Martínez writes, that Mexicans looking to migrate north crowded in Juárez, where Mexican government officials hurried to arrange two hundred jobs with the railroads in

Chihuahua. But the pay was such a pittance—1.5 pesos daily—that few accepted them, preferring to wait out the panic and hope for the higher-paying work in the United States to return. Not even desperate pleas from the mayor would budge them.

Like Victoria's father, Villa had worked as a miner in Santa Eulalia. That would have been sometime in 1899, when, journalist Paco Ignacio Taibo II writes, Villa had briefly tried to leave banditry behind, only to find that the clean life did not pay: The labor of miners and masons was too burdensome, the wages too meager. Although the guerrillero would not thunder through Santa Eulalia again until much later—reportedly, residents say, to collect a debt—scouts in its hills kept an eye out for him.

Villistas strode through the state, enlisting veterans of its past northern uprisings, and pillaging horses, cattle, and weapons from the nearby estates of wealthy Spanish, American, and foreign businessmen. Three years later, the bloodshed and unrest had not ceased—not after Villa had beaten back Orozco, not after Madero and his vice president were executed. Villa moved on to fight for Venustiano Carranza and assembled la División del Norte, likely the largest revolutionary army ever formed in Latin America. They roved across the land. The land. If Chihuahua had made fertile ground for blood and war, it was because it was born of it and now filled with Mexicanos who had lost their land but who had also taken it. And in this, too, was El Paso's story.

BEFORE VILLA AND his soldiers traveled back and forth through the mountain pass, what would become Texas to its east and New Mexico to its north and Chihuahua to its south had been home to hundreds of tribes. Not so much a nation but a house. Few stayed in one place; rather they roamed, moving from room to room with the rhythms of the earth, with the seasons, always in search of water, their societies and shared ways of life linked to pueblos that ran all through what would become the American Southwest and northern Mexico. Their land was considered so bleak and unwelcoming that the Aztecs reviled it and its people. The earliest Spaniards, migrating north in search of fame, youth, and gold, all but spurned it, too, until the sixteenth century, when they realized silver existed in what are now the cities of Chihuahua and Parral, near Santa Eulalia.

Don Juan de Oñate made his entrada into the region then, on a mandate from King Philip II of Spain to search for riches and settle the land. The Spaniard traveled up from southern Chihuahua with hundreds of soldiers and families, sheep and cattle. In a damning mistake, they tried to take a shorter route cutting across its desert dune seas, and the group ended up wandering for four days without shelter or fresh water, searching for "el paso por las montañas" ("the pass through the mountains"). To their relief, they came across the Rio Grande and followed its course to a place just outside of El Paso now known as San Elizario. There, on April, 30, 1598, Oñate gave a sermon thanking God for deliverance from the desert. He also took formal possession of the surrounding land, calling it Paso del Norte, and designated it an outpost on the Camino Real, or Spanish royal highway, that traced the old Indigenous trade routes from Ciudad Chihuahua to Santa Fe, New Mexico. The ceremony known as la Toma—the Taking—would initiate two hundred years of Spanish reign.

The brutal battles intensified in Chihuahua as they did in Texas and the whole of the American Southwest. Spanish, mestizo, and Indigenous military colonists pushed northward with the backing of land grants and promises of citizenship from the Spanish crown, proselytizing or maiming and lynching the Indigenous peoples who sought to fend them off. Long before mestizo rebels rose up against Porfirian soldiers in Tomóchic, believing themselves immune to bullets under God and la Santa, Tarahumara Natives had used the same town as a base against Spanish invaders and Jesuit priests. Tarahumara leaders turned their colonizers' stories of Jesus and Easter Sunday on their heads, historian Paul J. Vanderwood says, propelling their guerrilleros to their cause with the prophecy that those who died fighting would rise from the dead. In 1680, Spanish soldiers and Franciscan padres arrived in Paso del Norte, in retreat after the Tewa Pueblo leader Popé and other Native Americans attacked the governor's palace in Santa Fe, driving away the colonizers. They had in their company or custody—it has long been debated which—317 Tiguas who would eventually settle in Ysleta del Sur Pueblo, sitting just south of El Paso, on what were the southern banks of the

Rio Grande until the river changed its course. The Pueblo Revolt would separate the Tiguas in El Paso from their culture, as other Native tribes would regard them as brujos, or witches, for their perceived betrayal. But Native historians like Rick Quezada, who is Tigua, would later unearth historical records showing the migration of their ancestors to the borderlands was coerced, the result of war and dislocation.

When Mexico declared its independence, many military colonists in Chihuahua sided with the Spanish, whom they credited with lifting their prospects. After Mexico won and the Spanish monarchy and the missionaries were gone, Mexican political leaders, including Presidents Benito Juárez and Porfirio Díaz, relied on the colonists to stave off the dissenting tribes as Mexicanos sought to fortify their young nation's boundaries and identity. The people who remained in Chihuahua were largely of mixed Spanish and Indigenous heritage, mestizos and light-skinned Mexicans resembling the social and ethnic makeup of Mexico's urban middle classes. They formed a largely egalitarian society. Still, their military colonists hated the wandering N'dee—whom they labeled "Apache," meaning "enemy"—for returning the violence unleashed on their people. Mexicano military colonists were sung about in corridos, or ballads, and hailed as heroes. The Chihuahuan government rewarded their hate: 100 pesos for the scalps of male warriors, 50 for those of women, and 25 for every child.

Then Mexico itself began losing its land: first to Anglo settlers who in 1835 opposed its decision to fully outlaw slavery and revolted in the state that would become Texas, and then to the United States, which claimed half of its northern territories in the name of Manifest Destiny. After Americans captured the last legendary Bedonkohe leader, Geronimo, in 1886, the Mexican government no longer had any use for its seasoned Chihuahuan military colonists, only their land. No longer the "bulwarks of order," anthropologist Ana María Alonso has observed, like the N'dee before them, they became the victims of progress. Criminals and Indios. Enemies of the state.

THROUGH EL PORFIRIATO, the land barons of Chihuahua kept on Taking. Enrique Creel, the governor who relentlessly pursued Lauro Aguirre, went so far in selling off communal lands to foreigners and Americans that even Porfirian officials told him, privately, to stop. It was a form of territorial assault that, as historian Friedrich Katz describes it, he had first deployed against Tarahumara natives, most of whom could not read or write in Spanish and struggled to defend their claims in corrupt courts. His father-in-law, Luis Terrazas, grew so rich that it was often said he had once been asked if he was *de* Chihuahua, and he had retorted: "Yo no soy *de* Chihuahua, Chihuahua *es* mío" ("I am not of Chihuahua; Chihuahua is mine").

By the time the rebels rocked Mexico from end to end in the winter of 1910, the Terrazas family and their associates alone had amassed at least 8 million acres of land and 1.5 million cattle, horses, goats, and lambs, in a state where 95.5 percent of people owned no property at all, according to Taibo and others. Creel and Terrazas fled, and Villa gradually ascended to the governorship of Chihuahua, at the behest of others, for a brief time: one month, from December 1913 to January 1914, in which Villa, a teetotaler, banned his troops from drinking alcohol, confiscated the estates of Spanish elites and the Creel and Terraza clans, and began building an estimated one hundred schools. Villa managed to stabilize the state, but he left the larger questions unanswered, such as how to fairly redistribute the land.

The land. The land. The land. Revolucionarios could not decide whether loyal guerrilleros who had fought for it or penniless campesinos who would toil on it deserved the land. The elites had not entirely relinquished the takings they saw as earnings, and the hostilities kept climbing. Mexicanos turned on Americans and Europeans and the Chinese. Mexicanos turned on Mexicanos. The dead hung from trees. The dead were dumped into wheelbarrows and thrust into shallow dirt graves. The dead rotted in scorched deserts where coyotes and wild hogs preyed. Young men like Miguel, heeding Villa's calls or fearing the heat of his bullet, rushed to join his forces, while Mexicans made landless now left their homeland, too, disillusioned by the revolutionary cause and the violence. And so, across Chihuahua, those who had always survived in a place where few others could were once again paying for the land in blood. From these skirmishes famous men would build their names. But there are no corridos about Victoria or Miguel Martinez, no legends or Hollywood movies. They were simply two throwaway kids of the revolution who would spend about seventy years together, married until death, but not before they each headed north, five years apart, amid the revolution that would upend their country and their lives.

Ciudad Juárez, Chihuahua
1914

Along the border, El Paso and Ciudad Juárez sat landlocked and anxious. To the north, towering buildings, including a twelve-story concrete-frame skyscraper, now gleamed under the Texas sun. To the south, workers and refugees would have streamed past the Chews' grocery store, La Garantía, and the bullet-pocked adobe buildings of Avenida Juárez to the Santa Fe Bridge. As his fame and army grew, Villa transformed Juárez, his presence and army occupying it from corner to corner.

The Chews settled in a barrio somewhere in between a customhouse and their grocery store in downtown Juárez. In those bloody and war-torn years of revolution, the streets often smelled of smoke and gunpowder. Sometime around when their first daughter, Josephine, was born in late 1913, they would have reeked of beer and wine. That winter, Villa basked in international acclaim for a brilliant maneuver during the Second Battle of Ciudad Juárez. He had tricked the city's federal garrison into allowing 2,000 of his revolucionarios to enter hidden aboard a hijacked coal car: Villa's Trojan train. He then ordered all the stocks of alcoholic beverages from bars and cantinas in the city destroyed.

In January 1914, months before the outbreak of World War I, Villa defeated Orozco militia members and federal forces in the rural border town of Ojinaga in western Chihuahua. Some 5,000 people passed through the Juárez borderland into El Paso. They were federal soldiers and their families and others from Ciudad Chihuahua who had supported the wrong side and feared Villa's retaliation. Photos captured women, men, and children wrapped in rebozos, serapes, and blankets, dirt and exhaustion across their faces as they marched into Fort Bliss. The refugees had roamed through the desert for eight days, a journey longer than Oñate's and so arduous that one newspaper had called it a "spectacle of despair." As El Paso city council members and angry citizens worried about disease, social disorder, and the stress on the labor market, Hugh L. Scott, the district military commander, attempted to assure them the newcomers would be kept under heavy guard, in a tent camp well lit and enclosed by barbed wire.

Antonio Chew had opened his first business in the financial panic of 1907. Now he launched his second in the middle of a war. In the spring of 1914, he and his business partner, Joe Yat Look, formed a grocery firm selling general merchandise near La Garantía. Antonio was a thin, handsome man with high cheekbones and slicked-back black hair who often dressed in an elegant three-piece suit and tie. Herlinda's daughters remembered that he had feuded with a Juárez restaurateur for their mother's hand in marriage. Herlinda had always been so beautiful and popular that her aunts liked to tell her she was descended from an Aztec princess, given her Indigenous roots. As Antonio grew his grocery business, Herlinda worked in the theater across the plaza, translating movie subtitles into Spanish, and began helping Chinese immigrants with their customs cases.

Life for the Chinese in Mexico was getting harder as landless and resentful Mexicano rebels and workers turned on a Chinese business class with which they had long struggled to compete. Chinese merchants tended to be young men who arrived in Mexico with well-established Chinese networks. Many worked for abysmal wages or hawked goods on the street and yet managed to open their own stores and businesses by relying heavily on their commercial experience and the financial credit and business contacts of friends, relatives, prominent community leaders, and fraternal organizations.

The deadliest massacre against the Chinese had occurred only days after the First Battle of Ciudad Juárez, in May 1911, when rebel forces led by Emilio Madero, Francisco Madero's brother, descended upon Torreón, a bustling, cosmopolitan city in the northeastern state of Coahuila. After Emilio's army took the city, his guerrilleros and an unruly mob of 4,000 people ransacked the thriving Chinese business district, destroying businesses and slaughtering men, women, and children. One Mexican tailor saved seventy Chinese immigrants by misdirecting the hordes, while another rescued eight people hiding in a laundry, telling their attackers they were not there. The daughter of a Maderista leader sheltered eleven people in her home and told soldiers who tried to enter that they would have to kill her first. More than three hundred Mexicanos of Chinese and Japanese descent were nevertheless slain. Madero reprimanded his brother, ordered him to stop the violence, and distanced himself from the massacre.

But more than three years later, racist attacks were becoming more widespread and arbitrary. Chinese people were mutilated and hanged. Hungry Mexicanos pillaged Chinese-owned fields and local food stores. Villa and his allies—along with revolucionarios of every other faction looking to clothe, arm, and feed their armies—pressured or forced wealthy Chinese merchants to loan them funds, offer them contributions, and sell them food and goods at a loss. Anti-Chinese activists and politicians inflamed the airwaves and tabloids, arguing that Chinese people had monopolized the laundry and restaurant businesses, taking away work from Mexican women. The arguments were particularly effective in swaying poor Mexicanas already struggling to keep their families afloat as their men went off to fight.

Sometime in 1914, Herlinda became friends with a couple of Villa's own scouts who frequented the cantina next to La Garantía. One of those Villistas warned the Chews to take their family across the river because a raid on Juárez was imminent—and it was going to be "a bad one." Fearing for the safety of other Chinese in her Mexican city, Herlinda, by now well liked by the U.S. immigration agents at the Santa Fe Bridge, asked them if she could bring some of her friends and loved ones over the border whenever the fighting started. According to her daughter, Herlinda promised they would return when it was over.

"Well, I think they could arrange that. Just tell us how many people will come across?" the agent said.

"Oh, about two hundred," Herlinda responded.

The agent balked at first. "Two hundred? Do you know what would happen if they saw two hundred people going across the border? You'd start a stampede."

But they finally came to an agreement. Her group would wait at the border, and only when the first shot was fired would they be allowed to cross.

When the battle erupted, Herlinda arrived at the pass through the mountains. She had with her two hundred Chinese people. They ran across as bullets flew over their heads. On the other side, with anti-Chinese racism also raging, the only place that would take them in was the Gateway Hotel, whose staff Herlinda would remain close to for years. True to Herlinda's word, an *El Paso Times* article states, they all returned to Juárez when the onslaught had ended.

5

The Year of the Hunger

Ciudad Juárez, Chihuahua
1915

From what his grandsons can gather, Miguel Martinez must have arrived in Ciudad Juárez sometime in spring of 1915. He would have been eighteen or nineteen. The city was in ruins. Buildings were leveled. Soldiers were camped out in the streets, in homes, in the adobe haciendas of millionaires like Luis Terrazas. There was no food, not even for the horses.

It was the Year of the Hunger. Typhus epidemics tore through the country, and many Mexicanos were dying of starvation. The liberal aspirations of the revolution had long been drowned out by the perpetual conflicts and petty egos of revolucionarios. Villa had fought alongside Venustiano Carranza and Emiliano Zapata to topple the conservative dictator Victoriano Huerta, and then he had turned on Carranza as he and many other revolutionary leaders vied for power. It would be the deadliest period yet.

The Villista forces that had picked up Miguel in San Juanito had given him a horse and a saddle—and, true to his uncle's words, he had taught himself to ride as they marched north, exchanging fire with federales and other rebel factions along the way. They wandered up through the rugged peaks and the wide, golden plains of Durango and Chihuahua, stopping in places like Parral and Ciudad Chihuahua outside of Santa Eulalia until they finally made it to the borderland. Though he fought for Villistas, Miguel once told a grandson that he had not considered himself to be on any one revolucionario's side. He watched over himself, killed who he had to, and did what he needed to do to survive, praying to God he would live to see another fight—or, better yet, that there would be no fighting at all.

In one harsh battle that Miguel recalled, he was forced to drop to the ground under the mesquites as shots ripped through the air and men scrambled in all directions. After it was all over, he got up, and there in the dust was a weathered picture of el Santo Niño de Atocha, whose statues had been carried by Spanish explorers to the New World: a boy pilgrim wearing a feathered, wide-brimmed black hat, a long blue tunic, and a scallop shell on his red cloak. He became a devotee then of the Christ Child, the patron saint of the wrongfully accused and the oppressed, of children and of travelers like the one he had become.

Miguel and his fellow soldiers did not stay in Juárez long. The captain and his commanders led the troops out of the city through a narrow forty-mile stretch of farmland flanking the Rio Bravo. Almost a century later, when Juárez was wracked by violence again, over drugs and cartel turf, it became known as the "Valley of Death." But the guerrilleros in Miguel's time only knew it appeared endless. They walked for days across the chaparral and dry soil, passing mesquites, bighorn walnut trees, and the occasional cottonwood. What Miguel seemed to remember most, his son would say years later, were the pangs of hunger that rattled his insides. Just on the other side of the river, El Paso beckoned. There was plenty of work there, people whispered, and food to eat and no war.

More and more soldiers were abandoning rank, quietly slipping over the border in search of new and more promising horizons. Likely somewhere about an hour south of El Paso, near what are now the Mexican villages of Guadalupe and Práxedis Gilberto Guerrero—the latter named after a magonista—Miguel and a family he knew decided it was time they followed. But the couple's son, Juan, was marching with the troops at the head of the line. He was a teenage boy only slightly younger than Miguel and someone whom Miguel considered family. He agreed to retrieve him and meet Juan's parents along the Mexican side of the river overnight. Miguel walked for hours that day, past the masses of soldiers on foot, to where the captains and sergeants rode on horseback. When he finally spotted Juan, the troops were already setting up camp as darkness fell over the Chihuahuan monte. A captain started counting the men and put Miguel in charge of keeping watch over the horses. Miguel urged Juan to stay alert that night and not fall asleep so they could bail. But at midnight, when Miguel was done with his watch and tried to signal to Juan, the boy did not come.

Miguel crouched his way back to where the rest of the soldiers were lying on blankets and old serapes, and he found Juan with his eyes closed. He was too weak from starvation to move. Miguel picked him up and carried him away. With Juan in his arms, he walked all night along the Mexican side of the river, following the water's edge so as not to get lost. Near dawn, he finally found Juan's mother and father. The four embraced and then waded across the river to the United States.

On the other side, as the sun rose, they found more brush and sand and desert, and Miguel could no longer go on. He had not rested all night. He had not eaten a thing. He was dying of thirst. The desert of Chihuahua was scorched and extreme and inhospitable, as the earliest Indigenous nomads had known, and as Don Juan de Oñate had learned. Rain was scarce and evaporated almost as quickly as it fell to the earth.

Miguel told them to go on, dropped underneath a mesquite, and slept. He did not wake up until the afternoon. As his son relates it, an American was staring at him.

> "What are you doing here, boy? You're Mexican, right?" the old cowboy said.
>
> "Yes."
>
> "And where are you going?"
>
> "To look for work."
>
> "Do you want to work for me? I have plenty here."
>
> "Yes."
>
> "Seriously?"
>
> "Yes." Miguel nodded.

"Okay, you see those cows. I have three. Take care of this cow while I take these other two back to the ranch. But take care of her for me."

Miguel stayed and watched the cow. Not too long after, the man returned with a jug of milk and a pair of large gorditas. Miguel devoured them and then set out with the rancher to his house on the American side of the border. Miguel had found his first job in his new country.

THE WAY OUR grandparents and their parents remember it, the border that Miguel crossed was but a line in the sand. There were no long, winding processions of cars making their way over international bridges. No barbed wire. No politicians in Ohio or Michigan raising campaign money off fears over who or what may be coming across. Families could walk over the Rio Grande and have picnics on its banks, with relatives and their children from both sides of the divide splashing in the river's waters.

The earliest efforts to patrol and enforce the shifting dividing line between what would become Mexico and the United States came with the Spanish, who, after the Taking, set up presidios to defend their villages and the Indigenous communities they had evangelized against the N'dee. After the United States and Mexico went to war came the Splitting, and to secure the new border the U.S. military established Camp Calhoun in 1849, at the confluence of the Gila and Colorado Rivers, at what would later become Fort Yuma in Yuma, Arizona. The Gadsden Purchase, an agreement between the two nations that afforded the United States even more of southern Arizona and New Mexico, further modified the border a few years later. More strategic forts followed, including Fort Bliss in El Paso. Infantry and cavalry units, as well as Native American scout units, were expanded to walk the line. In Texas, historian Monica Muñoz Martinez relates, the military received backup from the Texas Rangers, who were known for their big Stetson hats, cowboy boots, and Colt revolvers that they tended to deploy at will and without mercy.

The U.S.-Mexico boundary was as quickly contested as it was drawn. The

United States sought to push it southward and Mexico northward, one side always fearing invasion from the other. With each struggle, the Mexicans became more Mexican and the Americans more American, and from then until Geronimo handed over his rifle in 1886, both waged warfare on the Native tribes that saw them both as invaders and did not recognize either of their boundaries but soon began to use them to their advantage, fleeing into one country to escape attacks or retribution from the other. The pursuers sometimes crossed borders, whether Washington or Mexico City authorized it or not, as did fronterizos, who were not yet quite fronterizos but becoming more so every day, caught in the liminal space between the formation of two nations and two national identities, each with its own magnetic center pulling the region apart.

As Villa and Zapata fought Carranza, the past and future met at the dividing line. Carranza fired back with weapons and techniques used in World War I: sophisticated machine guns, barbed wire, and trenches. Villa struggled to hold his renowned División del Norte together, as historian Friedrich Katz has documented, because most of his generals showed him little allegiance and refused to fight far from their native regions. His forces fractured into smaller groups that waged guerrilla warfare and retreated into the Sierra Madre of Chihuahua. At times, they had the help of N'dee and Yaqui natives, whose ancestors had forged their own escape routes into the mountains since the days of Spanish rule. When President Woodrow Wilson supported Carranza over Villa in late 1915, enraging Villa, Katz writes, the revolucionario focused on provoking an American invasion in an attempt to force Carranza, his enemy, into a hard place.

In calculated moves, in January 1916, his forces captured seventeen Americans from a Mexican train and massacred them at Santa Isabel in northern Mexico. Roughly two months later, on March 9, he did what the United States had feared since it had first invaded its southern neighbor in 1846: He led about five hundred of his ragtag rebels over the border, under the cover of dusk, into Columbus, New Mexico. For a couple of hours the invading guerrilleros plundered and fired, as surprised U.S. cavalrymen struggled to saddle up and hold them back. Villa had planned a small raid of the garrison to confiscate much-needed arms, ammunition, livestock, and dynamite. But the confrontation with the Americans escalated into a full-blown battle that took the lives of more than one hundred Villistas and seventeen Americans, including the pharmacist, the grocer, the hotelkeeper, and the married couple who owned the only dry goods store in town.

Walter H. Horne, one of the many East Coast transplants to move to El Paso because of his ailing health, had started selling photograph postcards of Mexican Revolution battles and rushed to Columbus that morning with his camera. He captured the smoky ruins, the adobe homes razed. An eyewitness recounted the horror in the streets and on the sidewalks where Villa's fallen men lay dead and dying. "Some twitched, some mumbled, most were sprawled in the abandoned posture of death," the person said. "Except for an occasional curse, they were left ignored. Later in the day they were gathered, stacked and burned."

But perhaps it was these lines in the handwritten testimony of Mary Slocum, the cavalry commander's wife, who weathered the attack with other Army wives and children in the one-story house of a lieutenant—the women sprawled on the floor, the girls and boys crawling under the beds, as shots pierced holes in clothes hanging against the wall—that captured just how much there would be no turning back. "When we came out of the house, the dead and wounded were everywhere," she said. "I did not know I could have such hate in my heart. I saw Mexicans horribly wounded and suffering terribly and did not care how much they suffered."

A headline printed in American newspapers the next day read:

Pancho Villa Must Die

El Paso, Texas
1916 to 1917

Where was Villa? In El Paso, the cables with sightings and knowledge on the revolucionario's potential whereabouts shot back and forth between officials in Washington and Fort Bliss, between generals along the border and other interested parties. They flitted in from Tucson and Nogales and Columbus, New Mexico. They shot across Texas, to Brownsville, Eagle Pass, Del Rio, and Houston. They carried information from Ciudad Chihuahua and Casas Grandes and Namiquipa and Guerrero and Torreón. There was one from an American millionaire worried about his mining company in Terlingua, writing from the Congress Hotel in Chicago.

Villa's attack on Columbus had been the first—and would be the last—military invasion by foreign forces on American soil since the British had burned down the White House and the U.S. Capitol during the War of 1812. One day later, Hugh L. Scott, who after the 1914 refugee crisis had ascended to the post of major general at Fort Bliss, fired off a memo with instructions from the president and secretary of war: The Southern Department of the U.S. Army was to organize a military force under Brigadier General John "Black Jack" Pershing to pursue the Mexican band that had invaded New Mexico. He was authorized to hire whatever guides and interpreters he needed and to deploy San Antonio airplanes for surveillance—the first time U.S. Army pilots and aircraft would ever be used for an operational mission. Commanders stationed at bases across the border, from Chihuahua and Sonora or within the fold of possible Villa operations, were to exercise the same military defense and pursuit tactics that they had wielded for years in cross-border raids along the U.S.-Mexico dividing line.

Pershing, a West Point graduate and the son of a general store manager from Missouri whose family had survived the Civil War, was known for his tactical proficiency and methodical planning. He also knew the bloody wars of the Southwest well. One of his earliest military assignments had been to lead the troop of Black officers within the 10th U.S. Cavalry Regiment, whom Plains tribes called buffalo soldiers for their dark, curly hair and fierce ways of fighting, as they helped run the Native Americans off their land. The assignment had earned Pershing, a white man, his nickname "Black Jack" before he went off to fight the last Apaches who refused to be displaced to reservations.

On March 15, 1916, to the cheers of crowds on a bright day in Columbus, Pershing set off into Mexico on Scott's directive. It would be called the Mexican Punitive Expedition. He had horses, field artillery, trucks bedecked with American flags, Texas Rangers, and a contingent of about 4,800 military men, including buffalo soldiers and Apache scouts from Fort Huachuca in Arizona.

The flurry of telegrams intensified across the borderland as the search for Villa continued for weeks and months. Villa was moving his command west and south of Boca Grande. He was following the river, his soldiers leaving their possessions strewn along the line of retreat from Columbus. Villa had captured Guerrero and Miñaca, killing 170 opposing soldiers. Now he was continuing south. He had killed some Americans. He was expected in Chihuahua on Sunday or Monday, where confidential sources believed he would execute foreigners. Where was Villa? He was variously reported moving north or northeast. His actual location on any given night was unknown. He was headed to Satevó. He might be in the mountains south or southwest of San Francisco de Borja. Reward recommended: $50,000 offered for his delivery (about $1.6 million today); $5,000 for any information that led to his capture (more than $166,000 today). He was said to have a gold crown on a left upper molar. A doctor indicated he also had an incomplete fracture on his right greater trochanter bone that would make it possible to identify his skeleton.

By early spring of 1916, the Pershing expedition had rumbled across more than 350 miles of dirt roads. Villistas were said to destroy garrisons. Villistas were said to fire on trains. Villistas had reportedly wrecked and burned rail lines and blown up the locomotive to Cuernavaca, fourteen kilometers from Mexico City, killing and injuring some two hundred passengers, including a member of the military guard. They were said to have sent a Carrancista general thirty pairs of ears as a gift that they had torn from the heads of Carrancistas. Tension was so high between Mexicans and Americans that many Mexican merchants refused to serve the military men they saw as gringo invaders, and the Carranza administration denied them the use of nationalized Mexican railroads. Villa was helped by his friends, just as he was by his enemies, who preferred to watch Chihuahua burn than deliver him to the United States. And burn it did. Pershing's men pushed through mud and sand as supplies dwindled. U.S. Army engineers built new roads into Mexico and rebuilt the bridges that Villistas had destroyed.

The most crucial aid to their survival came from Chinese and other Asian merchants who had tired of the abuse from Villistas and other rebel forces. In the larger towns, where they ran some of the most popular stores and cafés, they took the business of Pershing's military. They helped keep their canteens filled with boiled water to protect them from dysentery. Some even set up wagons and shacks made of twigs where they sold the troops comfort supplies—including soap, towels, tobacco, matches, candy, fruits, donuts, and pastries—as the dusty and weary soldiers wandered through the desert brush. Within months, more than three hundred Chinese people were working around Pershing encampments as merchants and tailors, cooks and launderers. In the El Paso and Ciudad Juárez region, Antonio Chew's grocery firm, Chew and Look, had become one of the largest wholesale suppliers, and his grandchildren believe it is highly likely that it was among the Chinese businesses stocking the many Chinese and few Mexican merchants traveling with Pershing's troops. The services were so welcome and essential that when Pershing headquartered his men at Camp Dublan that fall, he allowed the Chinese to build a modest "Chinatown" inside its perimeter. The base, which lay in Colonia Dublan, a couple of hours southwest of Juárez, soon housed Chinese stores, a few small cafés and barbershops, and a pool hall.

This incensed the Mexican rebels. Villistas slaughtered los Chinos out of Sinophobia, out of disdain for capitalists, out of resentment for their close association with the North Americans and Europeans they so distrusted. The anti-Chinese hatred ramped up further as Villa's forces began to dissolve, leaving many unemployed Mexicans to linger in poverty or migrate. In June and July, the cables went on. The reports circulating claimed the "Mexican mind" now believed that war was inevitable if Americans did not withdraw their soldiers. Mexican generals warned they could not ensure the safety of American citizens in Chihuahua because Mexican public sentiment had turned so much against the Americans. And where was Villa? Pershing's men still did not know. He was said to have been shot, punctured by a bullet that passed through the back muscles of both thighs without striking a bone. Yet a man who saw him four days later said he was on the mend: Villa could ride his horse again and had about 1,000 men. It was reported that he was gathering horses throughout the country. It was reported that he had split his forces into two marauding bands. It was also reported that he was riding on horseback with a stiff leg.

In El Paso, hotels like Paso del Norte, where patrons had gathered to watch the First Battle of Ciudad Juárez from the rooftop, popcorn and lemonade in hand, were still crawling with operatives and spies from different factions of revolucionarios and foreign governments. Now many were enlisted in the search for Villa. Felix A. Sommerfeld, a Jewish German secret agent who had worked for Madero near the Santa Fe Bridge and in la Junta's headquarters at the Richard Caples Building, drafted reports on Mexican consular agents in border states and tracked the shipments of arms. Not too far away, on the opposite end of El Segundo Barrio, Lieutenant Henry Ossian Flipper, the first Black West Point graduate and the first Black commanding officer of the buffalo soldiers, supplied a U.S. Senate subcommittee with information on the Mexican front. Flipper, who had been born enslaved in Thomasville, Georgia, had been dismissed from the military in 1882 when a white colonel accused him of stealing funds, a likely racist attack for which he was acquitted. But in the Southwest, where borders were drawn and redrawn, he had been able to reinvent himself as an engineer, surveyor, and translator. He even published a pamphlet on Estevanico, the enslaved Black Moor who traveled with the earliest group of Spanish explorers believed to have wandered through El Paso and the first man of African descent to traverse North America. It was titled *Did a Negro Discover Arizona and New Mexico?*

The military missives from the borderland that fall said an informant of Lieutenant Flipper's saw Villa in October with his own eyes. He apologized to Flipper because Flipper had been quite right: Villa was alive. He had arrived in San Isidro on a dummy train from Cusi. He had ridden into town carrying his crutch and gone into the main plaza at once. The band he brought with him had played, and many had shouted "¡Viva Villa!" as he gave a rousing speech. Villa reportedly said that Americans were coming in from every direction—that Carranza had sold out most of Mexico—and called on his beloved paisanos to join him in running the gringos out of the country. Some three hundred signed up but, to Villa, that had not been enough, and Villistas were said to have killed three men who refused. Many others were supposedly beaten, tortured, hanged, or burned with hot irons. The town, the informant went on, had been left desolate.

Miguel Martinez entered the United States through El Paso as a laborer that same month—on October 10, 1916—one of only two times we can say for certain he crossed into the United States after he first waded across the river; the other time being July 12, 1915. We know this because of two pocket-sized border crossing cards that have survived. One of those captures him in a grainy black-and-white photo. He is wearing a suit and tie and has a thin mustache and dark hair. The card says he is five feet, four and a quarter inches tall and that he has "two small scars on his left hand." Though it is difficult to make out the color of his jacket or the outline of his lips, his gaze straight into the camera is unmistakably self-assured and proud.

There is no historical consensus on why Villa did what he did. But there is no question he amplified the American fear of the Mexican. Americanos had dreaded an invasion from Mexico since la Santa had appeared in the borderland amid the embers of the earliest uprisings. They had feared it since los magonistas plotted to take down Juárez, not once, not twice, but three times. And they had especially feared it as late as 1915, when, during the worst of the revolution's violence, an anonymous group of Mexican and Tejano rebels had drafted a shoddy manifesto titled "Plan de San Diego." It had declared the creation of an army of Mexican nationals, Native Americans, and Mexican Americans to rebel against the United States. More clearly, it called for a race war and the slaying of every Anglo man over sixteen years of age to achieve la "Reconquista," or the liberation of Texas, New Mexico, Arizona, California, and Colorado. The reasons for the existence of the document have been as widely debated as Villa's motives for the attack on Columbus. Some historians believe it was purposely written with overzealous rhetoric to push the United States into backing one less radical revolutionary group over another—which the United States eventually did. (The plan was written in San Diego, Texas, but signed by prisoners in a Monterrey jail. Though Ricardo Magón's writing appeared to have a direct influence, he denied the connection, calling the plot a "bourgeois invention.") Nevertheless, it injected more racial animosity into a state already brimming with it.

For Mexican laborers like Miguel, these years marked a new reign of terror. The courts continued to churn with the cases of Mexican rebels and Chinese laborers. The line riders set up under the Chinese Exclusion Act in 1904—totaling only about seventy-five to seventy-seven officers at any given time—went after more Mexicans. Whether battles across northern Mexico were won or lost, historian David Dorado Romo and others say, often depended on whether revolucionarios could smuggle the arms and livestock their troops needed out of the major customs ports in El Paso and Juárez. Many bands of men, some of them rebels, some solely committed to banditry, exploited the profitable trade for their own gain or to seek restitution from Anglos for the injustices they had inflicted upon Mexicans and Mexican Americans in Texas. The border raids and livestock thefts committed against Anglo ranchers and farmers only amplified the perceptions of Mexicanos as enemies and criminals.

The cases enraged the Rangers, which, since the earliest days of the border's formation, had struggled to expand their influence in El Paso and West Texas, its limits too far out of reach, la conciencia colectiva too strong. Their treatment of Mexicans, particularly those with darker skin and who did not speak English, became harsher and more indiscriminate, historians say, the tactics more brutal and tainted by deep racial animosity. In South Texas during 1910 and 1920, a period now called la Matanza (the Massacre), Anglo settlers, including local law enforcement and the Rangers, killed hundreds if not thousands of Mexicanos and México Americanos along the border. Some photos capture Rangers—or "rinches," as Mexicanos called them—smiling or standing proudly beside the bodies of their bloodied and mutilated Mexican victims. One survivor recalled they had picked up his cousin from their farm because they "thought he was a bandit." They placed him in front of a cross in a cemetery a block away and shot him point-blank. "The 'rinches' just apprehended people and took them," the witness said. "We were afraid to challenge them because they were like big animals and they had guns."

And still the search for Villa continued. In November 1916, with typhus continuing to ravage the country, refugees arriving at the border warned that Villistas were occupying Santa Rosalía, Jiménez, and Parral. Mexico's working-class people were the most likely to have news of where Villa might be, operatives reported, but they were not talking. Their sympathies remained with Villa—or they feared his retaliation for "loose tongues." Villa took his revenge on the Chinese in late 1916 when his rebel forces attacked Chihuahua again. This time they seized the capital after three days of intense fire, and Villa allowed his men to kill more than one hundred Chinese people, including women and children. The cables reaching the borderland reported that Villa had launched an attack on Ciudad Chihuahua at eleven o'clock; that women were suffering abuse at the hands of Villa's soldiers; that Chinese refugees from Jiménez were continuing to relay the general massacre of their compatriots, Arabs, Spaniards, Japanese, and one American who was burned at the stake; and that more of Villa's rebel victims were arriving at the border with their ears cut off.

Where was Villa? Pershing never did find him. The Carranza administration wanted the Americans out of Mexico. And the American public wanted their soldiers to return. World War I was threatening to embroil the United States, and Pershing was soon called to Europe, where he would win his most famous battles. The Mexican Punitive Expedition officially ceased on February 5, 1917. But the borderlands—where Anglo Americanos turned on los Mexicanos and los Mexicanos turned on los Chinos, in lands wounded and bleeding since the Taking and the Splitting—had served as critical military training grounds for soldiers and combat pilots as troops engaged in battles with Villa's forces and both sides took heavy losses. The fate of border cities like El Paso and Juárez as militarized zones was sealed before Pershing and his men headed off to fight in France.

6

Of Lice and Villistas

IN THE FALL of 1913, as Villistas attacked mines and rail lines, camps and factories were once more shuttered across Chihuahua. Victoria Martinez's father, Ylario de la Rosa, jumped on the boxcars that rattled and roared and shook the earth as they moved through towns and cities on fire, tracing Indigenous trade routes worn and expanded by Mexican and Spanish colonists. Despite the war raging around them, the railroads had not stopped bringing hundreds and hundreds of Mexican blue-collar workers to the bustling mountain passageway by which El Paso and Ciudad Juárez remained so irrevocably linked.

El Paso stretched for miles at the foot of the mountains. With the arrival of rail, most of the adobe homes constructed in the traditions of Apache and Jumano tribes had been torn down—seen as obstacles to progress—and in their place rose bungalows and Queen Anne mansions of brick, wood, and stone. Hot winds blew through cypresses and mesquites. As the Mexican Revolution lumbered on, American and Mexican troops combed its borderlands. On the city's scenic overlooks, where one day teenagers would kiss into the night, cannons were now stationed, their barrels pointed down at its Mexican sister. But the desire for Mexican laborers across the American Southwest remained insatiable. Corporations needed obreros to operate machinery and traqueros to lay tracks and mineros to excavate silver and copper as far as Arizona, Colorado, and California. Wealthy families needed so-called domestics—women, young and old—to clean their homes, cook their food, and care for their children. Americans needed masons, farmhands, and gardeners, laundresses and seamstresses, shoemakers and shoe shiners, sales- and hotel clerks, factory grunts, bar hands, dishwashers, waiters, and more.

Ylario, who might have been one of thousands of miners across Chihuahua suddenly thrown out of work, or who might have simply felt the pull of the north, would have shuffled down Avenida Juárez with other workers to the inspection center at the Santa Fe Bridge as wagons and automobiles barreled down the dirt-paved roads. He would have heard the clanking of glass bottles and thud of crates inside shops, the hollers of Mexican vendors who sold corn, spices, and dried red peppers out of handwoven baskets. Like Herlinda and Antonio Chew, he might have caught the smell of smoke and gunpowder.

The mules that once carried fronterizos and well-dressed tourists south over the international line into Juárez and back north into El Paso over the Santa Fe Bridge had been replaced with electric streetcars. On the American side, John Mckiernan-González has written, medical and immigration inspectors monitored the bridge and railroad passenger cars. They distinguished "between upper- and lower-class Mexican nationals; between Chinese nationals, Chinese Mexicans, and Chinese Americans; and between Syrian nationals and Syrian Mexicans." Some they subjected to humiliating inspections. Most Chinese travelers they forbade from entering at all.

Once in El Paso, Mexicano workers hustled in manufacturing plants like the Southwestern Portland Cement Company and the Pearson box factory, in small packing houses like Swift and Armour and Morris, or in one of the many brick and mortar wholesale houses stocking cotton and woolen goods, hats, boots, and shoes, equipment for the agricultural and mining industries, furniture, and liquor. A wave of contractors and hiring agents would have met Ylario as soon as he left the bridge, near the Sacred Heart Church and the brick tenement on Third and Oregon where Teresa Urrea had lived. They hailed from farm agencies and smelting and mining companies, but mostly they came from America's biggest business at the time: the railroads, giants like the Southern Pacific and the Santa Fe, which competed for workers and saw Mexicans as essential to their expansion. The loud and rowdy crowds of agents hollered out pay and benefits packages in aggressive attempts to lure the most laborers to their crews.

"Come, I'll get you a job!"

"Come, come, I'll hire you!"

"Come, I'll get you a job!"

THROUGH THE BLOODIEST years of the war, Ylario joined the ebb and flow of Mexican traqueros who rushed in to fill the railroad jobs left behind in the United States by Chinese and Asian workers banned under the nation's Chinese exclusionary laws. Even as guerrilleros kept rising and falling and rising again, even under the watch of Rangers, line riders, and soldiers, Black, Mexican, and Chinese workers continued to pass through El Paso, as did Jewish, Italian, Syrian, Greek, Lebanese, and Slavic workers. As did Ylario.

But El Paso and its workers were on the brink of another foundational moment for the nation and its borders—one that in time would link the fate of the Martinezes and the Chews, as it would the fate of Mexican and Chinese laborers and later their American-born kin and all those "other" immigrants and children of immigrants caught somewhere in the space in between. Beginning in 1870, amid isolationism, economic downturns, and growing anti-Chinese racism in the West, Congress had begun to exclude full categories of people from entering the country. To fund its expanding migration bureaucracy and enforcement and to discourage immigration, it instituted and later increased a head tax on each immigrant—from 50 cents to $4, or from about $17 to nearly $134 in today's dollars. Over the next few decades, the calls from Americans for more stringent border restrictions would continue to build as an ascendant class of white nativists and eugenicists raised the alarm not only about the war consuming Mexico but also about the changing makeup of the United States.

To the far northeast, on Ellis Island, New York, then the nation's busiest port of entry, migration patterns were changing. More people were coming in—not from northern and western Europe as it had been for generations but from Italy and Poland, from across eastern and southern Europe, from the Middle East and Asia. These "new immigrants" were different, so went the pseudoscience in mainstream American politics, newspapers, and academic circles—the kind of racist and since disproven theories that had been spreading and evolving since Porfirio Díaz had heeded the advice of his Científicos. Nativists and eugenicists believed the newcomers could pose a threat to the white character and culture of the United States because of their inherent characteristics, mainly a lack of intelligence and physical fitness and a propensity for disease and criminality. As officials clamped down on Ellis Island, attention also turned to the *other* Ellis Islands, gateways into the United States that have not held as revered a place in its national mythos, though they have been no less significant to its origins: Angel Island in San Francisco, where mostly Chinese immigrants could be detained for weeks, months, or even years in conditions that many likened to prisons; and El Paso, a large and busy port of entry where people could move freely across a U.S.-Mexico border that Americans saw as "the nation's backdoor."

In the wretched winter of 1915, by which time Miguel Martinez would have joined Ylario in his comings and goings through El Paso (though their paths had not yet crossed), the alarm over Mexicans and other "undesirable" immigrants arriving at the southern border escalated even further with the rise of typhus in Mexico. The illness was miserable. It could be spread by lice carrying the bacteria and tended to appear in the form of a crusty, dark red-and-brown rash on the trunk of a person's body that multiplied into tiny red bumps across the arms and legs, chest, neck, and groin. Then came the chills, fever, and nausea, the convulsions, the vomiting, and diarrhea. The most severe cases ended in delirium, bleeding, and finally death. Venustiano Carranza, who became the nation's de facto leader as he battled with Pancho Villa, believed the typhus epidemic so grave and disturbing that he established public baths and barbershops that December to force people of "unclean appearance" to bathe. Civil authorities in Mexico City that same month began denying sick people entry to streetcars, churches, theaters, and other public venues.

There were strong public health reasons to limit the flow of travelers and migrants to help contain the disease. But flawed theories about race and genes also underlay the public fear. Even before the federal government ever stepped in to regulate the nation's borders, as Michael A. Schoeppner has chronicled, southern enslavers used racist tropes and fears of "contagion" in passing the first state immigration restrictions. They sought to prevent Black sailors from entering ports in Florida and South Carolina, Schoeppner points out, saying they could bring infectious ideas of Black liberty and autonomy that could lead to a "race war" pandemic. The arguments were particularly aimed at Black mariners from Haiti, where enslaved Haitians were close to overthrowing their French masters in what would become the only successful slave revolution in modern history.

For decades after that, he and historians like Alexandra Minna Stern have observed, white nativists and eugenicists, including eminent scholars at East Coast institutions like MIT and Harvard, continued to spout such rhetoric as they applied their "scientific" methods to what they saw as the "most pressing" challenges of the day: the "Indian race problem" nationwide; the "Black race problem" in the Deep South; the "Asian race problem" in the West; and the "Mexican race problem" in the American Southwest. At the nation's southern border, eugenicists believed Mexicans to be dirty, less intelligent, and racially inferior, or worse, contagious. As early as 1903, historian Mario T. García writes, the El Paso Medical Association contended that the "unrestricted immigration of Mexican 'peons'" was a potential health concern for the city and the entire country. The "most objectionable class" waded over the river, García reported the association argued, as it called on Washington to ban these Mexican workers for a year. (It did not. Their labor was too badly needed.) With the outbreak of the revolution, as historian Raúl Reyes (Ylario's great-grandson) has found, many now also regarded Mexicanos as a national security threat: criminals, political radicals, and anarchists at the edge of a "border revolution," out to overthrow the white man and reclaim the entirety of what used to be Mexican land.

In El Paso, concern over the disease and its potential carriers was especially high as more Mexicans came over the border. The city had boomed from nearly 15,000 people in 1900 to almost 40,000 in 1910, largely due to the migrations of Mexican laborers and refugees. The Mexicanos were rich and poor, miners, obreros, and campesinos, along with businessmen and clerics and intellectuals. They had been changing the demographics and political dynamics of the city. They had been opening up their own theaters and schools—their own Spanish-language newspapers for Mexicans and Mexican Americans eager to hear the latest about the revolution and still clashing over its ideals. Lauro Aguirre, who remained in El Paso, came to count more than twenty publications grinding out broadsides and reports alongside him, including those from new colleagues Silvestre Terrazas, another newspaper editor and distant relative of the affluent Terrrazas family of Chihuahua, and Isidra T. de Cárdenas, who launched the radical feminist newspaper *La Voz de la Mujer.*

In January 1916, when Villa and his guerrilleros executed the seventeen American citizens in Santa Isabel in northern Mexico, the racial and ethnic tensions in El Paso came to a head. Nine of the men had been natives of the city, and all of them had worked as engineers at ASARCO, home to Smeltertown, the labor camp near the border where Francisco Madero and his revolucionarios had once strategized. The night their disfigured bodies arrived at the downtown El Paso train station, brawls erupted in saloons and spilled into the streets, devolving into the city's first "race riot." Anglo men stormed into Chihuahuita and retaliated against all Mexicans, young and old. Mexicanos fought back, historian Miguel Antonio Levario has chronicled, with "sticks, bats, pipes, and anything else they could muster." The anti-Mexican rampage drew national attention as Brigadier General John J. Pershing declared martial law and troops swept through the streets to back up local police. After the turmoil, military and law enforcement officers embarked on a "clean-up" campaign, Levario says, rounding up "'suspected' Villa associates."

Sometime later, Claude C. Pierce, one of a dozen of the highest-ranking surgeons in the United States, arrived in El Paso. Pierce, who had cultivated his experience in the blood, disease, and "race betterment" theories of the day as a quarantine officer in Panama, had first been dispatched to the Texas border that winter to investigate a typhus outbreak in Laredo, Texas. Now an inspection officer at the Santa Fe Bridge had died from the fevers and El Paso was once again rattled.

Under pressure from authorities, Mckiernan-González writes, Pierce and other public health officials implemented measures to eliminate typhus at the facilities under their control. All Mexican male laborers detained at the hospital and city jail would now be required to soak in delousing "baths" of vinegar and kerosene. One at a time, Levario says, men at the jail were made to dip their naked bodies into tubs brimming with a solution some did not know was flammable. The plan went awry: On March 6, as fifty inmates were moved into a central courtyard and ordered to undress, the spark of a match inside the bathing room ignited the vapors above the vats. The place exploded. Patients and prisoners ran from—and through—the flames. Gasoline fumes mingled with the stench of burning clothes and flesh. Carmen Alonzo, seventeen and a nurse, was reported to have treated burn victims with skills she had picked up on Mexican battlefields. The body of Ocario Soto, one of the first prisoners dragged out and left to die, Levario says, emitted so much heat that some saw it blister the asphalt.

The firestorm led to riots around streetcars and assaults on Americans in Juárez—and an outpouring of empathy in El Paso. Mayor Tom Lea and El Paso judge Dan Jackson even convened a grand jury to hold U.S. officials like Pierce to account. But the proceeding was interrupted, Mckiernan-González has written, as the crowd in the courtroom became the first in the city to learn that Villa had gone on to attack Columbus. Once again, an angry mob formed and turned on the working-class Mexicanos they believed supported Villa. Once again, Anglo residents marched into Chihuahuita and attacked anyone who looked Mexican. In South El Paso and Juárez, meanwhile, the word was that Villa had invaded Columbus to punish the United States for setting his supporters on fire in El Paso.

And thus the next phase of health inspection measures at the border, Stern has said, would be connected with its militarization: U.S. officials would be on the lookout for ways to stamp out lice—and Villistas. The baths continued at the bridge and at the jail, and now public health officers drove around South El Paso picking up residents they believed looked like they had lice. As they took them to the bridge for disinfection, they fumigated or burned down their residences. Adobe homes, long seen as hovels where poor hygiene festered, were especially disdained. At the same time, Pierce and other federal health service and immigration bureau officials would spend $6,000 (roughly $181,000 today) expanding and retrofitting a shabby two-story redbrick building that ran along and in part underneath the Santa Fe Bridge with boilers and streamlined disinfection equipment—essentially, laundry machines. This time health inspectors planned to use new chemicals to disinfect every Mexican arrival for the lice that carried disease—not only poor and dark-skinned workers from the interior of the country. Among the city officials calling for tougher measures was Mayor Lea. In the many telegrams he sent to Washington lawmakers, he depicted a city overrun. "Hundreds dirty, lousey [*sic*] destitute Mexicans arriving at El Paso daily will undoubtedly . . . bring and spread typhus unless a quarantine is placed at once," he contended.

As the germ campaigns in El Paso unfolded, the nativist and anti-immigrant sentiments across the country continued to intensify. The United States was about to enter World War I, and as historian David Dorado Romo has found, Russian agents were circulating pamphlets, periodicals, and other propaganda along the Mexican side of the border with rumors that Germans were plotting to lead bombing raids from Mexican border cities like Juárez. There was so much fear—of Mexicans, of typhus, of socialists and leftist ideas, and now of Germans, whose lengthy immigration interrogations in El Paso were increasing alongside those of suspected Mexican arms smugglers and Chinese laborers. So strong was the anti-German sentiment in the United States that Americans decided to call frankfurters "hot dogs," Romo says, and sauerkraut "liberty cabbage." Few Americans dared own a dachshund.

For Ylario, like many other workers who rode the trains and kept the trains running, work in the north had always been temporary, a way to make a little money and go back home. But as the revolution dragged on, the body count piled up, and the harassment at the border increased, Ylario decided it was time to move his family to Texas for good. Horses and cattle and haciendas and power in Chihuahua kept changing hands, but the poor stayed poor and the rich stayed rich, as they say, and for families like his nothing seemed to fundamentally change.

On January 4, 1917, Ylario's wife, Tiburcia, and her children—Victoria, now ten, and her three younger siblings—took a train to Juárez from Ciudad

Chihuahua. They arrived at the Santa Fe Bridge four weeks before Pierce's new quarantine measures went into place, but they were still hosed down under the earlier fumigation processes tailored for Mexican laborers. Through much of the 1910s, Victoria would later recall, it was a running joke that you could tell who in downtown El Paso had most recently crossed the border by the state of their attire: wrinkled and worn. The giant laundering machines where health officers dumped people's belongings to sterilize them were known to ravage clothes and melt shoes. Historian Yolanda Chávez Leyva remembers her own mother, a Mexicana, had nightmares about the baths on her dying bed, even though she had never been subjected to them herself, likely because of her middle-class status and light skin.

LATER THAT JANUARY, on a Saturday, the new American public health mandate went into effect. People would no longer be allowed to enter El Paso from Juárez after dark without a special permit from the federal government, an attempt to keep El Pasoans away from the Juárez cabarets and gambling houses that American health officials dreaded as hot spots for typhus. The squat redbrick building at the foot of the Santa Fe Bridge had been divided into three corridors, with two large dressing rooms separated by a maze of showers and bathroom stalls running along either side of a wide hall of gas and disinfection chambers.

The new plan was to inspect *every* Mexican. But, sure enough, the first submitted to the quarantine order were mostly poor and dark-skinned laborers from the interior of Mexico—those considered, as Pierce put it, "vermin infested." People waited in a small yard encircled by a tall wooden fence before Mexican health inspectors divided them into groups. They led them into the plant, women down one dimly lit passageway and men down another. In high-ceilinged dressing rooms, they were forced to fully remove all their clothes. As their garments were sterilized, inspectors went to work checking people's bodies for lice. They shaved the scalps of men and boys who needed treatment; they doused the hair of women in vinegar and kerosene and wrapped their heads in towels. Then, under the watch of attendants, they marched the naked men and women into showers and sprayed their bodies down with soap, fumigation gases, and water.

No one did the "delousing" project offend more, perhaps, than Mexicana women, who filtered into the city every day to clean American homes as Americans accused them and their families of being unclean. On January 28, 1917, five days after Pierce unveiled the new measures, one of those domestic workers, Carmelita Torres, arrived at the edge of El Paso. Sources say she was seventeen—and that her route via electric trolley to the Santa Fe Bridge would have likely been a familiar one to her. There is little if any reliable analysis about her thinking or motivations that Sunday morning. The weakest, like the false narratives about Rosa Parks, speculate that she was sick of the disgrace; others that it was the spirit of the suffragette and Adelitas movements. Whatever it was, she refused to let officials subject her to the so-called baths.

No, no way, nohow. Carmelita protested and urged thirty other women to join her. Within an hour, the number had swelled to two hundred. By noon it was thousands of people, mostly young women, domestic workers like Carmelita, who flocked to the Mexican side of the border, where boot shops and emporiums and warehouses teemed with shoppers and workers. The protesters stopped trolleys on their tracks and lobbed insults and curses at immigration officials. They hurled mud, empty bottles, sticks, and small stones at anything and anyone attempting to crawl through the throngs of people to the American side. Women tore the controllers out of streetcars and wielded them as clubs or threw them in the river. They dispatched eight streetcar crew members back to El Paso on foot, one of them with a black eye and a bruised face. They shattered car windows. Mexican onlookers heckled those compatriots who tried to ignore the commotion as they went into the brick bathhouse to comply with the health regulations. One of those rabble-rousers shouted "¡Viva Villa!" and was promptly shot four times and killed.

Carmelita was described as "an auburn-haired Amazon" by the *El Paso Times* and a "red-haired girl" by the *Detroit Free Press*, one who—armed with a streetcar controller—proved to be a veritable "Joan of Arc" in a vigorous protest against a "vinegar and gasoline plunge." Those who knew their history might have said she had evoked the spirit of la Santa. American reporters portrayed male Mexican officials as weak in the face of girls while simultaneously painting the female rioters as menacing: One report said the women took on the Mexican soldiers called in to stop them, laughing in their faces as they grasped the men's horse bridles and seized their "sabers" and "whips." El Paso authorities called the women wild and dangerous and anti-American. Troublemakers. Never mind that many of the women alleged that health personnel were taking photographs of their nude bodies and that some of those pictures were believed to be plastered all over the walls of an El Paso bar. Never mind that the same kerosene fluid used at the checkpoint was said to have started the flames that engulfed Villa loyalists jailed in El Paso a year earlier.

The 1917 Bath Riots lasted three days. On the second and third mornings, hundreds of women once more rushed the border, halting the flow of trolley traffic, and were once more pushed back by Mexican federal forces. But the rioters ultimately failed to stop the medical inspections of Mexicans. Americans continued the measures for about forty years, the process growing more elaborate, the chemical pesticides deployed more dangerous. (The Nazis were so inspired by the baths, Romo has found, that they came to use one of the same fumigation gases later used at the southern border, Zyklon B, as an extermination tool in their concentration camps.)

For many historians, the expansion of the baths in El Paso marked the first in a string of national security measures. A month after the delousing stations opened, Congress, reversing a veto by President Woodrow Wilson, passed the Immigration Act of 1917, one of the most stringent immigration laws the United States has ever adopted to date. For the first time, all Mexican nationals were required to carry a passport to cross into El Paso. The head tax on immigrants was increased to $8 (almost $200 in today's currency), a move intended to restrict eastern European migration but that also applied to Mexicans.

The law reaffirmed the ban on contract laborers, making an exception for those who came in only for temporary work. It mandated new literacy tests, barring from entry immigrants over sixteen who could not read thirty to forty words in their own language. And it banned the entry of any immigrant of Asian descent from a newly created "Asiatic Barred Zone," which stretched from what is now Saudi Arabia and Afghanistan to the Pacific Islands and encompassed over half of the world's population; the only countries exempted were Japan, whose citizens' immigration had been restricted in a previous agreement with the United States, and the Philippines, a U.S. territory. Public health officials, in a public manual, outlined the "classes of aliens" that would be prevented from entering at all—including gay people, chronic alcoholics, prostitutes, disabled people, and anarchists.

The literacy tests would prove futile because most immigrants could easily read a couple of lines or be coached to do it. In El Paso, people had only to read twenty lines from the Bible in whatever language, and immigration officials enforced it with laxity. But at the Santa Fe Bridge some 127,000 people went through the baths in 1917 alone. Félix Urdiales, one man who crossed in that time with a U.S. passport, recalled that Texas Rangers were also stationed at the port of entry and that Mexican commuter workers from Juárez were subjected to the cleansing every eight days. To prove they had gone through the process, they received a receipt certifying when they had been cleaned.

As for Carmelita, it could be said that she was one of the first Mexicanas to disappear at the border. After Mexican military officers arrested her and transferred her to El Paso authorities, she was jailed and released because the protests had occurred on Mexican, not American, soil. No records or clues remain to indicate what became of her. Historians Stern and Romo, who unearthed her story, and Chávez Leyva, one of the most prolific chroniclers of Mexicanas and their lost histories, have long tried to trace her origin and whereabouts, but they are not sure Carmelita Torres was even her true name.

She flickered and vanished without a trace.

7

All Mexicans Must Go

Ciudad Juárez, Chihuahua
1917 to 1922

For Juarenses like the Chews, the days kept passing with uncertainty and unease. Villistas continued to march through war-torn streets, their conflicts with soldiers from other revolutionary factions at times breaking out into shoot-outs or all-out battles. The revolution had disrupted the trade with the eastern United States that Ciudad Juárez relied on, causing the price of food, gas, and all sorts of goods to spike. Medicine shortages were common. Many businesses shut down or were pillaged, by rebels, by bandits, by starving campesinos turned workers turned migrants turned beggars.

La Garantía was located on Avenida 16 de Septiembre, the bustling thoroughfare that had been named in honor of Mexican Independence Day—Mexican Independence Day 1888. That same day, Paso del Norte had also taken on its new namesake in tribute to former president Benito Juárez and the place it had held at the center of Mexican history. When President Juárez sought refuge in Paso del Norte, in August 1865, he had been governing on the move, just as José María Morelos y Pavón, an Afro-Mexican Catholic priest, had done during the Mexican War of Independence. Spanish royalist forces eventually caught up to Morelos and killed him. But his pupil, Vicente Ramón Guerrero Saldaña, went on to almost fully abolish slavery after he became Mexico's second president and the first Black president in North America in 1829.

All those decades later, Juárez, who entered the Mexican villa with an escort of Tiguas—and to shouts of "¡Ahí viene Juárez!"—was still trying to fulfill the promises for which his predecessors had fought and died, transforming Mexico into an egalitarian republic. He set up Mexico's national government at a federal post office building in the same downtown plaza where Chew would one day open La Garantía. As Porfirio Díaz, then one of his trusted generals, rose to fame by holding off the French, Juárez persisted in trying to implement the constitution of 1857 from the borderland. The document, which Juárez had helped draft, among other provisions, banned slavery, guaranteed freedom of speech, eliminated monopolies, and largely prevented civil companies and the Catholic Church from owning land.

Like the Mexican rebels and exiles in El Paso, Juárez infused Paso del Norte with his liberalism and brought it brief international fame, and Paso del Norte proved strategic for Juárez, putting him close enough to the United States, which was supplying munitions to his movement, and yet keeping him within the bounds of his country so he could retain his seat. But Juárez also left the city with the conditions that would make it ripe for revolt: He allocated huge portions of land to the liberal aristocrats who had aided him and to whom he was indebted—the future land barons of Chihuahua, whom northern guerrilleros like Pancho Villa would take up arms to overthrow.

Through the final years of the revolution, Mexicanos remained at odds over how to carry out Juárez's constitutional reforms and uphold the ideals of Mexicanos like Guerrero and Morelos regarding land, country, and democracy. As Venustiano Carranza and Pancho Villa clashed, a rift deepened between the largely middle-class and mestizo liberals and intellectuals who supported Carranza and his promise of a constitutionalist government—a "Mexico for Mexicans"—and the more populist and antiestablishment ideas of Villa and Emiliano Zapata, who remained his ally to the south.

The Chews would have been vulnerable. Villa continued to hold deep disdain for Chinese merchants, many of whom sided with Carranza over Villa and had helped Brigadier General John J. Pershing hunt him down. By the end of Pershing's expedition, hundreds of Chinese families had fled Durango and Chihuahua; five hundred Chinese had come under the protection of the U.S. Army; more than 3,000 Chinese refugees had sought asylum in the United States. Many left northern Mexico altogether and returned to China, weary of the anti-Asian racism on both sides of the border.

The Chews, from what their daughters recalled, continued to live near their store, about two blocks from a customhouse, in an apartment home with a courtyard. They would have now been in their twenties.

Herlinda Wong Chew, straddling two countries and three cultures, acted as an informal travel agent, booking train and steamship tickets for Chinese immigrants from the interior of Mexico to Guangzhou (Canton). She wore her hair in a bob and worked from her living room, which a news article years later said looked more like an office, with "white walls, a scrubbed floor, and sparse furnishings." There, she also taught young Chinese men aspiring to study in the United States how to speak English and read the U.S. Constitution in preparation for their immigration interviews. Her work had likely been how she had become well acquainted with the American immigration officials who had granted her and some two hundred Chinese residents temporary shelter during the Villa raid, a rescue excursion that led an El Paso newspaper to describe her as a "Chinese queen" and "refugee boss."

It must have been sometime in early 1917 (though it is difficult to say exactly when because the ship manifests appear to be lost to time) that Herlinda and Antonio Chew took a ship to Hong Kong with their daughter, Josephine, by then four, and their son, Antonio, one. Their grandchildren believe they might have been fleeing retaliation from Villistas as they trained their attacks on the Chinese. They also might have needed a respite from the war as Antonio was taking some serious business losses. Still another motivation for the trip could have been that Antonio was what many scholars have described as a sojourner, one of China's traveling sons who had migrated to the United States with the intention of accumulating some savings and eventually returning. In Antonio's village near the Pearl River Delta in Guangzhou, as the traditional Chinese family structure of the time dictated, Antonio would have been expected to send back regular financial remittances, to periodically return home, and—as he had not married before leaving—to bring home his wife, who would be bound to the authority of her husband's mother. Despite these harsh conditions, Herlinda, one of her grandsons believes, might have had her own reason for agreeing to return to China: After witnessing one uprising, she wanted to play a role in the aftermath of another, the Xinhai Revolution, which in 1912 had brought an end to the Qing dynasty and 268 years of imperial rule in her father's homeland.

Their journey there took about a month at sea—a "slow boat to China," as her daughters would joke years later. But Herlinda might have misjudged her husband's mother and her desire to ensure her son kept his commitments. Upon their arrival, as the family accounts go, her mother-in-law confiscated all the money they had brought with them and made her terms clear: Antonio was to end his sojourn, rejoin his family, and remain in his village. No, no way, nohow. In the spirit of the embers that had made her, Herlinda waged her own revolt. She "rejected outright the subservient role expected of her," her granddaughter said many years later, and "without any funds, she fled to Canton."

Once in Guangzhou, Herlinda took a job teaching English at a mission school. She was later hired as a tutor for the daughters of a wealthy Cantonese banker who was a close adviser to some of the top leaders of the Xinhai Revolution. As World War I and civil unrest grew worse, she realized her family needed to return to Mexico if they hoped to ever leave at all. Antonio joined her, and the Chews left Hong Kong on a ship on April 10, 1918, according to the manifests that have been found. They arrived in San Francisco a month later, and their daughter Grace was born that December.

In the time the Chews were gone, a period their grandchildren estimate could have been as long as fifteen months, Carranza assumed control of every Mexican state—except for Chihuahua, home to Villa, and Morelos, home to Zapata, and Mexicanos released the new constitution of 1917. Drawing from the earlier constitution and revolutionary debates raging since the first northern uprisings, it mandated land reform, secularized the Mexican state, set out worker protections, and held that all people were entitled to human rights regardless of race or gender. The war that wracked Mexico from the north to the south ended three years later, after Zapata was assassinated on Carranza's orders, and Carranza was assassinated soon after. Villa, who was granted a pardon and a ranch near Parral in return for retiring from politics, was killed in 1923.

To rebuild their country, Mexicans needed to reunify their society, and Mexican scholars and liberal elites embarked on an ambitious attempt to counter the eugenic movements of the era with their nation's own racial ideology, one rooted in the Mexican and Latin American history of mestizaje, or the racial mixing that had occurred when the Spaniards invaded the New World and colonized its Indigenous populations. In 1925, José Vasconselos, an educator and philosopher known as the "cultural caudillo" of the revolution, would publish *La raza cósmica* (*The Cosmic Race*). The essay challenged the white supremacy theories that ruled the globe by proposing that a "fifth universal race," composed of all the other races, would arise out of the Americas. He suggested that it was in fact Latin America's mestizos, a people of mixed Indigenous, African, Asian, and European ancestry, who were superior to "purebloods," and that Mexico, where some 90 percent of the population was mestizo, was free of racist beliefs and practices because so much of its population was already mixed.

La raza cósmica, he posited, would go on to erect a new civilization, Universópolis, which would transcend the traditional constructs of race, ethnicity, and nationality in the name of a common human destiny. But to do this, la raza needed to keep evolving—to keep getting better, in his view: Native Mexicans needed to become mestizos, just as mestizos needed to become "Indianized," until all undesirable traits were synthesized. In other words, he still believed in racial hierarchies. Whiteness was favored over Blackness and Mexicans over Indios, whom Vasconcelos cast as part of a Mexican past that had been glorious but was now past nonetheless. And in a Mexico for Mexicans, where did that leave Chinos Mexicanos like the Chews?

In February 1922, the Chew family packed up their belongings in Juárez to move to El Paso. At the time of their departure, the anti-Chinese racism in Mexico was beginning to coalesce into some of the most calculated and harmful campaigns yet. In the neighboring state of Sonora, then home to the largest Chinese population in Mexico, political activists organized cities to implement local ordinances levying discriminatory taxes on Chinese stores, as historian Evelyn Hu-DeHart has chronicled. They also tried to ban Chinese people from some of the very industries they had come to dominate, such as truck farming, laundry, and dealing in meats, fruits, and vegetables.

Before Americans feared the Mexican, Americans feared the Chinese. Under the Chinese Exclusion Act, the few Chinese immigrants allowed to immigrate to the United States could enter only through certain official ports, and El Paso was not one of them. So the Chews had to travel to Calexico, California, where they crossed on foot under the immigrant category of "merchants." They then took a train to El Paso on the same transcontinental rail line that Chinese workers and contractors, like Herlinda's father, had helped build.

Sierra Blanca, Texas, United States
1920s

Miguel Martinez was now in his twenties, too. After he had crossed the Rio Bravo, he bounced around Texas as he took whatever jobs he could find in quarries and on railroads. He ended up in Sierra Blanca, about eighty-eight miles southeast of El Paso. The small town was tucked into the bottom of a mountain and blanketed in white poppies, only a sixteen-mile trek from the U.S.-Mexico border. It was the final stop on the transcontinental line that ran all the way from California and had brought the Chews to El Paso. Most of its inhabitants—only a couple hundred or so—were Mexican laborers like him, along with their wives. They lived in empty boxcars, and Miguel and the other men would wrap rope around the edges of their homes to keep out snakes because the thinking was that they didn't like slithering up against the harshness of the fibers.

Victoria Martinez and her family lived in one of the railway carriages nearby. Her mother, Tiburcia, had been so upset at leaving all she had ever known in Chihuahua, the family lore goes, that she soon fell into a deep depression. Sometime in 1921, three years after making the journey through El Paso, she succumbed to a sickness. Some in her family surmise she likely caught the Spanish influenza that tore through the United States in 1918.

Others think it was her sadness that killed her. If anything, it robbed her of her defenses, of her very will to live.

For one thing, Texas was not a welcoming place—not for a Mexican. Back home, Tiburcia would have been able to pick up fresh oranges at the market and chat with her comadres in the plaza for hours. In Texas, white mobs could vanish a Mexican and no one would ask any questions. All of which is to say that, as Mexicanos like Victoria, Tiburcia, and Miguel passed through El Paso, moving across the border from one country to another, they crossed a line of time and space, from cosmic to inferior.

Victoria was only fourteen when her mother died. As the oldest, she became the matriarch of her family and the main caretaker to her sister and two brothers. Miguel was some ten years her senior, but he would later tell his grandchildren that he fell in love with their grandmother as soon as he first saw her. The two bonded, his grandson says, over the loss of their parents and their scars from the revolution.

On most days Miguel would get home from work covered in dust. He would wash up and put on fresh clothes before heading over to Victoria's boxcar. Miguel did not know how to read or write, but he would dictate his love notes for Victoria to a friend, who would write them down on small pieces of paper that Miguel would roll up and squeeze through a crack in her window.

Ylario was not enthusiastic about the courtship. He thought Miguel was too old for his daughter, who was still playing with dolls even though she was now running the household. But a justice of the peace in town took the father aside and persuaded him that perhaps this relationship was in their best interest. Miguel was a hard worker and a man with a good reputation who could take care of his daughter and help her raise her siblings.

They were married not long after Tiburcia's death, and Victoria and Miguel moved into a boxcar of their own. Victoria learned how to be a mother and a wife from the other women in town, she would tell her children and grandchildren many years later. They taught Victoria how to cook and clean and make tortillas. Sometimes they watched her siblings and her children so she could have a few hours to play with her friends. Victoria and Miguel had their first child, Little Miguel, when Victoria was fifteen. Lily and Camilo came next. Their daughters, Manuela and Maria, would be born in Chihuahua years later.

Of their children, Little Miguel was the most troublesome. One morning, when he was only three or four, he wandered out onto the main road leading out of Sierra Blanca while his parents worked, and an affable old white man, a hunter, picked him up in a rickety wagon. The stranger liked to set traps out in the sierra to catch coyotes and skunks. He would kill them with a club between their ears, skin and dry them, and sell their furs up in Dallas, where he made good money. With Little Miguel's parents nowhere to be found, he must have worried about leaving the boy alone in the brush and decided to take him along for the ride. Hours later, as the sun set, it seemed the whole town was out searching for Little Miguel: mothers, fathers, and children, and the single men who worked alongside his father, raking the countryside of West Texas. Many thought the boy had disappeared, that he would never be found again. Then they heard the rumble of an automobile.

Taca, taca, taca, taca. Little Miguel climbed down all smiles. Victoria was relieved, then furious. She scolded the boy and the old man at least twice her size.

Another time, Little Miguel burned down an entire garage. Like the other women in Sierra Blanca, Victoria used to stow the excess wooden planks of railroad lumber in that storage area so that they could burn them to heat their homes and the water they used to wash dishes and clothes. On a day when she was outside doing the laundry, she told Little Miguel to fetch her the gallon of petroleum from inside. He took it to his mother, but as he went back into the shed to return it, he became curious: What would happen if he used some of it to light a few papers on fire? He quickly found the answer as the whole garage was engulfed in flames—and out came the townspeople again to put it out: mothers and fathers and children and the single men who worked alongside his father, Miguel. Even as an elderly man, Little Miguel remained surprised his parents did not disown him right then and there.

Around the Martinezes, land developers and commercial growers were arriving in Texas in droves. After the end of World War I and a brief recession, the United States had entered an era of economic growth and mass production unlike it had ever seen. Inflation was down, the stock market was roaring, and Americans were building things: automobiles, appliances, homes, and skyscrapers with electricity. Texas growers, in pursuit of a "farm revolution," were expanding the state's agricultural industry, deeply rooted in chattel slavery and all that it implied, into a booming market enterprise. With the number of farms jumping, employers could not hire Mexicans fast enough to clear the pastures and ranchland that were needed for cash crops like cotton, wheat, and corn. First came the men, then their families. "Teams of men cleared dense countryside of mesquite trees and cacti covered in barbs and thorns, which choked the landscape and made farming difficult," Monica Muñoz Martinez writes, referring to Mexicanos. "Rows of crops soon replaced brush country."

The number of Mexican migrants who legally crossed the border, which had climbed all through the revolution, rose further: Historian Julia G. Young has tallied around 20,000 people every year in the 1910s to between 50,000 and 100,000 people yearly through the 1920s. Between 1926 and 1929, the number rose as Mexican Catholics opposed the new revolutionary government's efforts to enforce stringent restrictions on the public role of the Church. When Archbishop Primate José Mora y del Río, the Church's top spokesman, publicly refused to implement the 1917 constitution, calling it a socialist charter for secularization, some 25,000 Catholic partisans took up arms in the Cristero War. Violence consumed Mexico yet again, and instead of "¡Viva Villa!" the shouts in El Paso and Juárez barrios went "¡Viva Cristo Rey!" ("Long Live Christ the King!").

But if Mexico was pushing the eminence of mestizaje, the nativist and eugenics movements of the 1910s had only continued to grow stronger in the 1920s across the United States. To Americans, racial hierarchies had evolved beyond physical differences or biological hierarchy to encompass nationality and a complex set of cultural factors. Across Texas, as historian Trinidad Gonzales has examined, a rising Mexican American middle class was pushing to become fully integrated into white communities. They tended to know English, have citizenship, and were adopting an American way of life. But Mexican immigrant laborers were seen as a race apart or deemed "others." And a Mexicano or México Americano, particularly those with darker skin or who were less well off, could always fall into that category.

Just as Americans had rewarded the hard labor of Chinese immigrants with exclusion, they now thanked the Mexicanos with signs in restaurants and bars that read: NO DOGS OR MEXICANS ALLOWED. White managers and farm settlers, insistent that ethnic Mexicanos were beneath them in the social strata, ushered in what modern historians now call the "Juan Crow" laws of segregation, an informal system of measures that kept Mexican and Latino immigrants from using the same businesses, water fountains, buses, and other services as white Americans and would pave the way for the separation of white and Mexican students in public schools. Soon, even interracial marriages, long a part of fronterizo life, were prohibited.

And yet they still needed the Mexican worker. As white nativists and eugenicists argued for another round of sweeping measures to seal the nation's borders, a powerful farm lobby in Texas and across the American Southwest united to argue successfully that Mexican workers be exempt. During the 1920 congressional hearings on the "admission of illiterate Mexican laborers," according to political scientist Alexandra Filindra, Southwestern farmers and their congressional supporters conceived of an immigrant worker palatable to both the liberal and the socially conservative and eugenic sensibilities of the time. Farmers needed the hands in the field—and a suitable justification to bring Mexican laborers in. They argued ethnic Mexicans had certain positive qualities that made them "better" at labor than other immigrants. Young notes that ethnic Mexicans were, in the main, said to be "docile, taciturn, physically strong, and able to put up with unhealthy and demanding working conditions."

Perhaps more importantly, Young says, *temporary*: here only for a little while and far more likely—in fact, biologically destined—to return to Mexico rather than to establish a permanent life in the United States. What resulted was the trope of the migrant farmworker, "or the temporary Mexican," Filindra adds, a "new breed of peon." Between 1920 and 1923, as legal scholar K-Sue Park has written, the United States would even work with the Mexican government to provide a free return to Mexico for 100,000 people who had no criminal records and were willing to leave voluntarily to avoid spending time and money on their formal deportations.

The American nativist and eugenic movements hit their peak in 1924 when Congress passed the Johnson-Reed Act, the next expansive immigration measure following the last one, and one that Coolidge, who signed it, contended would "keep America American." It drew the support of the American labor movement and the Ku Klux Klan, which was experiencing a resurgence across the nation and in Texas—at the time of the law's passage, the state with more Klansmen in public office than any other. Under the law, the United States for the first time set annual quotas for each European country, established the Border Patrol, and opened the first official inspection center at the Santa Fe Bridge. The restrictions hardened the legal bounds of the "white race," historian Mae M. Ngai has stated, and rendered Chinese, Japanese, Indians, and other Asians racially ineligible for naturalized citizenship. Even as Mexicans were exempted from the numerical quotas altogether, she says, the methods the government used to enforce the quotas—the visas, the "baths," the border control measures and agencies—would work in tandem to transform Mexican immigrants into "the single largest group of illegal aliens" by the end of the decade.

In this caste-like system, Mexicanos were relegated to pico y pala—pick-and-shovel work—with meager wages, regardless of their training or level of experience. And the temporariness—an in-betweenness—would stay with Mexican Americans and Latinos more generally as it had with Chinese immigrants and other Asian Americans. They became perpetual foreigners—or, as Ngai terms it, "alien citizens," Americans whose citizenship and loyalty to country are always suspect. And so the Chews and the Martinezes would become two threads in the broader American fabric.

Violence followed. Despite their financial chokehold on the Southwest, or perhaps because of it, Anglo settlers and capitalists worried that Zapata-like revolts to redistribute their farmland could spread over the border. Texas Rangers lynched Mexican men and looted and burned the homes of Mexican and Mexican American families. A few days after the Johnson-Reed Act was enacted, Congress approved the funding for what would become the U.S. Border Patrol. Federal immigration officers would no longer wait for immigrants to come to them and inspect their documents at the border. They would actively pursue and "hunt them down," notes historian James Dupree, with the assumption that they should not be in the country to begin with. To police and pacify the new Mexican peon, the Border Patrol and immigration officials worked with the needs of American growers and industrialists in mind. If they needed Mexican workers to hustle on assembly lines or harvest cotton and wheat or mine more silver, they loosely enforced border laws and visa regulations. If they did not, they followed the letter of the law and launched deportation raids—typically before payday.

STILL, THE MARTINEZES remember their nearly fifteen years in Sierra Blanca as peaceful, possibly even some of the best. The prosperity of the decade had bypassed them as it had most Mexican Americans. They did not have much, and at least Little Miguel, as his children would say years later, appeared to like it that way. Their Mexican community was tight-knit. Neighbors knew one another. Families took care of each other's children, and Victoria had her own field of gravity that pulled people in. There always seemed to be someone over at the Martinezes' boxcar. Even a couple of the Border Patrol officers would stop by sometimes to pick up some of her egg burritos.

Then the elder Miguel injured the instrument most crucial to the Mexican and American worker, regardless of race, citizenship, or country: his hand. One afternoon at the quarry, the mill that Miguel and the other workers used to crush raw stone broke down. He was banging the machinery with a giant bar in hopes of getting it to function when he felt his hand being crushed. He lost three fingers and had to be rushed to El Paso by car. There were no ambulances in the isolated stretches of the West Texas brush country.

Though he quickly healed physically, he wasn't quite the same after that. He seemed to lose some of his confidence and became more withdrawn. To add to the hardship, sometime after he returned to the quarry, nativists seeking to curb the growing migrations of Mexicanos succeeded in pushing through the Undesirable Aliens Act of 1929, which for the first time made it illegal to cross the border unauthorized. A few months later, the stock market crashed, and the Great Depression swept through the United States. As the American economy deteriorated, white Americans claimed that Mexicans were stealing American jobs and were better off going back home. They were, after all, not permanent, not really American.

President Herbert Hoover promised "American jobs for real Americans" and allowed his secretary of labor, William N. Doak, to implement a program of local laws that banned the government from employing anyone of Mexican descent, regardless of whether they were legal permanent residents or U.S. citizens. There was no federal law or executive action ordering the mass deportation of people. But cities large and small launched illegal and unconstitutional raids to sweep up and remove Mexicans and Mexican Americans from the United States while the Hoover administration looked the other way.

In Los Angeles and Detroit, groups of plainclothes officers, brandishing guns and batons, rounded up hundreds of families in parks and public spaces. Private charities and corporations, such as the Southern Pacific Railroad and the Ford Motor Company, loaded people on trains to Mexico. Some Mexican immigrants left on their own, but many were tricked or coerced into repatriation—what economics professor Leo Grebler calls the "huge twilight zone between voluntary and forced migration." Across the country, colonias and barrios disappeared. By some estimates, between 355,000 and nearly 2 million Mexicans and Mexican Americans were repatriated through the 1930s, about 60 percent of whom were American citizens. The repatriations were billed as the "patriotic" way, the "humanitarian" way. All Mexicans had to go. That included the Martinezes.

8

The Search for Victoria

El Paso, Texas
2022

On a bright day in March, in the middle of another election cycle, I stopped in El Paso on my way to Santa Eulalia, Chihuahua. I was in search of Victoria Martinez and the pieces of history that had made our city who she was. Long gone were the bustling downtown factories and swanky clothing stores that Victoria and her family would have seen as they passed through the Pass. The old Caples Building, where la Junta had schemed and plotted against old Porfirio, sat abandoned, some of its windows broken and boarded up. An unfinished mural of Francisco Madero and Pancho Villa covered one of its walls. The Hotel Paso Del Norte remained a towering luxury establishment, with an emerald cap and an orange brick facade, but a Burger King now offered Whoppers on the site of the Roma Hotel and Emporium Bar, where Villa was known to down strawberry pop and ice cream in lieu of the alcoholic beverages he so despised. Lauro Aguirre's prolific newsroom—or propaganda shop; take your pick—had been torn down, along with most of the city's newspaper offices, both those in English and in Spanish, and in its place stood the offices of a Better Business Bureau.

On the other side of the Santa Fe Bridge, now several car lanes deep and winding over the mural-splashed concrete edges of the Rio Grande, people walked under the shadows of concertina wire into the bars and restaurants, pharmacies, jewelry stores, and leather boot shops lining the historic Avenida Juárez. The road still led into the plaza with the old mission founded by the Spanish, but the mission had long since been transformed into a towering cathedral. La Garantía, and the federal post office that once housed the Mexican national government when Benito Juárez had governed from the border in exile, had been replaced by small shops and a Michoacana creamery selling aguas frescas, or refreshing juices, and paletas de nuez, piña, and limón con chamoy (ices in flavors of walnut, pineapple, and lemon mixed with bittersweet fruit sauce and covered in chili powder). Nearby, vendors hawked clothes, wares, and yerbas buenas—good herbs, like the ones Teresa Urrea had used to heal—under the lolling tarps and trinkets of an open-air market.

My mother, Laura, and I climbed into a taxi that took us to the bus station and then boarded a bus to her mother's hometown of Ciudad Chihuahua. What we found there were traces of ourselves. The city had grown so much that there were entire stretches that looked almost identical to El Paso. Freeways curved into spaghetti bowls lined with Starbucks coffee shops and Walmarts and Petcos, and yet Chihuahua retained much of its character, its colorful adobe homes and eighteenth-century baroque buildings tucked into the golden mountains of la Sierra Madre that Villa had roamed. The last time I had visited I had been far too young to remember it, but it all felt familiar. Norteño.

Santa Eulalia was a twenty-five-minute drive to the southeast and had become a destination for Mexican tourists. The white stone church built in the town square centuries before Victoria was born rose on a hill. Not too far away, a small horror house captured the stories of its ghosts, and a UFO and paranormal museum in an adobe building painted black educated visitors on the history of a different kind of alien. At an hacienda-style building nearby, a former town president and cultural liaison launched into a story as soon as I told him my name. He said Santa Eulalia had almost been the capital of the state that the Spaniards had colonized as Nueva Vizcaya. That is, until Don Antonio de Deza y Ulloa, then its governor, cast the tiebreaking vote in an assembly of seventeen Spaniards that decided it would be Ciudad Chihuahua instead. "¡Por la culpa de tu pariente!" ("It's the fault of your ancestor!"), he said with a laugh.

There were no signs of Victoria. Not in the humble municipal offices. Not in the tiny library with metallic yellow bookshelves and a modest two-room museum on the city's mining history—its walls and shelves decked with old black-and-white photographs, hard hats, steel miners' lunch boxes, and white and purplish mineral crystals. Nor were there traces of Victoria's father. The few remaining records that Raúl Reyes, the Martinezes' grandson and a historian, had shared with me showed that his bisabuelito spelled his name Elario or Ylario, but the former town president now told me that it was more likely to be spelled Hilario in town records, if there were any. He said he would look but he made no promises.

We had hopes of searching for the rancho to the north of Ciudad Chihuahua, where my own grandmother had grown up. In the end, we found no remnants of her home either. But in Santa Eulalia and Chihuahua, I could feel something in me changing, the borders of my identity expanding. It might have been the first time since the El Paso shooting that I truly felt whole, and I wondered why, after all of my grandmother's stories of her childhood, I had never, not once before, thought to come back to the place where she was from.

My father, Mauricio, is from Puerto Vallarta, a beach town in Jalisco. My mother, Laura, was born in El Paso and raised in Juárez, in la Colonia Obrera, so named because it was mostly inhabited by obreros, or workers: welders, shoemakers, store clerks, and seamstresses—people who regularly crossed into El Paso, powering the bustle of its downtown stores and factories, before returning to their families at night. She learned about los Niños Héroes in school and, like all the other students, dressed up as a cadet in tribute to the boys on Mexican Independence Day. When my parents split, my mother, my sister, Bianca, and I moved back and forth between El Paso and various places in Southern California. El Paso always drew us back because it was home to our Mexican grandparents, Alicia and Arturo, and our three aunts, Alicia, Nora, and Bertha.

I must have started hearing the story about the boys when I was seven or eight. It must have been during the summer. It was always during the summer when my mother or grandmother would run errands across the border and return with the Mexican textbooks required for Juárez students. They would sit me down at the kitchen table and make me study. They did this because they did not trust American schools or teachers—"Too soft," my grandmother would say—and they wanted me to learn Spanish. They wanted me to know Mexican history as much as American history. They wanted me to know we were as much Mexican as American, as much from here as from there. Now in Chihuahua, I was realizing it was all one and the same: that to know El Paso, who she was and what made her, I needed to know its people—our memories, our stories, our families and their origins, including my own.

In Ciudad Chihuahua, the concrete towers of the pink stone prison where revolucionarios were once incarcerated were still pocked with bullet holes. Corridos played at the hacienda of Luz Corral, where Villa's first and most beloved wife (he is reported as having upward of twenty-five) lived out her best days. The Banco Minero, which the magonistas had once hoped to blow up, remained standing, as did the Spanish colonial home of Luis Terrazas, the balding aristocrat who had once claimed all of Chihuahua was his. Despite the ten-year war that tore Mexico asunder, the Creels and the Terrazas continued to own much of the wealth in a city where American capitalism was alive and well. I was told this by a long-lost friend of my mother's, Jorge Seyffert Terrazas, who had only revealed his full name then, telling us that he was a distant relative of Luis Terrazas himself. When he and my mother were both university students in El Paso, he went solely by Jorge Seyffert. Too much baggage came with the name Terrazas. It turned out his family detested Villa so much that he was not even allowed to set foot in Luz Corral's home.

At lunch, thinking of the younger generation of Chicanos in the United States who would use images of Villa and Emiliano Zapata as rallying emblems for Mexican American workers and to reclaim their identities as proud Mexican Americans, I asked Jorge's twenty-one-year-old son about his own thoughts on Villa. He looked up at me from behind black-rimmed glasses and responded without a second thought:

"Half of Chihuahua still loves him," he said. "Half still hates him."

When we returned to El Paso, I went over to my grandmother's to recount our travels through her hometown. Then it finally occurred to me to share with her a passage I had been reading about braceros. I asked her if my grandfather or great-grandfather had ever been subjected to the baths at the Santa Fe Bridge. She said they both had. It was the first time I had heard of it.

"Did they find that humiliating?" I asked.

"And if they found it humiliating, so what? It didn't matter." She laughed incredulously. "They had to work."

She remembered that she herself had not wanted to pass through the Pass or move to Texas for good. She would have preferred to stay in Juárez forever, like Tiburcia in Santa Eulalia. But my late grandfather, Arturo, could not shake the urge to pursue opportunity on the other side. He used to skip the border inspections as a teenager and wade across the Rio Grande to look for work in El Paso back when, as my grandmother would say, the border was but a line in the sand. When I asked my mother if he had ever said anything about these excursions or the border inspections, she remembered that he had once told her a story about a time one of the inspectors detected a mark on his body and warned him it could be cancer. His heart dropped and he silently prayed to God, she said, not that he would be free of cancer but that the inspector would let him pass.

SIERRA BLANCA, TEXAS
1931

AFTER HIS WORKPLACE injury, Miguel should have been offered a job for life at the quarry where he had worked for more than a decade. But he did not speak English—and he was Mexican—so he was not. As the forced migrations of Mexicanos started, plenty of other Mexican workers he knew began to give up hope of continuing to work in Texas. They were tired of living with the fear of deportation, the anti-Mexican hatred, the extreme poverty, and the lack of employment. They yearned to return to la madre patria. They yearned to return to Mexico.

Despite their legal green cards and status as "permanent resident aliens," the Martinezes decided that they had no other choice but to go, too. They packed up what they could, including some of their fancier appliances, like Victoria's sewing machine, and joined the mass of caravans of Mexicans and Mexican Americans clogging up the roadways back to Ciudad Chihuahua. Miguel had received about $500 in work injury compensation for the quarry accident, what would have been a settlement of more than $9,000 today, and he and Victoria hid it in a little pouch strapped to Little Miguel's belt. He had always been one for mischief, but the weight of this responsibility—the young keeper of the coin—was not lost on the eight-year-old boy, he would tell his nephew many years later. He guarded it like their lives depended on it—because they did.

On March 31, 1931, the Martinezes repatriated themselves to Mexico through the Mexican consulate in Presidio, about 250 miles southeast of El Paso, near what is now Big Bend Ranch State Park. A worn, typewritten sheet from the consulate lists the vehicle they were driving—a Ford sedan, model 1928, motor number 333372, license plate number G2-4515—along with the things they carried:

Trailer and one extra, used tire.
Extra tires, muy usadas. Very used.
Trunks of clothing.
Sewing machine.
Bundles of blankets.
Used stoves.
Chairs and empty buckets.
Axes and toolboxes.
Box filled with food supplies.
Jars with kitchen utensils.
Chicken coop with seven birds of poultry.
Boxes with more kitchen utensils.
Baskets with still more kitchen utensils.
Hunting traps.
Batch of stove pipes.
Table clock.
Oil lamps.

El Paso, Texas
1922 to 1930s

When the Chews arrived in El Paso—from its western reaches, because Chinese were not allowed into the city from its southern bridges—the Ku Klux Klan counted about 3,500 local members in the city and was experiencing a brief period of influence. Inside the famed Sheldon Hotel, near the Caples Building where Madero had once headquartered his revolutionary Junta, a Klan recruiter set up shop in the spring of 1921. The group opened Frontier Klan No. 100 that summer, and three Klan members took over the school board. By March 1922, even as concerns and protests among El Paso residents grew louder, some three hundred newly initiated Klansmen circled up to Scenic Drive in the Franklin Mountains to burn a wooden cross, as they would do several times more.

In El Paso, newspapers had once called for a border wall to keep out the Chinese, and city officials recorded the skin color of the Chews as "yellow." But the violence against the Chinese in El Paso and across Texas was less than in other parts of the country. No version of the notorious Anti-Chinese Leagues ever formed in the city. No citizens or politicians ever organized to force people out, and though some Chinese businesses had remained clustered downtown since the days when the first Chinese railroad workers arrived, the city did not have a traditional Chinatown because Chinese residents and businesses were not formally or informally confined to live and work in a certain area.

Within a year, the Chews opened the New China Grocery store in South El Paso, and then the New China Grocery Number Two, which Herlinda ran, on the corner of Overland and Stanton Streets downtown. By the close of the decade, they would have four stores. They would also be raising eight children, four girls and four boys. Apart from Josephine, Antonio, Grace, and Wellington, there would be Gloria, Fredrick, and Charles.

Herlinda tended to their stores and her "beehive," as she called the Chew clan in a letter to a close friend in San Diego. She also served on different boards, volunteered with welfare services, and was an active member of her Episcopal church. She appeared to have the same flair for camaraderie and hobnobbing as her father, often hosting or attending luncheons and events for various business and community groups. When she was not at a grocery store, school, or church, she was at immigration services. There, she translated the lengthy interrogations of Chinese immigrants detained at Angel Island who had American sponsors in the El Paso area, and interpreted for those completing their interviews at the Santa Fe Bridge, which the Chinese knew as the "Bridge of Sighs." She had kept building close ties with immigration officials on both sides of the border and in late 1928 even hosted two fine dinners, with a hired butler and private cook, for some of the top customs officers in Juárez.

All the talk and theorizing from eugenicists and nativists in the United States—over what made a person, what made some superior and not others, whether it was blood, race, and genes or physical traits, class, and nationality—had underpinned the first immigration laws, the labor system, and the first national security measures in Herlinda's new country. All were playing out in the ports of entry of her new city. But in her personal missives from these years, often witty and humorous, the emerging racial and ethnic regimes in the United States and in Mexico seemed far removed from the way she and many other people in El Paso lived out their identities in their day-to-day life: with pride.

Herlinda wrestled with the challenges of any mother, such as sewing dresses for her daughters—and convincing them to wear them—and reprimanding her younger children for the English curse words and "modern epithets" ("jiminy whiskers," "hot daddies," etc.) that they were picking up in the neighborhood. She also grappled with how to honor and instill in her children the culture, language, and tradition of all three of their heritages: Chinese, Mexican, and American. In December 1927, when she became the godmother of two Chinese babies of women in her circles, she approached their baptisms as she would those of her own children, going to great lengths to uphold Chinese and American customs as she helped the parents organize a major banquet with more than 150 Chinese and American guests. It was followed by a dance—on Antonio's dime—for their Mexican friends. Herlinda served as the hostess, mistress of ceremonies, and writer and interpreter of all the Chinese speeches.

By 1930, with the numbers of unemployed and impoverished El Paso residents swelling as a result of the Great Depression, American immigration laws were becoming so strict that Herlinda said it seemed easier to win the Chinese lottery than to get a visa. Back in her native country, the laws were also tightening. Mexico had begun trying to bar the entry of American Black people, whom its government now categorized as members of the razas no gratas. The anti-Chinese and nativist Mexican campaigns culminated in August 1931. Just as the United States was removing Mexicanos and México Americanos, politicians in Sonora—a state with a Chinese population of 11,000—revived laws that banned Chinese-Mexican marriages and imposed heavier burdens on Chinese businesses, requiring that they hire mostly Mexican workers and limiting what their stores could sell. Harassed by the immigration authorities, maligned by propaganda, and targeted by prejudicial laws, Chinos and Chinos Mexicanos began leaving Sonora in droves. It would be the largest expulsion of Chinese in Mexican history.

Some Chinese refugees, granted temporary American transit visas, sailed directly from Mexico to San Francisco, where they took ships back to China with Mexican wives and children and created Mexican barrios outside of their villages in southern China. Mexican vigilante groups rounded up others and shuttled them in trucks to Texas border cities like El Paso. With the Exclusion Act in effect, the United States bore the cost of deporting them to China.

Soon, Herlinda, like El Paso itself, was caught between a Mexico for Mexicans and an America for Americans. Even as Herlinda was helping Chinese immigrants in Mexico obtain travel visas to return to China, Mexican families and workers expelled from Minnesota and Kansas and Alaska, Detroit and Chicago and Los Angeles—where they had worked in slaughterhouses and on automobile assembly lines, on farms, in factories, and in the fisheries—were passing through the city on their way to Juárez and points south. Lauro Aguirre, the radical Mexicano journalist, had died in 1925, but if he had been alive, he would have been one of the members of the Spanish-language press on both sides of the border condemning the injustice. "¡El diablo nos está llevando!" ("The devil is taking us!"), the Mexicanos cried. In other words: Things are going to hell.

The Chinese in El Paso survived the misery of the Great Depression and expulsions, historians say, by pulling together. Families stepped in to offer food, shelter, and financial support to other families that fell into poverty. Neighbors became each other's source of relief. Herlinda and Antonio were known to rent train cars for some laborers and families who needed to make the journey to San Francisco, where they would board ships bound for Hong Kong or Antonio's native Guangzhou. They also made at least four trips to Guangzhou themselves to help others, including several Mexican women who had been deported with their Chinese husbands and were now in China, wrestling with a government that did not recognize their marriages.

By providing aid to those in need, the Chews were following in the steps of the city's Chinese merchants before them. The Chinese merchants of El Paso had been lifelines for Chinese immigrants since railroad workers established the first large Chinese grocery store near their lodging house downtown. They operated private banks and helped read and write letters for those who were illiterate. Their stores, patronized by Chinese and Mexican and American residents, as scholar Anna Louise Fahy describes it, sold the products that connected Chinese immigrants to their homeland, to their very identities.

During their journeys to China, the Chews would stay in Hong Kong for months at a time and enroll their children in local schools. Their daughter Grace later recalled that she looked forward to her first trip to China because she wanted to feel the Chinese part of herself that she had missed out on. The trip instead gave her a whole new appreciation for a city that had afforded her the freedom to be many parts of herself at once. "I thought that going there [to Hong Kong] I would, for the first time, feel what I really was," she said. Instead it was the first time she felt the brunt of "being a foreigner," the first time she could remember experiencing prejudice for her Americanness and her Mexicanness.

As the 1930s wore on, the Chews' businesses went "on the burn," their cash reserves rapidly depleted. Herlinda, now in her thirties, struggled to keep up her spirits. Serving on a welfare commission, she was faced with many of the same challenges that would boil up almost a century later in the middle of different crises: whether government aid was helpful or harmful;

whether the city could continue to afford the food, medical, and education assistance it was providing; whether more should be done to help immigrants with no lawful residence status. By 1934, needing a respite, she started planning what would become her last trip to China. When a friend suggested that she write a book about her life, she joked that it would be tragic but funny, too, as her Chinese relatives often berated her for having "too much of a sense of humor." She was still weighing all the parts of who she was. "What a mess it is to have an American-Mexican mind with Chinese dignity and tradition mixed up into a whole muddle," she mused.

Ciudad Chihuahua, Chihuahua, Mexico
1930s

Upon returning to Mexico, Victoria and Miguel bought their own little ranch outside of Ciudad Chihuahua, near Santa Eulalia, the place where Victoria had been born. She would have now been in her mid-twenties, he in his thirties. The family herded goats and cattle, and Little Miguel recalls that in their village, as in others nearby, they often met families from American cities such as Dallas and Phoenix and Denver. They had been loaded onto buses, trains, and trucks, some ordered by American officials and corporations, others of their own will, and dumped on the Mexican side of the border.

The Mexican government embraced the new arrivals—both Mexicanos and México Americanos—that the United States was spewing out, assuming that the industrial laborers would boost the workforce and revive the national economy. But many of the repatriated died from hunger and disease. Others, like the Martinezes, opted to buy several acres of land to grow crops and raise livestock rather than return to the quarries, mines, and factories. However, the old ways of the campesinos had been forgotten, and few knew how to work the land now. Some lost all of the savings that they had made north of the border as they tried to make ends meet.

It was said that in the trackless spaces of the Sierra Madre, where revolucionarios had fought and died among the mesquite brush and prickly bush, lay mounds of gold and silver. Men had craved the gold and died for it for centuries.

With the gold came the ghosts. In Victoria's hometown of Santa Eulalia, legend has it that an ancient caudillo wanders on his horse after night has fallen. He appears only to children and the inebriated, dressed in colonial garb. He was tortured and killed because he refused to divulge the location of the cave where he had amassed the gold he had taken from others. Now he has pledged to betray his secret only to those willing to sacrifice their first-born sons. Other spirits that wander Chihuahua are said to be wicked, such as those of old Porfirio's soldiers, some of whom lost their lives watching over the vast wealth concealed in the train cars headed to armies in the northern borderland.

Victoria and Miguel settled in Chihuahua, but the gold did not last. The Martinezes would speak little if at all of this time: too hard and painful to remember. But many decades later, before Victoria was diagnosed with Alzheimer's and her memory faded, she told her granddaughter-in-law Margarita that in Chihuahua she had feared the ghost of a mean revolucionario who haunted their fields. That was right before their situation became so dire that Victoria and Miguel ended up for a time in Ciudad Chihuahua, begging on the streets for coins.

Fort Worth, Texas,
2023

In the spring of 2023, I was still searching for Victoria's and El Paso's memory but also for the ghosts in the city's shadows. At a drab warehouse on the outskirts of Fort Worth, I found some of the El Paso court records I had been looking for, detailing the cases against magonistas, in dusty and worn leather-bound books. Alongside them were cases and cases against Chinese laborers: hundreds of men stowed away on pages worn and discolored, the glossy grayscale snapshots of some glued or stapled to their final judgments. In the dry language of the briefs, the defendants argued they were not "aliens" but men born and bred in the United States, in cities like Chicago and New York or, like Yee Gong, in San Francisco, "State of California, in the year 1888," but now "illegally confined and restrained of my liberty, at El Paso Texas."

One of the only reasons why we have an idea of where some of the earliest Chinese residents in El Paso hailed from is because historian Edward J. M. Rhoads walked through the graves inside Concordia Cemetery in 1973. Chinese people and businesses were not always counted in population statistics or directories. Immigration records cannot be entirely trusted because some Chinese immigrants were listed as business owners and partners solely in hopes of being granted exemptions from the Chinese Exclusion Act. Then there were the many who adopted the identities of others, "paper sons" and "paper daughters," born in China and holding fake documents claiming they were some American citizen's immediate family. A Chinese surname can reveal so much about a person—the specific area from which they emigrated, their cultural and socioeconomic background, who they married, and their family ties—and yet, many Chinese names were romanized and spelled so many different ways that attempting to untangle those roots is futile (Herlinda's father, Carlos Wong, actually went by Carlos Perez in Mexico). But by studying the markers of the Chinese buried in the Chinese section of Concordia Cemetery, Rhoads was able to reclaim a bit of El Paso's memory, discovering that most of the Chinese in the city, like Herlinda's father and her husband, had hailed from Guangzhou.

In 1939, Herlinda and Antonio were put to rest in another cemetery in the northeastern part of the city. She died of tuberculosis and lived out the final months of her life in Portland, Oregon. She had left in the hope that a change in climate would do her some good, but the disease had also stigmatized her, and she had not wanted to bring shame to her family. Antonio died of stomach cancer.

Back in Washington, I started reading about how the United States had agreed to allow American citizens who self-deported during the Great Depression to return. But the government forms that many Mexican Americans were handed before they left labeled them a burden on the state, complicating that very possibility. For many, the culture shock and adjustment to life in Mexico would prove traumatic. Little Miguel once recalled that some of the boys and girls he met in Chihuahua all spoke to each other in English. At school, their Spanish-speaking teachers did not understand what they were saying or know what to do with them. American-born children, historians Francisco E. Balderrama and Raymond Rodríguez have found, had "deep-seated scars of rejection by both cultures" that they said "would remain imbedded in their lives forever."

Many would not return until World War II, when Mexican American men would fight for their country despite the psychological wounds it had inflicted upon them. Some who did return were so traumatized that they did whatever was necessary to avoid reliving such an experience. They anglicized their names. They sought to marry people who were not Mexican. They chose not to live in Mexican communities. The scars of the forced removal were so deep, historians say, that they rippled for generations. Balderrama, who interviewed the direct descendants of the repatriation, told *Time* that "families locked away what happened."

And there it was: the reason why Victoria has not really, not ever truly, been found.

PART TWO

The Business of Drugs and War

I am among my own people, for . . . Mexico is a brown man's country. Do you blame them for fearing a "gringo" invasion with its attendant horror of color hatred?

—Langston Hughes

9

Homegrown Terror

IT WAS NOT even 10:30 a.m. and the pavement was already scorching hot the Saturday that a self-proclaimed white supremacist pulled into central El Paso to shoot Mexicans. Armando Vela, thirty-nine, a news photographer for *El Diario de El Paso*, remembers this because he had been lightly sweating and griping to himself about the heat. He was off from work that morning, on August 3, 2019, and happened to be shopping at the Sam's Club near Cielo Vista Mall when he decided to walk over to the Walmart across the street. He was stopped in his tracks when he saw people running through the parking lot in terror.

As he quickly scanned the site in confusion and shock, he realized some were pushing bloody victims out in shopping carts and on flatbed carts. His photographer reflexes kicked in. He took out his camera phone and started recording some of the earliest footage of the carnage. Paramedics hoisted a few survivors onto stretchers. On the burning asphalt, splayed on a white towel, an injured elderly woman howled in pain. "I saw people hugging their mothers, their sons," Vela would tell me later, catching his breath and fighting back tears, "and they were dying."

The Walmart, which sits off Interstate 10 in the middle of a busy commercial center, is within easy reach from the Paso del Norte International

Bridge and the city's other cross-border thoroughfares. On that day, as on most days, it was teeming with customers from both sides of the Rio Grande. Many were seniors who in the first days of every month tended to cash their Social Security checks at a small branch office of a bank inside the store before shopping for groceries. The man carried a semiautomatic rifle, which, he would later tell police, he had purchased online from a Romanian manufacturer and picked up at a gun store near the Dallas suburb where he lived. It was loaded with hollow-point bullets, which expand upon impact, creating larger wounds, and he would use it to strike fronterizos and passersby at America's gateway in the desert.

One of the first killed was María Eugenia Legarreta Rothe, fifty-eight, a mother of four from a prominent Chihuahua family who had driven in from Ciudad Chihuahua to pick up her teenage daughter at the airport and, with time to spare, had made a quick stop to run some errands. She had been walking to her car when the shooter opened fire and hit her. After he paused behind a parked vehicle to reload, he shot her again, this time point-blank.

Benny McGuire, a soccer dad, had been nearby, at the fold-out tables of the fundraising tent outside the front entrance. He and his ten-year-old daughter, Madison, were selling freshly made aguas frescas and chicharrones with other coaches and players from her girls' soccer team, EP Fusion. McGuire had been walking away when he heard the rifle blasts. He turned around in time to see a puff of smoke. "I looked at my daughter and said, 'Run!'" McGuire told the *El Paso Times*. "It just felt like time stopped."

Jorge Calvillo García, sixty-one, who had just arrived in his pickup truck with his son, Luis, and granddaughter, Emily, died shielding some of the girls. Guillermo "Memo" García, thirty-six, one of the team's coaches, was struck in the back at least three times as he also fought to protect loved ones. A second coach and other parents were hit, as by then hundreds of people, some dripping in blood, were rushing in and out of the store looking for places to hide. Several players and their relatives who had been passing out fliers ran inside into the bakery and crouched under the counter with employees. They heard the shooter enter the Walmart and the thud of bodies dropping to the ground as the crack of gunshots echoed across the store. As he came in, the man killed Alexander Gerhard Hoffmann, sixty-six, a German who had lived in Ciudad Juárez for more than forty years. He then turned his gunfire on a group of people huddled inside the bank branch near the checkout aisles, slaying nine.

They were Javier Amir Rodriguez, who had been on the verge of starting his sophomore year at Horizon High School, and at fifteen was the youngest victim; Margie Reckard, sixty-three, a Baltimore native with Nebraska roots battling Parkinson's disease; Gloria Irma Márquez, sixty-one, a Mexican mother and grandmother who, because of immigration complications, had been separated from one of her daughters for more than a decade; Leonardo Campos, forty-one, and Maribel Hernandez, fifty-six, a married couple who left four children behind; Ivan Filiberto Manzano, forty-six, a father of two and owner of a marketing firm in Juárez; Elsa Mendoza Márquez, fifty-seven, a school principal who was also from Juárez and had dashed into the bank while her son and husband waited in the car; and Andre and Jordan Anchondo, parents in their mid-twenties out shopping for one of their sons' school supplies. They died as Jordan held their two-month-old baby, Paul Gilbert Anchondo, who sustained broken bones as they fell.

With the bullets ringing, word of the bloodshed spread across parking lots and big-box stores and chain restaurants. About half a mile away, Ruby Luna, twenty-three, had been helping a customer at a Dillard's inside the mall when a frazzled man wandered into the clothing racks warning—wrongly, she would later learn—that a shooter was inside. She and three other employees took cover in a bedding stock room. The shelves were piled with sheets and blankets. Manny Quintana, who had been selling watches in the men's department one floor below, remembered shoppers were soon flooding in, screaming, "Get out! Get out! He's in here!" He helped direct them to the exits and then joined them as police officers, military soldiers, and SWAT teams swarmed the area and evacuated customers with shouts of "Hands up!"

The masses streamed out into the desert heat and a loud brightness filled with the blare of ambulances and sirens and the whirring blades of helicopters. Some ran with no thought or direction in mind but survival. Others desperately searched for friends and family members. People turned to each other and their phones for snippets of information, news mixed with rumors and conspiracy theories, videos of survivors fleeing gunshots, and pictures of unidentified armed men guessed to be the assailants. No one was sure where the killer was or if there were others. "The shooter is at the Cinemark theater"—so went the chatter of falsehoods. "There are two shooters and they are outside Cielo Vista Mall." "There are many shooters, clad in fatigues and riding in black SUVs."

At the Walmart, the killer turned away from the bank and walked through the checkout aisles, firing and wounding more people ducking behind shelves and counters and sprawled on the floors. A few whispered prayers beneath the tables of a fast-food restaurant within. Some hid in bathrooms and storage areas. An employee helped others climb into shipping containers. Adria Gonzalez, thirty-eight, had been arguing with her mother about the price of meat near the back when they heard what sounded like firecrackers ripping through the air. She ran to the front of the store as the killer shot the gun. "All I could see was he was like, 'Boom, boom, boom,'" she would tell me later, imitating his motions. Recalling the tips that her older brother would share with her from his military training, she snapped into action, ushering people out—some fifty survivors, an FBI agent would later tell her—to a hidden exit she spotted in the meat department. She carried two children in her arms.

Nine more people died inside near the checkout aisles. They included Arturo Benavides, sixty, an Army veteran and former bus driver; Angelina Englisbee, eighty-six, a Santa Fe native who only moments before had talked to her son on the phone and had sounded cheery; Raul Flores, eighty-three, and his wife, Maria, seventy-seven, who had been married for sixty years and were out buying air mattresses for visiting family members; Teresa Sanchez, eighty-two, a retired biology teacher; Adolfo Cerros Hernández, sixty-eight, and Sara Esther Regalado, sixty-six, another married couple who had stopped in from Juárez; and Luis Alfonso Juarez, a former ironworker who had become an American citizen after immigrating from Mexico and who, at ninety, was the oldest victim of the massacre.

At a temporary family reunification center, Stephanie Melendez recalls she was moved by the kindness of strangers who waited alongside her for news of whether their friends and relatives were dead or alive—people of all races, backgrounds, and nationalities. Melendez held out hope that her father, David Johnson, sixty-three, would make it, but her mother, Kathleen, already knew her husband was gone. She and their nine-year-old granddaughter, Kaitlyn, had been covered in his blood as he blocked them from the hail of gunfire. The grandparents had been babysitting the young girl and were standing in line with school supplies and a Disney *Descendants* outfit. When Melendez phoned her mom as they evacuated the store, all she could hear was her young daughter crying through the din of the chaos. "My mom just kept repeating, 'Kaitlyn was not shot. Dad was shot,'" Melendez said.

As the man left the Walmart, he paused to shoot at two more people who had driven by in their car and parked near the front of the store. He killed Juan de Dios Velásquez, seventy-seven, who attempted to put his body over that of his wife, Nicolasa Estela, when he realized the man was about to attack them. She was struck but lived.

García, the soccer coach, would die months later after multiple surgeries.

THE SHOOTER RETURNED to his own car and fled the lot. Then he came back to the scene about twenty minutes later and surrendered himself to law enforcement officers at a nearby intersection. He was taken to an El Paso police station, where he consented to two interviews, the first led by local detectives, the second by special agents with the Federal Bureau of Investigation. The man described himself as a white nationalist, a prosecutor later said at his plea hearing. In both interrogations, he confessed he had committed the shooting to, as the lawyer described it, "dissuade Mexican and other Hispanic immigrants from coming to the United States." He also pointed the investigators to a thumb drive in his car with information he wanted them to find.

The device contained a note to his family and the racist screed titled "The Inconvenient Truth" that he had written over several weeks and posted online only minutes before the shooting. The four single-spaced pages described

Hispanic immigrants as an "invasion," detailed a plan to divide the nation into territories by race, and claimed that white people were being replaced by immigrants and foreigners. They opened with the man expressing his support for another mass shooter who, only months before, in March 2019, had attacked two mosques in New Zealand, leaving fifty-one people dead. A third document on the flash drive was a copy of that killer's manifesto, "The Great Replacement," which promoted the white supremacist theory by the same name, often associated with Renaud Camus, a French writer.

The massacre in El Paso would illustrate a global rise in white extremism in the social media era and at a time when nativist and anti-immigrant sentiments were contributing to an appetite for closed borders and authoritarianism around the world. In the United States, that violence was part of a homegrown problem that had suffered from federal inattention through Republican and Democratic administrations as, for years, law enforcement agencies had tended to focus more on dismantling Mexican criminal organizations and foreign terror groups. When Donald J. Trump ascended to the White House in 2017, warning of a culturally changing America and rallying crowds with nativist cries of "Build the wall," he only further fanned the flames of conflict, as counterterrorism and national security scholars have documented. Like the theories of eugenicists and social Darwinists that had once spread around the world, white power and far-right-wing ideas reached beyond borders—this time with the help of the internet.

The ideologies of American white power organizations and foreign terror groups, like the Islamic State (ISIS) differ greatly: ISIS members have sought to create a caliphate, an autonomous region under an Islamic ruler in the heart of the Middle East. American white supremacists seek to build an all-white ethnostate. But the tactics their members use to recruit, radicalize, and push their most unstable followers to violence are similar. Through online channels, both kinds of extremists seek out those feeling disconnected from society and try to bolster their feeling that their way of life is under threat, that their political system is broken, and that the only way to right their grievances is through inflicting terror.

Domestic terror investigations do not entirely capture the scope of white power members' organizations or their racial and ethnic violence: One of the deadliest mass shootings to presage the El Paso massacre occurred in June 2015 when a twenty-one-year-old white supremacist attended a Bible study at an African American church in Charleston, South Carolina, and opened fire, killing nine Black parishioners. It was classified as a hate crime, not an act of terrorism or right-wing extremism, because law enforcement officials did not believe the charges against the killer aligned with such definitions as strictly outlined in federal law. Under the Trump administration, as Trump downplayed the dangers of white supremacist groups, resources shifted even further away from investigations into right-wing extremism, and the threat intensified, scholars have found.

In August 2017, several hundred men and women marched into the University of Virginia in Charlottesville bearing torches and chanting "Jew will not replace us." A day later, members of white power militias and organizations gathered at a nearby park for a unity rally organized by white supremacists who had been sharing racist content online, including memes supporting the use of Zyklon B, the gas used to kill Jews in Nazi extermination camps and sprayed on migrants in the El Paso "baths." As social justice protesters later marched through the streets, a self-avowed white supremacist intentionally plowed his car into the crowd. He killed Heather Heyer, a paralegal and civil rights activist, and injured thirty-five more people.

One year later, in October, a white nationalist shouting anti-Semitic slurs and armed with an AR-15 semiautomatic rifle and handguns killed eleven people at the Tree of Life synagogue in Pittsburgh. Only months before the El Paso shooting, on the last day of Passover, another white gunman following in the footsteps of the New Zealand shooter, attacked Chabad of Poway synagogue in Poway, California, near San Diego. He injured three and took the life of Lori Gilbert-Kaye, a congregant who jumped between the man and her rabbi. A few years later, in May 2022, a white teenage gunman also drawn to the Great Replacement theory opened fire at a supermarket in Buffalo, New York, killing ten people, all of whom were Black, and injuring three more. The stories of the victims, parents and grandparents out shopping for groceries or running quick errands, painfully echoed those of El Paso.

After the shooting at the Walmart, as I sat on a stone ledge on Scenic Drive in the Franklin Mountains, where cannons had once been pointed at Juárez below and members of the KKK had burned crosses, I thought about how the place where I was from needed to be explained to America every decade: about how it always seemed to enter the nation's collective consciousness through death and tragedy, border walls and boots on the ground, drugs and migrant caravans and national security, and not the vibrant mix of its people, the strength and labor of all those who had helped build the Southwest, coming and going through its mountain pass.

The inability of Americans to confront the uglier side of our history, to tell our story honestly—to remember the origins, both rich and violent, that had made El Paso, and thus our nation—appeared to me to be at the core of the cycle of violence, with blood spilled in defense of one of its deadliest myths: that such a pure white culture had ever existed on land so brown.

For three years I had borne witness to the escalating nativist and xenophobic rhetoric and antidemocratic strains that had been fueling more episodes of violence on both sides of the political spectrum, but more so, as counterterrorism researchers traced, on the right. I had first seen this strain of our politics on the rise when I became a state politics reporter for the *Los Angeles Times* in Sacramento in the summer of 2016 and one of my first assignments had been to cover a bloody clash between neo-Nazis and anti–white supremacists in which seven people were stabbed. I witnessed this political divide again at the "Battle for Berkeley" when, on a sunny, breezy day in the Bay, white nationalists and far-left protesters scuffled under clouds of pepper spray.

If I suspected El Paso's story needed to be central to the American story in the days I stood outside the Walmart memorial in my hometown after twenty-three people were massacred, I became absolutely certain of it in Washington, D.C., on January 6, 2021, when other political reporters and I were swept out of the Capitol Building through underground tunnels, alongside senators and staffers, as rioters brandishing Confederate flags and Nazi insignia trashed what is arguably the nation's most iconic symbol of democracy. And I was reminded of it yet again when, on the fourth anniversary of the Charlottesville terror attack, I stood on the same street where Heather Heyer was killed. At the makeshift memorial, which bore a heartbreaking similarity to the one in the parking lot in El Paso, people dropped off flowers and stuffed animals and some silently wept. Messages scribbled in chalk across a brick wall endured: *Gone but not forgotten. Never forget the summer of hate. Hope is action.*

A man who stopped to pay his respects turned to me as I looked on in silence. He told me that Heather's favorite color had been purple.

10

The Silence in Chuco Town

EL PASO, TEXAS
1940s to 1960s

IT COULD BE said that the embers of rebellion never quite faded in the back alleys of El Paso. Not long after the United States began to expel Mexicans and Mexican Americans through the Great Depression, a subculture emerged in the city among a young generation of Mexican and Mexican American rebels who rejected assimilation into the white American mainstream. They were called pachucas and pachucos, and they distinguished themselves by their defiance of societal norms and flashy dress and hairstyles. The men wore slicked-back pompadours and broad-brimmed hats and zoot suits, long coats with wide lapels, and high-waisted, loose-fitting trousers. The women donned red lipstick, pencil skirts, and jackets with shoulder pads, their tresses coiffed up high in curls or bouffants.

Pachucos and pachuchas listened to blues and danced swing. They smoked the occasional marijuana cigarette and spoke caló, a dialect of their making that mixed Spanish and English slang. Many moved to Los Angeles and nationwide, by themselves or with their families, following the well-worn paths of Mexican and Mexican American blue-collar workers who had been using El Paso as a crossroads since the U.S.-Mexico border had been drawn. Their fashion and movement went national, and El Paso gained underground fame as the home of El Chuco—or Chuco Town. Another story has it that it was in fact the Mexican workers who passed through the city who had given it and its pachucos the name. Residents of Juárez who worked at an El Paso shoe company in the 1920s and '30s, so goes the lore, could often be heard saying that they were headed "pa' el shoe co.," or "to the shoe co." Eventually, other Mexicanos repeated the phrase, indicating they were going "pa' Chuco" anytime they were crossing into El Paso.

Whatever the case, El Paso, or El Chuco, was the pass of the Mexican and specifically the Mexican worker: obreros Mexicanos, México Americanos, and fronterizos. Their migration was not so much unilateral but an ebb and flow, sometimes voluntary, more often, as it had been from the beginning—whether by imperial expansion, border enforcement, labor exploitation, or racial exclusion—out of necessity or outright coercion. The Martinezes and the Chews had lived through the revolution that had militarized the crossing and resulted in the vilification of its most constant crossers. Now their kin, like the Rubios, the Holguins, and the Mura'ls, would endure the expansion of measures, many racist and xenophobic, to inspect, surveil, and criminalize the people at the pass.

Not a full decade had gone by since the Mexican repatriations had ended when the United States began calling Mexican workers back. With so many American men going off to fight overseas during World War II, the country was once again in dire need of laborers, mainly in fields across the Southwest. To solve the shortage of workers, the United States and Mexico struck a deal in 1942 establishing the Bracero Program. It granted temporary permits for Mexican laborers to plant and harvest American crops. Over the next two decades, some 4 million men would register for the initiative in towns and cities across Mexico. Some 80,000 would cross through El Paso alone every year, joining the steady to and fro of all the other workers.

Sometime after 1945, the Martinezes' sons, Camilo and Little Miguel, moved to Juárez and joined the rhythm, finding work at the ASARCO copper smelting plant in El Paso, where Mexican families had once lived among the smokestacks of Smeltertown, nestled in the Franklin Mountains. Victoria wanted the family to stay close together, so after more than a decade in Ciudad Chihuahua and its rural outskirts, she and Miguel followed them to Juárez. They added to the flow of Mexicans going pa' Chuco nearly every day. Victoria went into cleaning houses, Miguel into keeping up gardens. Their second youngest daughter, Manuela, would babysit for relatives on the other side.

Like Herlinda Wong Chew, Victoria became a quick study in the U.S. immigration system. Mexican Americans were reintegrating into American society. The Second World War had exposed the horrors of the Holocaust, diminishing the eugenics movement that had sought to define them as peons (though not ending it), and Black soldiers returning home pushed for civil rights and the breaking of racial barriers after weathering the hypocrisy of prejudice and Jim Crow segregation even as they defended democracy abroad. The Chinese Exclusion Act had come to an end as the United States and China became allies, and so many Mexican American, Chinese American, and Filipino American G.I.'s were returning home from fighting for their country overseas that nativist fevers abated. Many Mexican American veterans were even feeling encouraged to participate in civic life, get better-paying jobs, and earn an education.

Victoria eventually obtained the legal means for her family to move to El Paso for good and helped other Mexican families come over, too. In 1952, Congress passed an immigration law ending the explicit racial bans on Asian immigrants. Although its provisions upheld the nation's controversial 1924 immigrant quotas, the new policy provided more legal avenues into the United States for workers with special skills as well as close family members of American citizens and permanent residents, including parents, like the Martinezes, who had U.S.-born children. In 1957, Victoria celebrated as Raymond L. Telles Jr., a decorated World War II veteran, became the first Mexican American mayor of El Paso.

BUT AS ONE global conflict ended, another started, and it would have deadly implications for Latinos, inside and outside their new nation's borders. The United States and the Soviet Union, which had fought together as allies against fascism and German and Japanese expansion, entered a Cold War rivalry that would play out in bloody struggles, not on each other's territories but across Latin America and developing countries around the world.

In a throwback to Mexico's history, American corporations, under dictators they helped install, had bought up massive amounts of land in countries such as El Salvador, Guatemala, Nicaragua, and Honduras. As the United States opposed the Soviets' communist regimes, it came to see virtually any leftist movement in the region for social change, land reform, and independent economic development as a threat to the economic growth it sought to foster through its capitalism and market-based economies. The ghosts of Zapata, of Villa, of la Santa lingered in the minds of Americans who may no longer have recalled their names but had not forgotten the fear of revolts—now on land that had been Latin American before it was American, Spanish before it was Latin American, and Native before the Americans, Latin Americans, and Spanish had existed on that land at all.

The United States staged its first major Cold War intervention in Latin America in 1954 when the Central Intelligence Agency supported a right-wing coup against Jacobo Árbenz Guzmán, the democratically elected president of Guatemala. The United States saw Árbenz as a communist threat for, among other actions, legalizing the Communist Party and nationalizing the plantations of the United Fruit Company. Once the U.S.-backed president assumed office, he immediately began rolling back land reforms that had benefited poor campesinos and voting rights for illiterate Guatemaltecos, which included most of the Indigenous Maya of the Ixil communities in the country's highlands.

As the United States moved to stop Latin Americans from rising up over the land its companies owned south of the border, Americans sought to subjugate the Mexicanos who worked that land to the north of it. In Texas, the farm lobby, which had long held powerful sway in Southwest politics, was now wrestling with Mexico as the nation demanded better pay and working conditions for its braceros. The fights worsened as a number of agricultural contractors flouted regulations, allowing more immigrants from Mexico to enter without lawful work authorization. About a year before the United States helped topple Árbenz, it launched the notoriously racist Operation Wetback, the nation's largest mass deportation project since the last one, named after an ethnic slur that Americans called Mexicanos who entered the country unlawfully by wading across the Rio Grande. Immigration officers and local officials in El Paso and cities along the border used military tactics to corral anywhere from 300,000 to 1.3 million people—mostly Mexican and Mexican American workers, some of whom were American citizens—and load them onto buses, boats, and planes. Once again, cruel racial stereotypes of "dirty" and "disease-bearing" Mexicans were used to justify the brutal means, and people were dropped into unfamiliar parts of Mexico, where they struggled to rebuild what they had lost. Hundreds of others died of sunstroke and sickness in custody. Once again, the rhetoric seemed to harm perceptions of all Latinos in the United States, regardless of nationality or citizenship.

THE MARTINEZES, MUCH older now, on solid legal footing, and familiar with the cold treatment of Mexican workers in the United States, escaped the brunt of the deportations. They bought a little house on Tampa Avenue in South Central El Paso in 1955. It sat near a freight company and an old refinery, on one of those quiet and wide open streets where they could see the Franklin Mountains from their driveway. The house was painted the color of corn silk and had the look of a shoebox, with a flat, walnut-colored roof and decorative wrought iron bars over its windows. A short brick wall curved around a couple of Italian cypresses and an Afghan pine. Their home became a meeting point, a playground, a harbor within a harbor for their children and grandchildren.

Inside, it was cozy, with old mahogany furniture and flower-patterned couches. The cabinets were decked with family photographs and saints, including a small altar to el Santo Niño de Atocha, the elder Miguel's patron saint since his revolutionary days. If one of their children or grandchildren needed a place to lay up or put themselves back together after suffering a hard knock in life, they took them in. If one of them needed a bit of cash, Victoria would persuade Miguel to go into the savings they kept under lock and key in a slim wooden chest in their closet. No one dared borrow what they could not someday pay back.

Victoria was round-faced and petite, a spunky viejita who wore long, flowing skirts and chaste button-up dresses that fell to her ankles. Her graying brown hair was often pulled back in a tight bun, a few flyaways caught in the mountain breeze, a pair of wide, clear-rimmed glasses over her eyes. In photos, she is often captured flashing a grin or laughing, and perhaps it is the trouble that Little Miguel was known to get into or the stories I have heard of Victoria herself that color my view, but there seems to be a twinkle of mischief in her eye. Miguel, whom she called her viejito, was usually at her side. He was a tall and thin brown man with a large, balding forehead and neatly creased trousers that Victoria likely ironed for him.

The Martinezes insisted on family, church, and tradition. Victoria and Miguel had raised her three siblings together, as well as five children of their own, and nearly every Sunday and major holiday, after mass, their very large, very rambunctious family would gather at their house for brunch, barbecues, or pachangas. Mother's Day and Father's Day were holy. The smell of carne asada and grilled hamburgers and hot dogs would waft through the backyard as primas and primos and tías and tíos arrived with their children and their children's children. The tables would fill up with pots of menudo, tamales, and chili, large plates of macaroni, and bowls of salads—all kinds of salads: potato salad, carrot and raisin salad, watermelon and fruit salads.

There was a special order to the night. The girls ate first, then all the boys, then the adults. Afterward, the children would play jacks or baseball or do jigsaw puzzles in the backyard. The women would sit around with Victoria, laughing and catching up. A radio was usually blasting corridos (Miguel's favorites remained those about Pancho Villa), rancheras, Tejano music, and border blues and rock. It would not be long before someone started dancing or pulled out a guitar.

"How's your boyfriend doing?" Victoria would tease her granddaughters. "Next time you go to the movies, I'm going to come with you and sit right between you two."

As they got older, one of those boyfriends she would tease her granddaughters about became her son-in-law, and just before dawn he would crash the Martinezes' celebrations with his rock band to serenade the head matriarch after their gigs at quinces and weddings were done. Victoria would make a big fuss about how wild he was, but everyone knew she enjoyed it—so much so that she began leaving a long extension cord hanging out from one of the windows so that the young men could plug in their amps and guitars should they happen to show up.

About her children and grandchildren, Victoria seemed to know everything: their love interests and heartbreaks, what made them tick, what they wanted out of life. But just as their children and grandchildren knew not to ask for money they could not pay back, they knew not to ask about their grandparents' pasts. Such questions were seen as prying, and prying was a sign of disrespect. Victoria and Miguel, like many Mexicanos of their generation, were private people who buried the most painful memories of what they had witnessed—a war, a depression, a repatriation—in a deep silence. There is only one other kind of silence I can think of to describe it: the deep void of sound in a famous southeastern corner of Victoria's native Chihuahua, la Zona del Silencio. In this region, where meteorites tend to fall with more frequency, the landscape produces a silence so vast and profound that, before the existence of satellite communications, as legend has it, radio receivers could not even detect or transmit hertz waves. It is a silence that can be found only in a few earthly locations: the silence of a remote land of space and aliens, carried from one generation to the next.

"¿Y eso para qué lo quieres saber, mi'jo?" Raúl Reyes recalls that his grandmother Victoria would say. "Why do you want to know that, son? What is past is past. We made it through. What matters is we are here now."

THROUGH THE NEXT few decades, the Martinez family kept growing, and so did their city. After the United States had entered World War II, war industries boomed in Texas and military installations were built or expanded across the state. That included Fort Bliss in El Paso, which buzzed with soldiers. The development of military technology and air combat changed the way wars were fought, and this eased the tensions that had long embroiled land borders in the United States and across western Europe. Cities along the U.S.-Mexico dividing line settled into a dynamic synergy.

El Paso and Ciudad Juárez became two vibrant centers of trade and commerce, each benefiting the other despite their different characters. Whereas El Paso could be quiet, straitlaced, and uptight, its conservative roots running as deep as its liberal ones, Juárez, its louder and more cosmopolitan sister, had a freer spirit. The strong and steady stream of people, labor, and ideas that had coursed between them since their split produced its own distinct border culture, one that Chicano scholars would later call a "third space" but was as much a part of the American fabric as the pachucas and pachucos who danced and smoked their way to rebellion.

Because of the ebb and flow of its workers, its hybridity and position at the crossroads of theories of mestizaje, El Paso was more open toward racial mixing and less stringent on enforcement of its segregation policies than most of the American South. The Black population in El Paso consisted mostly of agricultural, industrial, and railroad workers, along with a few middle-class professionals. It was relatively small well into the twentieth century, but mighty. In 1914, a few years after he moved to the city to escape the lynchings of Black people in east and central Texas, Dr. Lawrence A. Nixon helped found the first chapter of the NAACP in the state. He went on to file a legal challenge that worked its way up to the Supreme Court, and in 1944, it ended the practice that allowed the state and the Democratic Party to deny Black people primary votes. It would be one of the first victories of what would become the Civil Rights Movement. More than a decade later, Thelma White, a valedictorian at segregated Douglass High School, would go on to challenge the racial exclusion of Black students at Texas Western College, now the University of Texas at El Paso. The lawsuit would clear the way to make the school the first desegregated undergraduate institution in the state.

Still, rigid racial and ethnic codes and mores persisted. Many Black soldiers stayed within Fort Bliss, and Black communities tended to concentrate in East Central, Northeast, and East El Paso. The city was predominantly Hispanic but ruled by a white elite minority. Poll taxes kept many Black and Mexican American voters from the ballot box. Interracial marriages were not granted, and Black people were barred from theaters, restaurants, and most white and Mexican bars. In this zero-sum game for power, Black and

Mexican American residents were often pitted against each other, and tensions could and did erupt.

El Paso was the home of Jim and Juan Crow, of the military and the Border Patrol, of persecuted conservative Catholics, many of whom had fled the Cristero War. Like the magonistas, some had been chased down for neutrality violations as they organized protests against Mexico's new revolutionary government from cities in Texas and Arizona. (In one case, three prominent Catholic lawyers from El Paso had defended a Mexican immigrant who was arrested in Tucson after he tried to incite a Catholic uprising with the help of an exiled Catholic bishop, other Mexican migrants, and Yaqui fighters.)

Juárez, on the other hand, was deep in its años dorados, its golden years, as elder fronterizos recall them, a mini Las Vegas on the border offering glitzy dining, aromatic cocktails, and the very finest shows. The streets where revolutionary soldiers and federales had plodded through, occupying worn and damaged tenements, had been revitalized. Investors had bought out residents and refurbished humble adobe houses and buildings into large, multistory music venues, casinos, bars, and restaurants, with stages, terraces, and patios lined with colorful Mexican tiles. These places drew professional dancers and big international bands. Outdoors, mariachis played on street corners, vendors hawked flowers and cigarettes, and so many people came and went at all hours of the night that any given dawn could look as busy as a midafternoon. As electric billboards came into fashion, the glow of neon lit up the town.

There was the Big Kid's Palace, the Silver King, the Coney Island, and the Black Cat. There was also El Mint, where patrons sipped on mint juleps for 60 cents a pop (about $10 in today's currency). El Molino Rojo, or the Moulin Rouge, showcased nude cabaret dancers. La Fiesta, a nightclub designed in old colonial, missionary, and pueblito Mexicano styles, featured a monumental Aztec Stone of the Sun hanging over its stage and hosted top international acts like Earl Grant, Frank Sinatra, and Nat King Cole. Then there was El Chairmont, the Turf, the Gem, and El Submarino. There was La Cucaracha, El Follies, Waikikí, and the majestic El Palacio Chino, which had the look of a theater and was the only venue in the city where at the beginning of every function the stage swiveled up from the floor and rose high above ground level, giving all spectators a good view.

The golden era had begun in the roaring twenties, shortly after the end of the Mexican Revolution. First, Texas banned liquor, gaming, and prostitution within ten miles of all American military training camps, like Fort Bliss, spelling the end for all 265 of El Paso's legal saloons. Then the Eighteenth Amendment ushered in Prohibition across the country. Many bars, saloons, and distilleries nationwide did not bother engaging in temperance debates. They packed up and moved south of the border. Juárez seemed to transform overnight. High rollers and celebrities barreled into its streets, including its two main boulevards, Avenida Juárez and Avenida 16 de Septiembre, where Antonio Chew's La Garantía had once stood. In 1926 the city celebrated the opening of Coliseo Juárez, a massive coliseum for fairs and events, including sports competitions and horse and dog races. On opening day, 8,000 people packed into the stands to watch boxer Jack Dempsey knock out four opponents in a row. At the most high-end venues and gambling spots—like el Tívoli Garden, el Keno, and el Central Cafe—the waiters wore crisp white jackets and black bow ties. The glassware and chandeliers were imported. The linen tablecloths draped above the floors just so. The dress code was upscale, la fiesta sin fin (the party endless).

The Great Depression and the end of Prohibition hurt the scene somewhat in the 1930s, but American soldiers reenergized it and kept it blazing through World War II, the Korean War, and Vietnam, as did El Paso shoppers in search of cheaper gasoline and medications for purchase without a doctor's prescription, and American couples looking to separate from their spouses under a Chihuahua state law passed to generate hefty sums of revenue by making divorce proceedings swift, loose, and inexpensive. If Vegas was a wedding destination, Juárez was the spot for los divorcios al vapor—divorces that evaporated marriages as quickly as steam. In January 1961, Marilyn Monroe was captured making her way back into El Paso in dark shades and a black suit after divorcing playwright Arthur Miller in a Juárez courtroom, where she appeared tired and upset, a black flower pot hat shading her golden curls. Elizabeth Taylor and Richard Burton ended one of their torrid unions in the city a few years later.

The jaunt over the border was more than a good time. For many fronterizos, it was a break from the silence. For Black Americans, that U.S.-Mexico dividing line had long symbolized freedom. Mexico had started trying to outlaw slavery since it first declared its independence from the Spanish in 1821, long before the American Civil War, and almost immediately, enslaved Black people had fled American plantations to reach it. In the 1950s, a neighborhood of Black Mexicans, or Blaxicans, emerged in downtown Juárez, according to anthropologists Howard Campbell and Michael Williams. Its formation was driven as much by the draw of Mexico, its history, entertainment attractions, and more pliable racial attitudes as by the desire to escape the harshness of Jim Crow.

In Juárez, there was segregation in the Mexican entertainment districts, rules that were informal and mostly went unspoken but that patrons abided. Black people were not allowed into certain bars frequented only by white foreigners and some affluent Mexicans. If Black men were seen hanging out with Mexican women on main streets, there was a high chance Mexican police would harass them. But in la Mariscal, the raunchy red-light district near the city's central plaza, which most Black residents lived in and around, Black business owners and performers fueled a thriving Black jazz and blues scene that the pachucos of the previous decade would have died for—and there, nearly anything went. The Black-owned venues, the most popular of which was Club 77, catered to a largely Black crowd but plenty of white people and Mexicans, too. Gay boys could kiss gay boys. Juárez trawlers, whether Black or white, as anthropologist Howard Campbell has documented, could take on whole new identities: Michael, a white guy from Chicago, could become Miguelito. Charles Kelly, a Black man from Detroit, could become Carlos.

From the moment the border between El Paso and Juárez had been etched with sticks and stones, Mexicanos and México Americanos had been made to conform to the black-and-white binary that was the American caste system, even as it suppressed and contradicted the mixed social, racial, and cultural roots of our families. The Treaty of Guadalupe Hidalgo had classified Mexicans left on land that had once been Mexican as white, and until 1920 a handful of states, including Texas, had even recognized "alien voting rights" for Mexicans. But despite this "fragile legal claim to whiteness," as scholars such as Laura E. Gómez have termed it, the majority of Mexicanos and México Americanos would remain relegated to a space not unlike the borderlands many inhabited, a place somewhere in between. An off-white.

Like the pachucos who replaced the magonistas loitering in El Paso's downtown bars, some Mexicans and Mexican Americans had attempted to eliminate the borders of whiteness altogether. Before the Teresita Rebellion, Catarino Garza, a journalist, led a small group of armed rebels against Porfirio Díaz in the northern Mexican uprising credited as the earliest harbinger of the Mexican Revolution—a cross-border revolt in South Texas that rallied under the banner cry "¡Libre fronterizo!" Through the revolution, many Mexicanos born on different sides of the river organized as a united front against the discrimination they experienced in the United States. But as eugenics and nativist movements took hold and vigilante groups and the Texas Rangers unleashed racial terror across much of Texas—massacres such as those of la Matanza—some Mexicans and Mexican Americans became convinced that they needed to fight, in social, legal, and political realms, to be seen and treated as white because to be seen or treated as Black or otherwise meant the seizure of their land and property, lynching, violence, or death.

At the end of the First World War, a group of Mexican American men, most of them returning veterans from middle-class families, launched some of the largest campaigns to obtain Mexican civil rights and political power in South Texas and formed the League of United Latin American Citizens. In 1946, their organization became part of the successful class action lawsuit that challenged the racial segregation of Mexican Americans in California public schools. The case ruling, which found it unlawful to forcibly separate Mexican American students by their ancestry, skin color, and Spanish language, strengthened the landmark Supreme Court decision in 1954 that desegregated Black and white schools. But the plaintiffs argued the discrimination had been based on ancestry and language, not race, because the census legally classified Mexican Americans as racially white.

And yet, the 1954 court ruling that came as Árbenz fell in Guatemala and Mexican men were rounded up along the borderland would supercharge the Civil Rights Movement that would propel many Mexicans and Mexican Americans to reconsider their relationship with Blackness. Some would find new radical ways to combat the silence, to reclaim their Black, mestizo, and Indigenous origins, to find solidarity in la Raza. Again the movements would not be without their flaws. Women tended not to be included in leadership ranks. The empowerment found in theories of mestizaje would belie its uglier chapters of racism and forced assimilation for native Mexicans. But along the borderland, in those years, la conciencia colectiva was once more rising.

And Juárez continued to lure people in. Langston Hughes, on a lecture tour across the United States, took a day trip to the city in 1953. Roberto Ávila, known as "Beto" in Mexico and "Bobby" in the United States, was toasted at the Kentucky Club in 1954, the same year he became the first Mexicano to win an American League batting title, hitting a .341 average for the Cleveland team. Ernest Hemingway and Luis Miguel Dominguín, a Spanish bullfighter, turned Club 15 near the downtown cathedral into their home base when they spent one hot summer month in the city in 1959, on a world tour in commemoration of Hemingway's sixtieth birthday. The heat, it was reported, left them no choice but to drink copious numbers of Cruz Blanca chelas and bottles of Juarez Whiskey Straight American.

Before he obtained national fame, Texas blues legend Long John Hunter in 1957 scored a regular gig at the Lobby Club, or el Lobby, where he led the house band for thirteen years. He was known to play two guitars at once and perform stunts on ropes that hung from the ceiling. Etta James and a then-unknown Buddy Holly were said to have attended his shows. One story had it that James Brown hopped onstage in the middle of a break—and was promptly dressed down by Hunter's fans. Hunter's hit "El Paso Rock" was likely to have streamed out of the radio playing at the Martinezes' little house on Tampa, just as it did out of radio stations in Del Rio, Texas, where Billy Gibbons, frontman of the Texas trio ZZ Top, grew up listening to him. Gibbons would later call him El Paso and Juárez's gift to the blues. As he put it, "It didn't get more Texas border boogie than that."

As a child in those years, Victoria's granddaughter, Margie Martinez, did not know that her grandparents had once been forced out of the United States, and she was too young to understand when American officials booted out Mexicans again. Racism and colorism were the kinds of matters Mexicanos and México Americanos did not talk about. What she did know was that at her old school, where most of the kids were Mexican, they made fun of her because she had brown skin and did not know how to speak Spanish and that at her new school, where most of the kids were white, some wouldn't talk to her because she had brown skin and was Mexican. Yet, echoing Herlinda's granddaughter many years later, she told me El Paso had always let her feel pride in her binational, bicultural identity.

She recalled she had Victoria's independent streak, and the two always seemed to be up to something—like the time they persuaded the priest to allow Margie to perform her first Holy Communion months before the first catechism class even convened for the year. In the Catholic tradition, children—usually older than Margie was at the time—had to be well versed in a number of Catholic teachings before they could receive the body and blood of Christ. Margie didn't know much about the Eucharist, but she really, really wanted to try one of those little wafers everyone else got at mass.

"She wants to try the Eucharist, Father," Victoria told the priest. "Might it be the Holy Spirit calling her, Father? At least, let her take the Communion test."

Finally, the priest obliged, figuring Margie, who was about five or six, would never pass the test anyway. But Margie spent the next few weeks studying, learning the Seven Sacraments, the Ten Commandments, and every prayer that was asked of her by heart. She passed, and at the next wedding at the church, there was Margie, an honorary flower girl, so that the priest could host her first Holy Communion ceremony at the same time.

"My mother would say, 'That spoiled girl is always with her grandma,'" Margie remembered.

11

American Dreamer

San Gabriel, Durango
1964

Sabino Rubio was born just outside the Mexican town where Pancho Villa may well lie dead and buried. Four years after Villa attacked the New Mexican town of Columbus, the guerrillero negotiated his truce with the Mexican government and retired to a simple life just south of Chihuahua, in the northern Mexican state of Durango, where he had been born. He had never truly trusted anyone, not even his closest friends, and in retirement his paranoia did not dissipate. He tended to always travel with an escort of at least fifty armed fighters whom he had personally selected during his fight with Venustiano Carranza to form his famous cavalry of bodyguards, Los Dorados, the Golden Ones.

But as the threats to his life decreased and the costs of his security detail became too high, Villa shed his guards. On July 20, 1923, the old former general had only a few men with him when they were ambushed in Parral, in southern Chihuahua, after visiting some friends and one of Villa's many ex-wives. Villa had been at the wheel of his black 1919 Dodge roadster when, at the intersection of Benito Juárez and Gabino Barrera, a pumpkin seed vendor suddenly lurched forward and saluted them with a shout of "¡Viva Villa!" The move was a signal to an assassin that Villa was in the front seat, and before Villa could even return the battle cry, the spray of bullets rained down on his car. He was hit nine times. He and an aide died instantly.

Villa's killer, Jesús Salas Barraza, a man whom Villa had once pistol-whipped in an argument over a woman, was sentenced to twenty years in prison but was released after a month. Villa was buried a day after his slaying, his coffin dragged to a cemetery in Parral by two black horses. A military guard and band and a dour procession of thousands of people followed closely behind.

There was no peace for the revolucionario. Three years later, grave robbers desecrated Villa's tomb and made off with his skull, believing they could sell it in the United States, where bulletins had once offered hefty rewards for his head. A furious Mexican president demanded that Villa's remains be moved to Mexico City after that. But locals say the governor of Durango switched out the bodies and that the real Villa still lies six feet underground in an unmarked grave in Parral.

As a young Sabino grew up, people continued to gather in Parral every year on the anniversary of Villa's death for a celebration in his honor. The town remained the largest pueblo near Sabino's rancho of San Gabriel, a quiet hamlet of no more than one hundred people who lived scattered in squat adobe homes among the cottonwoods and rolling chaparral of Durango, right on the border with Chihuahua. Long gone were the revolucionarios who had roamed the open prairies. Long gone, too, was the adventure that Sabino was sure those men must have had. His life was all work, tilling soil and herding cows. He was around eighteen or nineteen and restless.

After the end of the Mexican Revolution and the Cristero War, the National Revolutionary Party (Partido Revolucionario Nacional) had assumed control of Mexico and installed a socialist-capitalist government. It took back ownership of private-owned farms, ranches, and plantations across the country—that is to say, most of the rural property in Mexico—and converted them into ejidos, communal lands where community members had rights over the fruit of their toil, though ownership remained in the hands of the Mexican state. But through the Bracero Program, many of these farms and ranches languished as most young and able men went to el Norte to work in American fields, leaving women and older men to tend to the communal lands and rely on their remittances.

Sabino's rancho had not been as hard hit as most, but it was small. Many of its residents were tied by blood or bond, and everyone seemed to know everyone else and their business. Sabino's father was a generous yet stern vaquero who kept him and his sixteen younger brothers in line. The young men rose with the sun to sow chile, maíz, and frijoles on his family's parcel of land. Out in the fields, the air was fresh but life was slow and money hard to come by. There was not much else to do but to go to church. The only stores were small commissary shops. There were no electric lights. No cars or trucks or paved roads. The only way to get around was by horse.

Sabino set his eyes on what lay north, far beyond the isolated mountain ranges and golden grasses of Durango and Chihuahua, and on a hot summer afternoon in 1964, when a town meeting was called inside San Gabriel's only schoolhouse, it was as if the good spirits in the sierra heard his prayers. On most days, in the large adobe building, one teacher taught alternating classes for students in grades one through four. But on this day dozens of campesinos crammed inside. They filled the long wooden benches and stood against the walls.

A town foreman soon called the meeting to order and alerted the room that San Gabriel had just received a letter from the government of Durango, offering its men the chance to join the Bracero Program in the United States. The initiative was well-known in rural areas like San Gabriel. Though word had it the trips up north were long and harsh, and men could go hungry and sleep on concrete floors for days, many believed it was all worth it for what felt like the opportunity of a lifetime: a chance to earn a solid living wage and power an important sector of the American economy. Some sold their chickens, pigs, and cows to make the journey.

In Durango, as Sabino recalls it, each municipality in the state's rural areas was given a quota to fill, based on the number of field hands that agricultural growers estimated they needed on American farms. From San Gabriel, the number was sixty: sixty opportunities for him to leave the slow ways of the rancho behind, the slow ways revolucionarios had once died to defend; sixty opportunities to earn some real money. Sabino needed only one.

The room buzzed with excitement as men eager for the jobs scribbled their names on thin strips of paper and a volunteer collected the scraps in the cup of a sombrero. Another man stuck his hand inside and gave the batch a good mix before he began to pull out the slips and read each name aloud. It was like a lottery, and Sabino would never forget winning it.

"¡Sabino Rubio!" the foreman's voice thundered. Sabino, a tall, lanky teenager in boots and a vaquero's hat, stood in the crowd with his dad, friends, and cousins. He was elated. He would never look back.

El Paso, Texas
1964

When the United States and Mexico started the Bracero Program during the Second World War, Camp Bliss was constructed within Fort Bliss. At first the internment camp, a detention facility to house "suspected enemy aliens," held twenty-nine of the roughly 120,000 Japanese and Japanese Americans who were wrongfully imprisoned during the war. The prisoners lived in a stockade on rocky terrain behind a double barbed-wire fence and were watched from above by armed guards on elevated towers.

Within two years, it was phased out and converted into a camp where Italian prisoners were held to relieve the demands of El Paso area farmers, who were so short on hands in the region's surrounding cotton fields. But the Italian prisoners were phased out after complaints from the cotton farmers that the Italians were poor farmworkers. And so, after D-Day, military officers brought in German prisoners instead. These workers were better received, but one year after the war ended, the camp was closed and the Germans were gone.

In contrast, the Mexican braceros never stopped coming.

The chosen from San Gabriel were sent to Durango, and within a week or two the men were notified what day they were to report to the contracting center in Ciudad Chihuahua. Soon, Sabino was on a bus there with about a dozen other men. They registered at the laborers' station, then took another bus north to a depot in Ciudad Juárez. Mexican police officers greeted them upon their arrival. They assembled the men into lines according to where they came from and led them through the streets for a mile or two to the international bridge—pa' Chuco—campesinos turned into workers turned back into campesinos, now on someone else's land.

Sabino remembers that a couple of skyscrapers dotted the downtown El Paso skyline. But he did not get much of a chance to take in the view. At the checkpoint, American officials performed a quick inspection of their documents, then shuttled them along the U.S.-Mexico border to the Rio Vista Bracero Reception Center in the small city of Socorro, just south of El Paso. The facility, which sat on a desolate stretch of ranchland, was a collection of adobe barracks with arched gable roofs, porches, and covered breezeways fashioned in the style of an old Spanish mission. The farm had housed indigent residents during the Great Depression and later elderly people and neglected children. Now the reception center was one of five along the border and processed thousands of braceros a day.

By the time Sabino arrived that sweltering summer of 1964, the staff at Rio Vista had churned out nearly 800,000 contracts in the thirteen years since it had first opened its doors, dispatching braceros to worksites in Texas, New Mexico, the northern and central plains, the upper Midwest, and the Rocky Mountain states. The braceros who passed through its corridors hailed from ranches and pueblos all across Mexico: Chihuahua, Zacatecas, and Veracruz; Michoacán, Durango, and Tamaulipas. One group of Indigenous Mexican laborers, only one of whom spoke Spanish, had at one point come from as far south as the state of Yucatán, where Mexico twists into the shape of a boot that kicks into the gulf. The freshest recruits tended to arrive in white, baggy cotton pants and shirts, straw hats, and huaraches. The veterans walked in decked out in western wear: jeans, boots, and cowboy hats.

Once at Rio Vista, Sabino and his group from San Gabriel joined hundreds of other aspiring braceros making their way around the quad to different stations at each of the buildings. A central PA system crackled with announcements, and staff members gave out instructions with bullhorns. First, they organized Sabino's incoming group into four or five lines and led the men to a large, open barracks supported by wooden beams and topped with a low-pitched roof. They ordered them to strip off all of their clothes under the shelter and then sprayed each of them down with small silver canisters filled with lindane powder. Inspectors told the workers the insecticide would kill off any lice and ticks and ensure they were clean. Call Carmelita!

"Ahí no habia distinción" ("There was no distinction"), Sabino recalled years later. It did not matter if you were from a popular pueblo or a little-known ranchito like his own. It did not matter what color your skin was or whether your family was a little better-off. Every Mexican who wanted the work was subjected to the process.

Before Sabino had boarded the bus to Juárez, officials in Ciudad Chihuahua had let him know what to expect once he arrived in El Paso, so Sabino wasn't too surprised by the demands of the gabachos, who now herded them like cattle. But once he was standing there naked in the open air, surrounded by dozens of other nude men, he felt exposed and strange. The dust reeked with a musty odor and slightly stung their skin. It made their eyes water and itch. It turned their bodies, faces, and hair white. It was not uncommon for at least one bracero to joke, "Well, I guess we're gringos now."

Sabino laughs now at how ridiculous it all was. But back then he did not dwell on any of it, did not give the inspections so much as a second thought. He focused on the light streaming in from the outside, on the work that lay ahead, and of course the money to be made. The American Dream. Drenched in the chemicals, the men were escorted to the bathrooms, where they showered and dressed in fresh clothes. They had their photographs and fingerprints taken. Medical staff with the United States Public Health Service tested their blood, snapped X-rays of their chests, and gave them cursory physicals. Then they were taken to the mess hall for a quick lunch that included beans, rice, chili con carne, and a small bar of laxative. Apparently, their new bosses not only wanted their outsides clean but their insides clean, too, Sabino recalled. The laxative looked like a piece of chocolate, and Sabino thought it was dessert. But one of his friends who had already worked a season as a Texas bracero stopped him before he popped it in his mouth.

"Te va a dar torzón" ("It will give you a stomachache"), he told Sabino. Sabino heeded the advice and threw it away.

Not all of the men who arrived at the center were selected. An infectious disease made one ineligible, and Department of Labor employees were looking for specific traits in their workers—mainly youth, servility, humility, and docility. The ideal candidate was a lean and muscular man between his twenties and forties, someone whose hands were callused and face was wrinkled and damaged from the sun. White-collar workers and other Mexicanos drawn to the program by the prospect of building a nest egg to bring back home, however paltry, would rub their hands with stones or chalk to make them look hardened. Immigration officers like Socorro Pérez, who typed out passports at Rio Vista's fingerprinting station from roughly 1955 to 1957, could sniff them out. "If their hands were very smooth, that meant they were not workers; they were just out here for the adventure or to stay here," she said in an oral history interview. But Pérez also noted that some men's hands were so worn down from the manual labor that they no longer had readable fingerprints: The unique markers of human identity had been erased.

Outside the dining hall, small buses waited to take the new field hands to farms across the country, their destinations mounted above their front windows. Individual American growers and representatives of major growers' organizations like the El Paso Valley Cotton Association and the Artesia Alfalfa Growers Association picked their men by size and appearance, a process that historians now say carried reverberations of antebellum slave or modern livestock auctions. The old-timers knew which places had the better pay and conditions and which to avoid—such as those near Pecos, Texas, which had been so discriminatory in the 1950s that Mexican Americans and braceros had not been allowed to sit on the main floor of the local movie theater.

Sabino, who had never traveled beyond Chihuahua and did not know any better, found himself aboard the bus headed exactly there. Over the next three and a half months, he picked cotton across the Texas oil country, first in Stanton, then in Pecos, later likely in Midland, though he is not exactly sure. The farms were giant bustling enterprises far removed from his ranchito outside of Parral. Buses and trucks moved in and out of the worksites daily. Neat, rigid acres of blooming white cotton fields stretched for miles in all directions. He worked alongside dozens of braceros, their backs hunched from sunrise to sundown, often six or seven days a week. He worked for whichever gabacho grower in the valley needed it, the farmers shuttling him and all the other workers from parcel to parcel. At night, Sabino slept on bunk beds in sheet-metal barracks with about forty other men. On their infrequent downtime, they cracked jokes, listened to the radio, and cooked their own meals in a wide, communal kitchen with rows of gas stoves.

The American Dream was coined as the United States kicked out Mexican and Mexican American families like the Martinezes. Historians and economists credit the writer James Truslow Adams with popularizing the phrase in his 1931 bestseller, *The Epic of America*. In his book, Adams ruminated on the Great Depression as he tried to figure out where the country went wrong. Like Teresa Urrea, who had warned her masses of followers that money and avarice warped people's relationships and goals, Truslow argued against the worshipping of material gains. To Adams, the American Dream was part of a liberal vision in which government could be a force to fight big business, and the United States would be "a land in which life should be better and richer and fuller for every man, with opportunity for each according to ability and achievement."

His symbol of the American Dream at the time had been the Library of Congress. But perhaps it is the earliest mention in print of the words "American Dream" that most fits its legacy: a 1930 ad for a $13.50 marked-down bedspring from an American mattress company.

Federal government campaigns had long sought to encourage Americans to consume and participate in the capitalist economy as a bulwark against the Russian Revolution and the specter of communism. Presidents Warren G. Harding and Calvin Coolidge saw homeownership in particular as a way to bind the American people to the political system and ensure economic and social stability, and Coolidge went so far as to describe it as a patriotic duty. That became especially true through the end of World War II and the cold war that the United States was fighting in Latin America and beyond. The material benchmark of the American Dream became the single-family house and all the appliances that came with it. Pushing the myth, marketers and companies such as General Electric, Kelvinator, and others established the dream house as what returning G.I.'s should expect from their country after serving abroad.

Braceros like Sabino not only bought into the idea of the American Dream but also helped it flourish. On weekends, in towns and cities like Pecos, Texas, Mexicanos filled banks, post offices, and downtown stores, like Penneys and Woolworth's. Many sent part of their earnings back home to Mexico, but a lot of it they spent on flour, beans, and other groceries, on tablecloths and dish towels for their wives. When the season ended, Sabino and other men hopped on buses back to their towns and pueblos in Mexico with gifts for their families. The American Dream was Levi's jeans and sewing machines, radios and bicycles, baby strollers and high chairs and jewelry for their relatives. Not "¡Tierra y Libertad!" but "Goods and Liberty!"

Sabino would have done it all over again. For many braceros, despite the prejudice and hardships, and the baths with dangerous chemicals, the job was a point of pride, a chance to serve the United States, as critical and patriotic a duty as any wartime post in the military. But in November 1960, CBS had aired the documentary *Harvest of Shame*, hosted by Edward R. Murrow, exposing how low wages and poor working conditions harmed Hispanic men like Sabino—and how their employment was affecting the jobs of American-born agricultural workers. Among those watching the evening segment was President Kennedy, who was so disturbed that braceros were negatively affecting the wages and working conditions of native-born farm laborers that he pushed until his assassination for the program to end. On December 31, 1964, under his successor, Lyndon Baines Johnson, and against the protests of farmers, Congress finally did eliminate it, and Sabino became one of the hundreds of thousands of men left without a permit to work legally in the United States, though he was no less drawn to the dream.

12

The Deportation Machine

El Paso–Ciudad Juárez
1965 to 1970s

Sabino Rubio returned to San Gabriel after his Bracero journey, but El Chuco called him back. Like it had Carlos and Antonio. Like it had Hilario and Miguel and Little Miguel. Sabino had gotten a taste of the adventure and promise of opportunity and higher wages on the other side of the border, and the pull of the north was too strong to resist. Plus, Americans' demand for migrant labor had not subsided. They depended on it.

Rubio moved into a cousin's home in Ciudad Juárez. He legally crossed into El Paso with a permit card that allowed Mexicanos to travel anywhere in the United States within twenty-five miles of the U.S.-Mexico border for a short period of time. Then he worked illegally because the card did not authorize Mexicanos to work, but Sabino did so anyway. As soon as he was past the border checkpoint, he stowed the document away in an inside pocket, he recalls, and prayed to God no border agent would stop him again and find it once he was deep into the deserts and scrubland of the Southwest.

In New Mexico, he fixed roofs with a baseball cap and a bandanna shielding his sweaty brow from the hot desert sun. Across Texas, he helped build highway overpasses, often in the winter, bundled up in layers of sweaters and coats in futile attempts to stay warm in the freezing temperatures. Those were the worst. He always preferred the heat to the cold. He helped build a bridge in Amarillo and another that connected the Midland airport to Interstate 27. He worked all along Interstate 10, helping Americans move from one place to another faster and more efficiently even as he was constantly on the lookout for la migra curtailing his own movements.

Mexican workers, as scholars have written, were beginning to constitute the largest group in the stream of illegal migration from Mexico and Latin America, as the United States expanded a system of border and immigration enforcement laws and measures that would in time criminalize their labor, no matter how much the United States relied on it. At the height of the Civil Rights Movement, President Lyndon Johnson signed the Immigration and Nationality Act of 1965 at the base of the Statue of Liberty. It was the culmination of a decade of activism by descendants of Jewish, Irish Catholic, and Asian immigrants who sought to abolish the nation's system of quotas that had been crafted through the eugenics movement and discriminated against newcomers based on nationality, race, and ancestry.

Civil rights activists helped champion the law, which replaced the quotas with a process of sorting immigrants into preference categories based on family relationships and skills, redefining who could belong in the United States. But the 1965 act, as historian Mae M. Ngai has described, would usher in inclusion along with even greater exclusion. It left numerical limits on hemispheric immigration intact, effectively cutting the number of visas available for Mexican immigrants to 20,000 per year. With the Bracero Program coming to an end at the same time, millions of seasonal migrant workers who had been part of an institutionalized network of American labor were rendered undocumented. And as the law set in motion the demographic changes that would fundamentally transform the face of the nation, with increases in immigration from Asian, African, and Latin American countries, a conservative and right-wing backlash would mount. Its scapegoats would be Mexicanos.

Deportations or the fear of them became part of Sabino's everyday existence. He learned to stay alert for immigration officers even in his downtime. He watched out for their green uniforms on job sites and in grocery stores and as he drove to and from work. He did not always manage to avoid them and lost track of how many times officers sent him back to Mexico, only for him to return. Though it had been a criminal act to enter the country without authorization since 1929, that law was seldom enforced.

The paved roads and concrete overpasses that Sabino was helping build across the Southwest were rising in El Paso, too. The border region was continuing to grow. In Juárez, when he was not out looking for work across the Southwest, Sabino hung out with his cousin and old friends who had by then also moved up from San Gabriel. He started growing closer to Estela, the sister of a friend's wife, a pretty girl with big doe eyes and light brown hair whom he had known from afar for years.

Estela was the middle child of seven children who had grown up in a close-knit family on another ranch just north of Parral. When she was fifteen, she and her family moved to a small hacienda on the fringes of Ciudad Juárez where there were not yet many homes and the streets were still unpaved. She could not have been more thrilled. The people in the city were as warm and convivial as those in her rancho. People greeted each other on the street, and as Little Miguel Martinez had said of his Mexican community in Sierra Blanca, they looked out for one another and their children. Yet in Juárez, life was even better: She no longer had to chuck wood into an iron stove to make tortillas or haul buckets of water inside from a nearby river to wash dishes or clothes. There was electricity, and appliances ran on petroleum. There were dances and big-box stores with garments on display where people much richer than her could buy all sorts of nice things.

Within a few years, she started making the trip to El Paso to work as a nanny, and, like Sabino, she tucked away her passport card once she reached the other side. She would leave on Sunday, live with the family who paid her to babysit during the week, and return on Friday evening. It was not a hard job. She slept in an extra bedroom in a small apartment, and the children were easy enough to handle. But El Paso was a much harsher place culturally, she recalls. People did not seem to coexist or associate with their neighbors the way they did south of the border. The only El Pasoans she really talked to other than the children were her own employers, who every week promptly picked her up and dropped her off at the same downtown plaza that fed into the Santa Fe International Bridge. Like Sabino, the only reason she kept on crossing was to work: She made $10 a week, what would have been roughly $100 today.

Estela and Sabino hit it off sometime in 1967, the same year El Paso completed a wide concrete bridge with four car lanes to replace the modest crossing at the Santa Fe. After years of land disputes over the shifting course of the Rio Grande, President John F. Kennedy had signed a 1963 treaty returning about six hundred acres of land to Mexico in his Cold War strategy to improve relations between the United States and its southern neighbor. Some 5,600 residents, mostly Mexican American, were displaced as engineers rechanneled the river and modernized what would be dedicated as the Paso del Norte International Bridge.

Estela admired how hard Sabino worked and that he could tough it out in the United States. If Mexican men were not willing to do that, she said, it was very hard to make it in Juárez, where employers paid too little. Soon the two were married and had their first daughter, Blanca, in September 1969. Susan and her twin brother, Robert, were born two years later. Their daughter Sylvia, who for years would be the only one in the family with American citizenship, was born in El Paso a year after that. The youngest, Brian, would come along many years later.

The Rubios moved into a small, humble ranch named el Pajarito (the Little Bird) that Estela's family owned in Juárez. Her parents lived in the main house in the front, and the Rubios occupied the small bungalow in the back of the property, which was surrounded by a tall brick wall. Blanca and Susan helped take care of their grandfather's chicken coop, and their young uncles, then in their late twenties, worked in the watermelon fields. Their part of town was still mostly farmland, and the girls could see the rows of crops stretching into the distance. The area was so flat that, driving around, they could look across the border into Juárez's sister city stretching deep into the mountains on the other side. On the rare occasions when they had a little savings, the family made visits to downtown El Paso to grab a burger or shop at the giant JCPenney where braceros and traqueros and revolutionaries once wandered. For the children, those trips were simply fun weekend excursions. A treat. They had no idea they were crossing into another country or that a border divided El Paso and Ciudad Juárez. It all seemed to blend together: two cities, one all-encompassing culture.

The people of the borderland had muchas tranzas (many tricks) to get by—side hustles, not always up to code but often necessary to make ends meet, in a region where Mexican and Mexican American working-class families grappled with social, legal, and political mores and codes designed only to hold them down. In those days, the Rubio sisters' uncles and cousins used to head over to El Paso every week to buy used goods at pawnshops and thrift stores. They would load them up in the beds of their trucks to resell at their tienditas, or small shops, back in Juárez. The items were nicknamed "la falluca," as the sisters remember it, because the secondhand stuff casi siempre fallaba (it almost always failed). But it was more affordable for many, and it helped their uncles support their families.

Their dad continued to bend the rules, too. Estela took care of the children as Sabino continued to cross the border. He would head off for a few months at a time to build roadways and come back when he felt the heat of the Border Patrol or a job was finished.

Winnie, Texas, United States
Late 1976

As 1976 rolled around, Estela had had enough. She didn't want her children growing apart from their father. So, when Sabino found work on a roadway construction project in Winnie, Texas, a small farming community just outside of Houston, the family packed up all the things they could fit into an old van and moved with him.

The Rubios settled into a modest one-story home they rented in the Mexican part of town. Winnie, population roughly 1,500, was composed mostly of white families, and many of the few Hispanics around were Tejanos who had papers, spoke English with a Texas drawl, and seemed to act more like gabachos or white people than the Mexicanos they knew back home. The

Rubios, on the other hand, were undocumented working-class Mexicans, part of an even smaller group of Latinos who tried to lie low and lived in the silence—who, once their labor was done, retreated to the margins.

Over the next three months, they picked up on an unspoken code. Mexicans—because the gabachos tended to call all undocumented workers Mexican regardless of their countries of origin (and because most were indeed Mexican)—shopped on their own side of town. Mexicans did not leave their homes much if they did not have to go to work or school. Mexicans always kept one eye out for la migra and another for local law enforcement, because one never knew which one could spell the end of their American stay.

Coming from a place where Mexican culture had been so vibrant, where they had never had to hide a part of themselves, Estela was soon feeling cooped up. Blanca (then six) and Susan and Robert (four) struggled to make friends. Blanca and Susan were light-skinned with blond hair. They could have passed as Tejanas or maybe even white girls, yet they were the only Spanish speakers in their classes. Blanca's teacher in particular seemed flustered. She often left the child in a corner with crayons and pages from a coloring book. As Blanca picked up English on the playground, she began trying to sit with other students in class, but her teacher kept relegating her back to her corner. She could not speak well enough to advocate for herself, nor could her parents.

Beyond their inner world, the deportation machine had continued churning through the 1970s on the backs of Mexican laborers like Sabino, in what historian Adam Goodman has called "the dawn of the age of mass expulsion." El Paso and border cities functioned as revolving doors as border agents continued to apprehend people in the borderlands but also began targeting millions of immigrants in the nation's interior, many of whom had lived in the United States for years. The annual expulsions, according to Goodman, tallied more than one million on average between the 1970s and the late 2000s, and rarely dropped below 900,000 in any given fiscal year. Criminal prosecutions under the 1929 criminal entry law cost too much time and money. So, officials often skipped the process altogether. Deportations tended to be fast-tracked, without due process, and were lightly described as "voluntary departures." Mexican workers kept coming back, as

Sabino had been doing for years, only to be caught again. The repeated apprehensions angered border officials but also helped them clamor for more funding and officers, bulking up the American immigration bureaucracy. All the while, American employers had their labor demands met.

Under the unwritten rules of the time, the Texas Rice Festival that was held in Winnie every fall to mark the start of the rice harvest should have been off-limits. Mexicans certainly did not go to the giant celebration that was organized by mostly white farmers and drew families from all over the county and across Southeast Texas. The Rubios knew attending might be a risk. But they decided to go regardless. Sabino and Estela thought their children could use the distraction of a good time—and they could, too.

On a chilly October afternoon, the Rubios piled into their old van and drove down to Winnie Stowell Park, where a merry-go-round, a Ferris wheel, and other rides were spinning. People ate cotton candy and played carnival games for stuffed animals. The fairgrounds were packed, and festival officers would later boast that the crowds were the largest in the seven years that the event had been hosted. The celebrations featured auctions, an antique car show, frog races, a rice cooking competition, eating contests, flag ceremonies, and performances by Dixieland bands, street dancers, baton twirlers, and gospel choirs. An agricultural youth group had also gathered contributions from businesses and local volunteers to build a large wooden barn for the festival's first-ever livestock show.

Every festival, young beauty contestants competed to be crowned senior queen and junior queen and for all sorts of pageant titles: Miss Congeniality, Miss LaPetite, Miss Sugar 'N' Spice. A Farmer of the Year was to be named and rice-industry leaders honored for such achievements as producing new varieties of rice, increasing rice yields, and developing better methods of fertilizing fields and controlling weeds, insects, and plant diseases. That year the nominees for best farmer included B. J. Jones, sixty-four, the owner of 1,316 acres in Liberty, who had started out as a tenant farmer with his father in 1932 and had developed a sturdy rice drainage system; Robert Horn, thirty-eight, who kept his 1,800 acres in Nome well stocked with the latest technology; and Henry Hirasaki, thirty-five, the chairman of a rice and soybean committee in Orange County, where he owned 2,500 acres and followed good land management based on the teachings of his grandfather, who had started farming rice in the 1900s.

The festivities were to be capped with a Christian mass to mark the harvest and a parade featuring military and high school bands, floats, antique cars, and beauty queens atop combine "chariots." But the Rubios would not get to see or enjoy any of it—not the prized cows or bulls; not the trail riders or crowning of the queens or the Little Wranglers Rodeo; not the "lavish praise" that a *Beaumont Enterprise* article said was heaped on the rice industry's "heroes." As soon as they arrived, the children needed to use the restroom. Estela hustled all four of them inside the nearest facilities as Sabino waited near the doors. Standing out there alone in the crowds, he suddenly began to feel uneasy. It was quickly dawning on him why all the other Mexican laborers stayed home. Most of the families coming in were white. There did not seem to be another brown face like his in sight. That was when he noticed two men in forest green uniforms in the distance and moving in his direction. He had been in this situation many times before, and he did not second-guess who they were. He instinctively started walking, then picked up the pace, desperately trying to lose the border agents in the swarms of people without drawing too much suspicion. But they remained behind him, and he began walking faster. It was all in vain. They caught up with him and pulled him to the side.

"Sir, can we see your papers?" one of them asked. Sabino's heart started pumping harder. La migra. La migra. La migra. It was always on the brain and around every corner. He could feel the hot stares of onlookers. He could feel all the borders, the taking and sorting and separating of people, land, and labor, closing in.

"No tengo papeles" ("I do not have any papers"), he replied.

"We are going to have to talk to you more seriously," the officer said.

As Estela and the children exited the bathroom, her heart sunk at the sight of the two border agents talking to her husband. They rounded up the family and escorted them off the grounds. She can't recall anymore if her children cried. All Blanca can remember is the terror in her parents' eyes.

The memories of family members differ on what happened next, but one thing is clear: They were deported.

Estela and Sabino are almost sure the immigration officers granted the family permission to return home to pack before driving back to Juárez. The children say they did not return to their Winnie home and left everything behind, the reason for a gap in their baby pictures. Susan is certain of it because she had been saving up her allowances in a bottle filled with dimes and quarters—almost $10.

She never got to spend the money.

13

Young Fronterizos

El Paso–Juárez
1970s to 1980s

Blanca Rubio says she will always remember the date she returned to the United States: August 16, 1977, the day Elvis Presley died. She was seven, and the country was in mourning. After the Winnie deportation, Blanca and her family had their border crossing cards taken away, but her aunt had similar permits for her son and two daughters, who were roughly the same age as Blanca and her twin siblings, Susan and Robert. The three of them piled into her car, and her aunt presented the cards to the agent to get the children across the Paso del Norte International Bridge. They did not include identification photos, and few questions were asked.

Their mother, Estela, recalls the Rio Bravo waters were low enough for her to walk across with the help of a young man, a neighbor and friend of the family, who knew where along the border and at what time to cross to avoid la migra. She paid him about $5, what would have been between $26 and $30 today, and met her sister and children on the other side. The Rubios then made their way to the downtown El Paso train station, a redbrick building with Spanish colonial touches and a green spire that had stood in the same place since Mexican intellectuals and exiles had streamed into the city in 1906. Elvis Presley himself had been welcomed there in 1958. Now

Blanca, Susan, and Robert were the next generation at the crossroads that moved people in all four cardinal directions across time.

Estela and her children boarded a train to downtown Los Angeles, where they were to reunite with Sabino after spending months apart. The brush with immigration agents had not stopped Sabino from heading over the border again. The pay in Juárez had simply been too meager to sustain his family. Besides, he liked the United States. The manual labor en el Norte was grueling and exhausting and at times frustrating. The sun, the dust, and the wind showed workers little mercy. Racist gabachos called Mexican men like him a mojado: a wetback. But at least one could get ahead if they put in the work. To Sabino, his children's chances at a better life already seemed so much greater than his own had ever been in San Gabriel.

Sabino now not only worked illegally after losing his border crossing card; he crossed illegally, too, by cutting through the Rio Bravo. Despite the expanding immigration laws and increasing number of officers patrolling the border, there remained desert areas that were sparsely surveyed, and the cycle of deportations continued. On most days the river was so dry that the water reached only up to his ankles. Only once or twice after heavy rains did he have to wade across. Even so, he had grown wary of the dangers of crossing back and forth. When he finally found a permanent job at a carpet factory in Los Angeles, he and Estela decided he should take it. Over the next year, he saved the money he needed to buy his family their train tickets and bring them over.

Estela had been on edge as the date of their departure approached. So much maneuvering. So many moves that could go wrong. But once on the train, she recalls, she felt strangely calm. A fellow passenger, a Mexican American woman who spoke Spanish, chatted her up and warned her that an immigration agent typically boarded the ride at some point to do a quick inspection but that he only tended to check the restrooms. Sure enough, some miles into the ride, the agent appeared. Estela did not panic. She and the woman kept talking in Spanish as her children, wrapped in blankets, napped in their seats and on the floor. As soon as he hopped off, Estela's new friend turned to face her with a wide smile on her face.

"Ya la hizo" ("You've made it"), she said.

The train continued chugging west, down the rail lines that Chinese, Mexican, German, Irish, and Italian traqueros had once helped build and maintain, as she and the children once more left the borderland that had made them who they were, fronterizos, border dwellers with feet in two places. It was the beginning of a much longer journey for Blanca and Susan and who they would become.

IF THE SINGLE-FAMILY house was the material benchmark of the American Dream, then El Paso was the sheer embodiment of it. The city that the Rubios left behind was sprawling now, suburbia in the desert, with a couple of short downtown skyscrapers and art deco towers cutting against the Franklin Mountains, and an interstate running straight through, all the way to the Pacific Ocean. On the side of one of those peaks, the El Paso Electric Company had assembled more than 450 light bulbs shaped into a giant star that often lit up the night sky. The border region had only continued growing. Manufacturing jobs had stagnated in the rest of the country, but not here, not where wages were so low, unions were all but nonexistent, and the steady stream of Mexican shoppers drove a constant demand for workers, the workers' rights campaigns of los magonistas lost to time and forgotten.

José Alfredo Holguin and his four brothers and two sisters lived just on the other side of the river, in a two-story home on a dirt road where two colonias collided on the western edge of Ciudad Juárez, one just as humble as the other. Old cars bumped along the rocky, unpaved hills, and many residents, like their grandfather, constructed their homes block by block, using the mountainous terrain they shoveled from the earth and transformed into adobe with sun and water. Their neighborhood, like the one where the Rubios had lived, was quiet and sparsely populated. Families owned chickens and goats and relied on horses and donkeys to haul their goods in carts. It afforded what so many other Mexican pueblos across la República Mexicana did, Alfredo would recall years later: a simple kind of ranchero life.

Like nearly everyone else in their barrio, Alfredo's father, Roman Holguin, raised chickens and rabbits, along with a couple of pigs to roast during

Christmas festivities and on New Year's Day. He was originally from the small town of Jiménez, near la Zona del Silencio, in the southeastern reaches of Chihuahua. For some time he had operated heavy machinery, tractors, forklifts, and road graders. Like Sabino Rubio, he also helped to clear and finish roads, but these ran all across Chihuahua, Durango, and Coahuila, including the highway connecting Ciudad Juárez to Torreón. When that work dried up, he became a driver for one of the city's bus companies, and it seemed there was always some bus or other large motor vehicle parked outside the Holguin home.

Perhaps it was for this reason that the Holguin brothers, from a young age, were fascinated by the mechanics and functioning of things, and would one day open their own transportation business. As boys, they used sticks and twine to make the bodies of toy cars and attached old bottle caps as the wheels. They drove the tiny contraptions down the dirt paths that wound around their colonia. As they got older, they would roll each other down those same roads inside old bus tires from their father's vehicles, and when they really wanted to give each other or their parents a scare, they jumped on the backs of buses for fun, hanging on for dear life just to see how far they could go. All of which is to say the Holguin brothers were vagos, wild ones.

In what was likely their most reckless venture, Alfredo and his younger brother Roman Holguin Jr. would visit one of their uncles who was a tinsmith and lived at the top of one of the tallest hills in their colonia. Roman recalled that they would help him tear off the hoods of old cars, which he would use to fashion into tin for bathtubs and containers. Then they would use the leftover scraps to slide down the dirt hill from his garage. It must have been some five or six stories high, but this did not faze them. When he told me about these times on a cold winter night decades later, Roman said it was important to understand how good they and other Juárez children had it in order to understand how bad things would become. Alfredo and Roman could stay out for hours playing with all their friends on the street. Roman recalled spinning tops and bouncing marbles and playing long games of los encantados, or freeze tag.

The Holguin brothers liked learning in class, but they would not make it past middle school. The books and uniforms cost too much. Instead, they went into business with their father, distributing water and petroleum to other colonias all over Juárez, on streets named after dead and gone revolucionarios, out of his beat-up pickup truck. The business did not make much money, but it did provide them with the basic necessities: food, clothes, and potable water. At night, a teenage Alfredo strummed away on his bass guitar and snuck away to play gigs whenever he could. He must have dreamed of a life like that of Juárez's native son and world-famous crooner, Juan Gabriel, or "Juanga" as fans lovingly called him, who had just shot to superstardom and was making Mexicanos on both sides of the border swell with pride. Roman only wished he could be more like his older brother: self-assured and bold.

The Juárez of their youth remained all neon and flashing lights—not quite the international tourist destination it had been a decade or two earlier, but a place where Mexicans and Americans could hit the streets to go to the theater, listen to old balladeers and mariachis, and dance in vibrant clubs to merengues, salsas, and cumbias or pop, rock, and electronic. There remained only a few spots from the city's truly golden years, like el Kentucky, but now there were Salon Mexico and the ElectriQ Discoteque. There was Chihuahua Charlie's, El Chamuco, and Manhattan. As Roman spoke of the brightness of those years, I could picture it clearly. I remember these decades as if I had lived them because my mother's family would talk about them so often. After she and her brother and sisters moved to El Paso from Juárez as teenagers in the late 1970s, they had continued to return to Juárez with their friends all through their young adult years. They would party the night away and meet up in the early hours for bowls of pozole at some twenty-four-hour joint or other before heading back over the border together. Sometimes, after her split from my grandfather, even my grandmother and her boyfriend would join them if they were out on the town, because if there is one stereotype about Mexicanos that many of us will gladly accept, it's that we know how to have a good time.

But the Cold War had not ended and now another war was starting. Following the civil rights era and a rise in recreational drug use in the 1960s—by hippies, children in slums, veterans returning from Vietnam—Republican president Richard M. Nixon declared the national "war on drugs" in 1971. He pushed for higher prison sentences for the use of certain drugs, created the Drug Enforcement Administration, and poured funding into drug control agencies. He and federal officials framed the effort as a response to increases in heroin addiction and narcotics use among college students, describing the issue of American drug abuse as "public enemy number one." Yet the policies would wreak havoc on Black and Latino neighborhoods, which, as they had been in the past, were often wrongfully perceived and portrayed as more prone to the abuse of illegal substances.

In a 1994 interview, which was not published in *Harper's Magazine* until more than two decades later (and after he had already died), John Ehrlichman, Nixon's domestic policy chief, seemed to suggest that targeting certain demographics had been their motive all along. He told journalist Dan Baum that the Nixon campaign actually identified two enemies, "the antiwar left and black people." "We knew we couldn't make it illegal to be either against the war or black, but by getting the public to associate the hippies with marijuana and blacks with heroin, and then criminalizing both heavily, we could disrupt those communities," he said. "We could arrest their leaders, raid their homes, break up their meetings, and vilify them night after night on the evening news. Did we know we were lying about the drugs? Of course we did." (Ehrlichman's children questioned the veracity of the report, but Baum stood by it, likening Ehrlichman's admission to atonement.)

The war on drugs gained new momentum under Republican president Ronald Reagan, who entered the White House in 1981 on the votes of evangelical Christians, neoconservatives, and other voices of the New Right unsettled by the social reforms and cultural changes of earlier decades. He was a man of profoundly conservative values, respected for his pragmatism and experience in moderate politics. As a former radio host and Hollywood actor, he had a folksy, well-honed way of speaking and a penchant for soaring rhetoric about the nation's ideals. For Latin America and a growing Latino population in the United States, the Reagan Revolution of free-market conservatism, tough-on-crime policies, and a hardline approach toward illegal immigration would have long-lasting implications.

Shortly after Reagan took office, he promised to continue America's tradition of welcoming people from all over the world, which, as he would reiterate time and time again, he saw as one of the most important sources of the country's strength and greatness. But he also pledged to increase controls on who could enter the country and to crack down on drugs. He gave more funding to the DEA, much of it for investigations aimed at curbing the flow of cocaine, which traffickers were funneling in from Colombia through Mexico. He also sought to impose higher mandatory minimum prison sentences for the possession of certain narcotics—laws that would result in tougher punishment for holding fewer grams of crack, which was spreading through Black neighborhoods, than for amounts of cocaine, which was more commonly used among white Americans. At the same time, in schools and television ads, First Lady Nancy Reagan oversaw the "Just Say No" campaign, underscoring the dangers of drug abuse.

The antidrug initiatives dovetailed with the Reagan administration's escalation of Cold War interventions in Latin America, where the United States had continued to back a string of right-wing military governments since it had helped knock down Jacobo Árbenz in Guatemala in 1954. The push led to an eruption of dirty and civil wars. Military dictators sought to deregulate their nations' banking systems, roll back land reforms, remove barriers to trade, and privatize their telecommunications, energy, and transportation industries. In the reign of chaos and terror that transpired, millions were tortured, disappeared, or killed as wealth, natural resources, and property were concentrated under a handful of elites and multinational corporations.

In Chile, the United States backed the brutal Pinochet regime. In Argentina, it provided some support to the military junta that ousted Isabel Perón. In Guatemala, the military dictatorship it helped install unleashed a series of attacks on the Maya Ixil and other Indigenous groups that amounted to a genocide. In Nicaragua, it buttressed a Contra army that aimed to oust the left-wing Sandinista government. In El Salvador, it spent billions fighting left-wing rebels from the Farabundo Martí National Liberation Front, or FMLN. The list of nations where Americans intruded continued.

As more Latin Americans fled, many followed the same paths that Mexican workers traveled to head north—to pass through the Pass, pa' Chuco. Once in the United States, the refugees, most Salvadoran, tended to find safety in many of the same poor and segregated neighborhoods where Black and Mexicano families lived, but the young turned on the young. Some Black, México Americano, and Salvadoreño youth found protection and camaraderie in gangs, in a nation that ignored, scorned, or criminalized their existence, and violence flared up in cities like Chicago and Los Angeles. The bloodshed helped the next wave of anti-immigrant activists amplify fears of lawless Mexicans—and now a wider and more diverse swath of Latinos—ideas that had often percolated in the American mind since the U.S.-Mexico border cut El Paso and Juárez in two, and especially since Pancho Villa and his Dorados kicked up dust across Texas, New Mexico, and Chihuahua. As historian William Anthony Nericcio wrote of what Americans thought of Mexico's civil war, "Villista, Carrancista—to them, all Mexicans were 'greasers' and were labeled as such on their postcards." Dangerous criminals and bandidos.

As early as 1981, the Select Commission on Immigration and Refugee Policy released a set of recommendations to deal with a flow of immigrants and refugees it described as "out of control." And just as soon, the battle lines were drawn between staunch anti-immigrant groups pushing for tougher border enforcement and a burgeoning pro-immigration movement. Those who wanted to restrict migration warned it had been increasing since the Immigration and Nationality Act of 1965—not only from Latin American nations but also from many others, such as Japan, India, Korea, Haiti, Congo, and Somalia. An international left-wing community of church groups, human rights organizations, and activists fought to provide sanctuary to migrants fleeing Central American civil wars and to highlight the United States' complicity in the conflicts. At home, a crop of Latino civil and immigrant rights groups that had been steadily expanding since the civil rights era argued in favor of relief for Mexicano and Latino workers, who, like Sabino, had been caught in endless cycles of "voluntary departures" and employer abuse.

In El Paso and Juárez, where hundreds of the activists had gathered for cross-border conferences in the 1970s, young Chicanos now cruised in souped-up lowriders through the downtown streets where their descendants had once toiled in brick-and-mortar businesses and small packing houses. Latino civil rights leaders in the city, and across the Southwest, were trying to forge new solidarity among the growing populations of young Latinos, which had grown much more culturally, racially, and ethnically complex, though their social, political, and economic struggles remained inextricably linked. South Texas Hispanics rarely saw themselves as allies of the young, proud Chicanos of Southern California. Mexican Americans in Arizona felt they had little in common with Puerto Ricans in New York or Cuban Americans in Florida.

The activists were hardly in smooth alignment, their wrangling as intense as the infighting had been among the revolucionarios in Francisco Madero's camp—so many disparate interests and approaches at once in sync and at odds. The League of United Latin American Citizens had once sought to build political power by encouraging Texans of Mexican descent to learn English, become naturalized citizens, and adopt an American way of life. Now it was being tested by newer groups that had come of age during the Chicano rights movement, when Mexican Americans turned to bolder ways of embracing their dual identity in an American society that made them feel so invisible—and to nationalistic movements that at times led to the exclusion of other Mexicano immigrants and other Latinos.

But at the core, many believed, the Mexican American communities of the Southwest—like the Latino diaspora across the whole of the United States—all carried the weight of Spanish colonization, American imperialism, and the modern-day fear of the Mexican. And some activists had learned hard lessons from the past. Through the 1950s, fierce wage competition and divisions between Mexican migrants and Mexican American laborers had initially led a few Mexican American civil rights groups to back President Dwight D. Eisenhower's Operation Wetback, only to reverse their stance after the deportations began devastating not just Mexican families but Mexican American families, too.

On November 6, 1986, Reagan finally signed the Immigration Reform and Control Act. It introduced new civil and criminal penalties for employers who hired undocumented workers, increased funding for border security, and created pathways to citizenship for farmworkers and undocumented migrants who had entered the United States before 1982. It would legalize the immigration status of roughly 3 million people, many Mexican

American, including Sabino and Estela Rubio. It would be celebrated and derided.

THAT SAME YEAR, Raúl Reyes had captured a video that would become one of the final traces of his grandparents, Victoria and Miguel Martinez. The Martinez family had grown so large, it had splintered. With time, as tends to happen with many families, brothers and sisters, aunts and uncles, had gone their separate ways. Victoria's second oldest son, Camilo, had died from cancer in 1980, likely caught, Raúl believes, from all those years he worked at the ASARCO smelting plant. Those still alive did not seem to come over to the Martinezes' little house on Tampa as often. Sunday and holiday gatherings had become quiet affairs. But Raúl and his wife, Margarita, continued to visit with their son, Clifford, after mass and menudo at their favorite breakfast spot.

Victoria and Miguel had taken in Raúl and his mother, Manuela, without any questions or reproach when Manuela had done what many Mexican American women could not even fathom in the Mexican Catholic households of El Paso in the 1950s: left her husband. And it had been Victoria who kept him from slipping through the system in schools where, as the Rubio sisters also recall it, mostly white American teachers did not expect much from Mexican American students, especially brown-skinned young men.

On Mother's Day 1986, with Raúl recording on a clunky video camera, bright sunlight streaming in through the windows, his wife, Margarita, in a white sundress, stood over the salt-and-pepper-haired Miguel. He was rocking on a worn plush recliner, as Victoria wrapped her arms around their son, Clifford, then three, on a nearby couch.

"How did you two meet?" Margarita asked.

"Oh, she was so pretty, I wanted to snatch her away and make her my wife," Miguel said.

"To hell with that; what you mean, snatch me away?" Victoria playfully objected. "I wouldn't let you. You would have had to do things the right way to be with me."

Miguel died four years later, and Victoria six years after that. She had been forgetting people, places, and things, and often left a burning pot on the stove, or Margarita would come across a bag of sugar that her mother-in-law had left in an odd place. The tape would become even more treasured after she and Raúl lost Clifford on the Fourth of July in 1995, when, at age twelve, he fell in a pool at a relative's house unnoticed and drowned. Raúl threw himself into his work to avoid dwelling on his grief and began digging into the lives of Mexicanos and México Americanos like his abuelitos. He would eventually come to share the video with their daughter, Brooke, once she was old enough.

On the other side of the border, the Holguin brothers, now in their late teens and twenties, occupied the third space that was fronterizo life, the transnational tides flowing in and out around them, through El Paso and back. Alfredo had married a young woman from his neighborhood in 1981 and had his first son soon after. He and his siblings lost their father three years later. The brothers tried to keep their petroleum business going, but soon Alfredo started looking for other ways to make money. He began crossing into El Paso to collect cardboard and discarded food from American restaurants that looked to be in good condition. He would recycle the cardboard for change and resell the food in Juárez at a profit. Like Sabino, he eventually moved into the carpeting business and learned to install flooring.

When he had earned the funds he needed to buy a passenger van, Alfredo called up another one of his brothers, who was working as an undocumented laborer in Albuquerque, New Mexico. He sold him on the idea of opening their own transportation company. Soon they had made enough to acquire a small bus, and then a couple more, and Alfredo brought some of his other brothers to the fold. They could not see it then. They were too young and the future looked too promising, as one of those younger brothers, Alberto, remembers it. But the movement of drugs to American consumers north was going strong, and no war or law or ad campaign was going to stop it—not when there were big profits to be made.

14

Hold the Line

El Paso–Ciudad Juárez
1993

BEFORE ANY WALL or fence lined the nearly 2,000-mile border running from the Pacific Ocean to the Gulf of Mexico, the tiny force of line riders created to keep out Chinese laborers saw themselves as the nation's "Southern gatekeepers." Most were white men who observed a "frontier justice" not unlike that of the Texas Rangers as they sought to protect the United States from the intrusions of Asian laborers and other immigrants excluded under the nation's earliest immigration laws. Frank W. Berkshire, a Kentuckian and vocal progressive, rose through the ranks of these officers as a Chinese inspector before he took control of the Bureau of Immigration and Naturalization in 1907. He moved to El Paso a couple of years later, and in time rose to become the first federal immigration official to command the entire U.S.-Mexico boundary from the border instead of from Washington, D.C.

To the place that Americans saw as the nation's back door, in the heat of the eugenics movement, Berkshire brought an East Coast bureaucracy and set of liberal reforms. Progressives like him, historian James Dupree explains, had arrived at the same conclusions as racist white nativists: that unchecked access into the country was a threat. But unlike those nativists, who wanted to keep "unassimilable" or "undesirable" people out, progressives believed they needed to limit the flow of people crossing American borders in order to address social ills such as poverty, sloth, and certain moral maladies. Under Berkshire's watch, the line riders gradually became a more disciplined organization, with new hierarchies and border stations that abided by more rules and structure. Over time, Berkshire began to conceive of an entirely separate law enforcement body to detect and capture immigrants who sought to circumvent the nation's ports of entry—one that would include paid patrol inspectors, guards, cooks, and clerks, along with vehicles, wagons, and horses. He got his wish in 1924 when Congress approved the funding for his vision two days after enacting the nation's controversial system of immigrant quotas. And la migra was born . . .

When it was founded that May, the Border Patrol was composed of mostly white working-class men who did not own land and saw the job as an opportunity for upward mobility. Twenty-four percent of the force had been transferred from the Mounted Guard of Chinese Inspectors. One of those, Jefferson Davis Milton—the first officer appointed, or the "father of the Border Patrol"—was the son of a Confederate governor in Florida and had made his name in the bloodshed to settle the American West. In the beginning, Latinos made up only a minuscule fraction of the agency, recruited as early as the 1920s for their ability to speak Spanish. But by 1989, Latinos and Latinas had come to make up almost 36 percent of its agents. Despite the often fraught nature of the job—as Mexicans and Latinos became the focus of anti-immigrant vitriol and the illegal immigration debate—many Latinos began to see it as one of the few viable professions to earn a good living, particularly as many sought a way out of poor barrios and tended to be shut out from opportunities to go to college. In El Paso, which since its Old West days had gained a reputation as home to some of the toughest lawmen, the title also carried respect and, for some, even glory.

Silvestre "Silver" Reyes, the grandchild of Mexican immigrants who fled the violence of the Mexican Revolution, was the eldest of ten children born in Canutillo, a small rural community northwest of the city. He joined the Border Patrol in 1969, the year after he lost complete hearing in his right ear when a mortar landed near his foxhole during combat in Vietnam, where he served as an Army helicopter crew chief. As the national outcry over illegal immigration began to mount under the Reagan administration, Reyes assumed control of the McAllen sector in 1984, becoming the agency's first Hispanic sector chief. Overseeing the Lower Rio Grande Valley in South Texas, he noticed many immigrants coming from Central America were sent home by plane, which added to the cost of deportations. So he began experimenting with what a *New York Times* article would later call a "wall of officers." For years the Border Patrol had centered on finding and deporting immigrants without lawful American residency. Reyes focused on attempting to prevent people from entering in the first place. He deployed his agents to the border, or the "line," in the parlance of the Border Patrol, and ordered them to block people from coming across.

Reyes implemented the strategy for only six weeks, as it required a large budget to cover overtime pay for the constant presence of officers at the line. But in his view it worked, and when he was reassigned to El Paso in 1993, he decided to try his approach at a much larger scale. Washington superiors turned down his funding request for the idea, and in his telling he had a financial officer dig into his sector's internal budget to make it possible. If Reyes was especially determined, it was because he had been tasked with ushering change in his new region after the last local head had retired in turbulence. There had been disputes and shootings, charges of abuse, and a lawsuit filed by plaintiffs and Latino civil rights organizations against the Border Patrol for racially profiling El Paso residents. Agents had tended to harass Hispanics to show their papers, according to court records, in their pursuit of unlawful Mexican border crossers.

The El Paso corridor stretched from western Texas to New Mexico and encompassed the nation's second-busiest crossing after San Diego. Like other points along the border, the timeless mountain pass was seeing another rise in Mexicano workers crossing. The trade and economic policies that had often been intertwined with the antidrug and anti-communist interventions in Mexico and Latin America had wracked the region with severe financial crises, spurring high inflation and currency devaluations. Some countries had plunged further into debt as they borrowed from American institutions, the World Bank, and the International Monetary Fund. Against this backdrop, Reyes launched the operation that would reorient border policy for decades to come: toward a concept that would become known as "prevention through deterrence."

On September 19, 1993, under the glaring desert light, four hundred Border Patrol officers assembled a blockade that stretched for twenty miles. The chain of agents in hunter green uniforms and SUVs stood watch for two weeks, twenty-four hours a day. Reyes justified the heavy law enforcement presence, as politicians had done and would continue to do for generations, by tying crime with the rise in migrants, though studies over many years have found that immigrants are less likely to commit crimes than people born in the United States. People who attempted to evade the wall of officers were soon picked up, driven sixty miles west, and abandoned in the rural town of Palomas, Chihuahua, where Pancho Villa and his revolucionarios had once crossed before attacking Columbus, New Mexico. The deportees would have to find their way back to Juárez through the hostile Chihuahuan desert, a journey as arduous as Don Oñate's.

Reyes initially named the initiative Operation Blockade but changed it to Operation Hold the Line at the behest of Mexican and American officials who felt the former sounded too militaristic. And protests rocked both sides of the line. Catholic bishops in southern New Mexico, El Paso, and Juárez railed against the inhumane treatment of migrants and the harm to the relationship between the two sister cities. The chamber of commerce in Ciudad Juárez called for a boycott of El Paso retailers. Operation Bridge Builders, an activist group formed in response, urged El Pasoans to reject the "self-proclaimed saviors with guns and riot gear." Hundreds of Juarenses gathered at the bridge locally known as el Puente Libre and cried, "¡Viva México!" and "¡Queremos trabajar!" ("We want to work!").

Still, Washington officials, at first skeptical of Reyes's strategy, embraced it after the agency's apprehensions of migrants in the El Paso sector dropped by 72 percent over the next year. Mexicanos, Salvadoreños, Guatemaltecos, and Hondureños had not stopped crossing the U.S.-Mexico border. They had simply moved on to do it in farther and even more remote locations, but federal immigration officials called Operation Hold the Line a success and planned to introduce it in other sectors. The push even garnered the support of President Bill Clinton, who had clinched victory in 1992, breaking the streak of two Republican presidencies, and was tacking to the right on crime and immigration.

All the while, the end of the Cold War and dissolution of the Soviet Union had brought the United States a whole new set of geopolitical considerations. Clinton had won on a platform centered on fortifying the nation's economy and trade relations as the world became more interconnected. He continued a push under his Republican predecessors, Ronald Reagan and George H. W. Bush, to build closer ties with Canada and Mexico as he worked to implement the North American Free Trade Agreement (NAFTA). The landmark treaty, which had been signed in 1992 with substantial bipartisan support, eliminated most tariffs on goods traded between the three countries, included provisions to safeguard intellectual property, and, through side deals, sought to implement labor and environmental protections. But, above all, its goal was to integrate Mexico into the global economy and open it up to new markets as the nation had largely sought to protect its state-run industries from the pillaging it had suffered by American and foreign investors since the days of the Mexican Revolution. American and Mexican officials also believed that economic development in Mexico could alleviate their friction over illegal immigration, as more opportunities down south could keep Mexicanos from illegally migrating north.

In 1994, as American federal immigration officials launched Operation Gatekeeper (the next iteration of Operation Hold the Line) in San Diego, new maquiladoras, or factories with tariff exemptions, began opening or expanding in Ciudad Juárez and all along the Mexican borderland. Auto and meatpacking plants, electronics and garment factories. Ford and General Motors. Hewlett-Packard, Philips, RCA, and Whirlpool. Dell, Delphi, and General Electric. Making and assembling mobile phones, televisions, radios, and computers. Washing machines and refrigerators. Microchips and semiconductors. Seat belts. The stuff of American Dreams. The low-wage factory jobs that Mexicanos had sought in the north for decades as they passed through Chuco Town came south in droves.

NAFTA was supposed to bring the border region into a new century, accelerating the growth of maquiladoras, which had started as far back as the 1960s. But the shifts began to devastate the industrial belt and Midwest of the United States just as the largely white factory workers who had opposed the trade agreement in those parts had feared. And as companies moved their operations south and over the border, many brought their anti-worker practices with them, crushing unions and depressing wages for the Mexican workers who rushed to fill them. In Juárez, those tended to be young, working-class Indigenous and mestiza women from some of the city's poorest barrios.

At first, NAFTA seemed like a boon for the Holguin brothers. As more maquiladoras opened, they expanded their routes and fleet of ruteras, or small green-and-white buses, as more workers needed shuttles to and from their jobs at the industrial parks. Soon it seemed the entire Holguin clan was pitching in, with brothers and wives, children and cousins serving as drivers, mechanics, and office administrators. Alfredo and three of his brothers—Roman, Luis, and Alberto, or "Beto"—would meet at their small business office and garage next to Alfredo's home before embarking on their rounds at about the crack of dawn. As they bought more ruteras and hired more drivers, they began to spend more time together at the business, working the radios or talking shop inside whatever bus happened to be parked in their lot in need of maintenance.

They tended to arrive around 8:00 in the morning and not leave until late at night. Midnight could strike and they would still be out there, catching up on each other's families, brainstorming ways to innovate and broaden their services, and debating politics, whether lamenting the city's corruption or railing against abusive police officers. Often they would have breakfast, lunch, and dinner delivered. They would watch their children go to and come back from school and chat with them, their friends, neighbors, and cousins, and whoever else dropped in. Sometimes it was so cold, the windows in the buses would fog up. At other times, it would be so hot, they would be sitting there sweating through their shirts.

The Holguins were too overtaken with the grind, too focused on staying ahead of their competitors, to realize that organized crime was evolving around them. After the Drug Enforcement Administration and the U.S. Coast Guard increased their crackdown on Colombian cartels through the 1980s, Mexican traffickers took on a bigger role in the cocaine trade. Planes full of bricks began arriving in Mexico, turning the nation into a crucial transportation hub. At first, Colombian cartels handed off refined cocaine to Mexican middlemen, who would take it over the U.S.-Mexico border and leave it in stash houses for Colombian criminal groups working within the United States to pick up later. But in 1989, the same year American drug enforcement agencies busted Colombians with about twenty-one metric tons of the drug in a single raid, Mexican smugglers reportedly held back shipments to extort the Colombians for delinquent payments, and the Colombians ended up forfeiting a large chunk of the wholesale American cocaine market to Mexican criminal organizations.

Soon, Mexicanas started disappearing. Many worked at the same maquiladoras the Holguins' ruteras shuttled factory workers to and from. They were found beaten and raped. They had been shot, stabbed, or strangled. Sometimes their bodies had been mutilated. Sometimes there were disturbing patterns. Some had been abandoned with a puncture to their left breasts or slashes across their faces or injuries to their eyes or genitals. Some girls and women were never found. The remains of others had been dropped into tubs of acid or burned or dumped in the desert—bones and body bags in what were once cotton fields, now dirt lands littered with broken glass bottles and crushed cans.

Alma. Laura. Esmeralda. Maria. Mayra. Veronica. Merlín. Rosa. Virginia. There were dozens. *Teresa. Idali. Lupita. Luz. Cynthia. Jocelyn. Paloma. Lorenza. Gladys. Patricia. Guillermina. Gloria. Elizabeth. Angelica. Miriam. Adriana. Ignacia. Olga. Guadalupe. Rosario. Sandra. Rocio. Soledad. Leticia. Susana. Perla. Victoria.* Then there were hundreds. Some were identified. Some never were. The murders at the hands of bad boyfriends and abusive husbands, drug cartel members, and copycats went unsolved.

They were women like Claudia Ivette González, twenty, who, before she went missing, liked watching the Dallas Cowboys with her best friend and plastered her room with Backstreet Boys posters. She was last seen after she had arrived a couple of minutes late at an American maquiladora, where workers assembled car seats and electrical systems, and was turned away in the darkness. They were women like Silvia Elena Rivera Morales, seventeen, a single mom who sold jewelry, burritos, and Avon products to neighbors, mostly on foot, and disappeared on a business call. And like Lilia Alejandra García Andrade, seventeen, who, before her body was found, was last seen kicking and punching men who in broad daylight pushed her into the back of a white van and drove off.

The women tended to be young and pretty, at times as young as twelve or thirteen, with brown hair and coffee-colored eyes. Many were Mexicanas and Centro Americanas who, like Claudia, worked in las maquiladoras. In some cases, in a Mexican society where beauty standards often favor European features, they had pale or light brown skin. Most if not all came from humble working-class families. Initially, their murders and disappearances from barrios with unpaved roads, adobe homes, and shoes hanging from electric phone lines garnered little coverage. But as the numbers of snatched girls and women mounted, the details from the scenes became more heinous, and the police gave their families few if any answers, their mothers and loved ones began going to the press and taking to the streets. They drew national and then international attention and a wide network of feminist and human rights activists. The cases became known as the "Juárez femicides," and they were the first outward sign that something in El Paso's sister city was going very wrong.

For me, they would also lead to the moment when it all started, the reason why I first began trying to understand our southern border and how it shaped us. By the 2000s the number of crimes had dropped but not stopped, and neither had the public outcry. I must have been about sixteen, the same age as many of the victims, when I contacted some of the mothers, as I was working on a series of stories about the Juárez femicides for my high school newspaper. I did not have a driver's license yet, so I asked my grandmother to drive me over to the home of Josefina González Rodríguez, Claudia's mother, where she and Eva Arce, Silvia's mother, agreed to be interviewed. It was there that I learned how Claudia, Silvia, and Alejandra had disappeared, where Eva took me outside into a yard flanking a barren desert lot and pointed to home after home on the same block where a family had lost a mother, a daughter, or a sister, and where Josefina led me down a narrow hallway into her daughter's room. It looked exactly as she had left it and eerily similar to mine on the other side of the U.S.-Mexico dividing line.

Toward the end of our conversation, Eva told me her daughter had been such a hard worker because she wanted more than anything to get ahead, to be somebody. I had been somewhat wayward in those years, a mostly A student but mouthy with my own single mother and angsty, a bit of a wild one—a vaga. Mostly, consciously or not, I was angry: angry that my parents had split, angry that we always seemed to be on the verge of financial collapse, angry that other families seemed to have their acts together better than mine. Confronted with my privilege that day, I remember I realized then I could no longer squander it. If Silvia had been taken, her death could not be in vain. She would be somebody to me, and I would try to become someone better for her and for Claudia and for Alejandra.

There were different theories circulating about what was driving the crimes. One was that the city belonged to la Línea—what locals called the Juárez Cartel in those years and which was said to encompass influential members of society, drug traffickers, and corrupt Border Patrol and law enforcement officers on both sides of the border—a line stretching from Juárez to places as far as New York and New Jersey. When a particularly large load of product reached its intended destination, the criminal group reportedly kidnapped and raped women as a form of celebration. Other sources believed they were more than a way to mark their victories but sacrifices, part of satanic and other occult practices that some drug cartel members religiously followed. In a string of still more cases, police arrested maquiladora bus drivers, some of whom admitted to the killings, but information also came to light that some of these confessions had been obtained under torture and coercion. Photos of some of the men captured burn marks on their abdomens and genitals.

On our way back to El Paso, I told my grandmother I had been in touch with Mario Escobedo, one of the defense lawyers, who, along with his son, twenty-nine-year-old Mario Escobedo Jr., had represented two of the bus drivers whom they believed had been wrongly accused in the murders of Claudia and ten other women. The two had been calling out the police and government for making scapegoats out of the drivers when, one night, two cars chased Mario Jr. through the city as he dialed his father in panic. His vehicle was riddled with bullets, and Mario Jr. was shot point-blank in the head, what doctors called a "bala de gracia," a bullet of grace. His father agreed to speak to me, but every time I phoned at the arranged time, my calls would go unanswered. My grandmother asked if I knew the name of his law practice, and I happened to have the office address with me in a ratty spiral notebook. She drove me there, parked right outside its white wooden stairs, and told me to go up there and knock on the door. When I looked at her, stunned and with nervous hesitation, she looked me dead in the eye and told me to be braver. It seemed the conversations with the mothers had also stirred something in her.

When Mario Sr. saw me standing there alone, a skinny little thing in a JCPenney blazer and jeans, carrying a clunky tape recorder and a notebook, he let me in. He took me into his dimly lit office lined with bookshelves, and from behind a gleaming mahogany desk, in his soft, gravelly voice, he began to tell me of the last night he had heard from his son. Mario Jr., he said, had shouted into the phone that he was being followed by vehicles he had never seen before and that he believed the men inside were going to kill him. The father recalled he heard a round of gunfire and a crash. Desperate, he climbed into his truck and drove to where his son had mentioned he had been, but he was too late. The men in the vans turned out to be police officers who claimed they had mistaken Mario Jr. for a fugitive and given chase, but many critics of the Juárez police—local newspapers, human rights activists and lawyers, and privately, even some law enforcement officers—called it a police execution.

Roughly two decades later, as I sat with Roman Holguin in El Paso for lunch, I asked him if he recalled the maquiladora bus driver cases and whether he or his brothers had ever feared that they could be blamed for the deaths of missing Mexicanas. He said he recalled being afraid for his sisters, one of whom had worked in a maquiladora herself, making piñatas, long before women started disappearing. But, standing outside the gates of their old transportation business in Ciudad Juárez later that evening, Beto argued they had not thought they would be accused of the murders—not then. They were too trusting in their government, too confident that if they did not stray into illicit activities—that if they abided by the rules and did not veer off the set routes of their buses—the government would leave them alone. "You can call it an innocence," he said.

Los Angeles, California, United States
1990 to 2000s

The year Operation Gatekeeper came to California, Blanca and Susan Rubio became young American citizens, with their American-born sister, Sylvia, then only four, technically serving as their sponsor. They were now in their twenties. As in El Paso, thousands of Latino immigrants marched in protest in downtown Los Angeles. But the television news was dominated by the images of hundreds of Mexicanos crossing la frontera at a time as onlookers on the Mexican side cheered them on. On the other side, with a recession and unemployment rates hitting the state hard, Mexicano and Latino workers quickly became the targets of Democratic and Republican politicians who blamed them for rising crime rates and accused them of draining state resources.

Governor Pete Wilson, a Republican and former U.S. senator from California, won reelection that fall with campaign ads featuring menacing music and blurry black-and-white footage of Mexican immigrants running across a border checkpoint near San Diego. California voters, including many Mexican Americans and Latinos, worried about the arrival of new immigrants and their children falling behind in school, approved a series of anti-immigrant ballot initiatives, the most notorious of which was Proposition

187. The measure called for a state citizenship database to screen immigrants and barred undocumented immigrants living in the state from obtaining health care, public education, and other social services. The other two proposals passed outlawed affirmative action programs and required that children speak only English in schools.

The focus on illegal immigration was also beginning to consume Washington. Newt Gingrich, a rising Republican House member from Georgia, noticing its potential as political red meat, seized on the issue as part of a slate of Republican priorities; he abandoned congressional norms and began developing the aggressive, no-holds-barred tactics that would be adopted on both sides of the political aisle. On his way to becoming House speaker in January 1995, as historian Julian E. Zelizer has traced, he used floor speeches televised on fledgling C-SPAN to speak unfiltered to Americans, control political messaging, and obstruct the legislative process. Top congressional Democrats followed in near lockstep. Senator Dianne Feinstein of California joined Republicans like Wilson in zeroing in on the people crossing the border. "I say return them to their own country wherever that country may be," she said.

After throwing his support behind Operation Hold the Line in El Paso in 1993, Clinton approved Operation Gatekeeper in San Diego in 1994. It was followed by Operation Safeguard in the Tucson sector later that year, then Operation Rio Grande in the McAllen, Texas, sector in 1997. Just four years after Operation Hold the Line began, the Border Patrol's budget had swelled from $362 million to $727 million and the number of its border agents increased from 3,991 to 6,848. And by 1996, under the banner of curbing crime and drug use, Clinton had signed a sweeping package of laws that escalated the fusion of the nation's immigration and criminal legal systems: It expanded the number of deportable offenses, made it profitable for cities and counties to lock up immigrants, and increased coordination between federal law enforcement and immigration forces. The efforts would translate into long sentences and mass incarceration for generations of Black and Latino men in the United States and into millions more American dollars to boost border security and combat the underground flow of drugs, guns, and money.

In those days, Sabino often worked nights, taking three buses to the carpet factory in the City of Industry. Estela cleaned homes. Their Pico-Union neighborhood grew rougher with the years as gangs and shootings became commonplace in Los Angeles. Yet the Rubio sisters remember they were especially tight as a family, and that in itself was a privilege as the families of some of their friends—who often spent the night in their one-bedroom apartment—were fractured by immigration woes, detentions, deportations, or imprisonments. Money was scarce, but the Rubios looked forward to weekend trips to the beach, picnics in the park, and Fridays at the local market, where the children would wander through the booths and shops and Sabino would let each pick out one small trinket as a gift.

Blanca, as is so often the case with the oldest child in immigrant families, assumed the role of protector and translator, even though she detested her Mexican accent and dreaded talking to doctors, dealing with clerks at convenience stores—even ordering pizza. When her parents were away or at work, she enforced curfews. At Christmas, she wrapped the presents. In high school, like me, she had struggled to find her way. Expectations weren't high for a Mexican American woman from Pico-Union, especially not as the anti-immigrant and anti-Mexican rhetoric heated up with the immigration battles of the 1990s. After a high school counselor dissuaded her from applying to universities—"Oh, honey, you're just going to get married and have children," she recalls being told—she enrolled in community college but soon dropped out and began working at a statewide association for human resources professionals. But colleagues, seeing her potential, persuaded Blanca to return to school.

Blanca and Susan wound up graduating from East Los Angeles College on the same spring day in 1997, and they later completed master's degrees at Azusa Pacific University in Azusa, California. While in college, Blanca became the youngest member to serve on the water board in Baldwin Park and then took a post as a schoolteacher in 2000. She dove into her work in education, realizing it was the chance to help Latino students in a way her own unhelpful guidance counselor and teachers back in Winnie, Texas, had not. Within three years she had been elected to the school board.

With time, the bulk of the state's anti-immigrant measures were blocked in the courts, and the xenophobia eased as Mexico's financial crisis cooled and migration slowed again. The English-only statewide proposition in particular came to generate wide opposition from Latinos as many families discovered it had not improved access to education for their children and had even harmed it: In some schools, Latino children were now being held back, ridiculed, or quietly segregated for speaking Spanish. But the anti-immigrant rhetoric that had over the long term subtly and not so subtly shaped the identities of Latinos did not entirely dissipate. As it had time and time again, it only ebbed. Pundits and commentators, taking a page from the Gingrich playbook of political theater, continued to arouse fears of Mexicans, migrants, and invasions on the budding Fox News network and in the ecosystem of conservative radio stations across the country. They would grow in intensity and gain in reach after Islamic extremists crashed commercial aircraft into the World Trade Center on September 11, 2001. Although most of the hijackers in the terror attack—the deadliest on American soil—had entered the country legally with visitor visas through the northern border, the southern border became a center of attention. The United States reassembled immigration enforcement under the new Department of Homeland Security, and funding for border agents, detention facilities, and surveillance technology across the Southwest ballooned. Immigration training facilities for Border Patrol agents began to resemble paramilitary camps, and the goal at the southern border was no longer simply prevention; it was "zero tolerance"—meaning not a single unauthorized crossing would be tolerated.

Through it all, Susan had not had any intention of following her sister into politics. She was a teacher, as she had always wanted to be, but she found herself on the front lines of every social, emotional, and economic struggle facing families. She could often tell which children in her mostly Latino classes had not eaten, which had slept in their cars, which were falling in with the wrong crowds. At Blanca's urging, Susan decided to tackle those issues through public office. She was elected city clerk of Baldwin Park in 2005 and four years later successfully ran for a seat on the city council.

But there was one student neither Blanca nor Susan could prevent from falling through the cracks. Unlike his sisters, their brother Robert was moved to a special education campus when he failed an English aptitude test upon their arrival in California. He grew emotionally withdrawn over the years, and eventually he and the family lost touch. Blanca felt that she had failed in her duty to protect him, and in speaking up for others, the sisters would later often say, they were speaking up for him.

15

Mexicans in Exile

CIUDAD JUÁREZ, CHIHUAHUA
2008

THE DRUG WAR came to the Holguins in early 2008. Alfredo Beltrán Leyva, one of the top bosses of the Mexican drug trade, was captured that January in the western state of Sinaloa as he attempted to flee in an SUV with an assault rifle, two suitcases holding $900,000 in cash, and eleven luxury watches. Eleven of his hitmen were nabbed in mansions in Mexico City the next day. The men, along with the caches of automatic weapons, rifles, and grenades seized, were presented before reporters, a show of force by the government of Mexican president Felipe Calderón as he took on his nation's drug lords.

Only two years earlier, shortly after taking office, Calderón had vowed to use all the powers of the state to bring to heel criminal syndicates that had not only withstood American antidrug efforts to quash them but had become more expansive. He began by deploying 6,500 Mexican soldiers to target the top cartel in Michoacán, his home state, and then went on to dispatch tens of thousands more military personnel across Mexico to replace those police forces that he saw as corrupt. With American aid, he also began to topple drug queens and kingpins, like Beltrán Leyva, and to ship them to maximum security prisons in the United States for prosecution.

The approach seemed promising. Plucked out of their bastions, severed from their connections, their handover was hailed as the start of a new era of cooperation between Mexico and the United States. Major players of the Mexican underworld would land on American ground over the next decade to face charges, from Texas to New York to Colorado to California: la Barbie, el Señor de los Cielos, la Reina del Pacífico—the roll call of nicknames as varied as a card game of Lotería. But disappearances and homicides quickly began to skyrocket in Mexico as rudderless criminal organizations splintered into smaller and even more vicious offshoots, competing over increasingly fragmented turf. The result would be a fifteen-year conflict not quite officially declared a war yet a war nonetheless, and one far deadlier than the Mexican Revolution itself.

As for Beltrán Leyva, he was known as el Mochomo, or the Desert Ant, and the power vacuum his arrest left within the Beltrán Leyva Organization would help bathe Chihuahua once more in blood. Beltrán Leyva and his brothers had formed the BLO back when Mexican drug traffickers had come to dominate the wholesale cocaine market. Working alongside their cousin, Joaquín Guzmán Loera, or el Chapo ("Shorty"), the head of the Sinaloa Cartel, they had spread out across much of central Mexico, as well as into Sonora and Tamaulipas in the north, with branches in human and weapons smuggling, money laundering, murder, kidnapping, and extortion. But once Beltrán Leyva was gone, old rivalries resurfaced between the Beltrán Leyva brothers and Guzmán, who they believed had given up Mochomo to the Drug Enforcement Administration.

When the Calderón government launched Operation Chihuahua against the cartels in the state that March, the Beltrán Leyvas and the Guzmáns were fighting with each other and the Juárez Cartel, or la Línea, over the coveted trade routes out of Ciudad Juárez into El Paso. Los Zetas, which until then had served as the paramilitary wing of the Gulf Cartel in Tamaulipas, had also begun moving into the state from the east, on the verge of breaking off as an independent organization after Gulf leader Osiel Cárdenas Guillén—el Mata Amigos, or Friend Killer—was extradited to the United States in 2007.

As the hostilities picked up, warnings went out to businesses large and small across central Ciudad Juárez. If their owners wanted to keep their doors open and stay safe, they would have to pay derecho de piso, protection money. Different criminal groups and their gangs of enforcers hustled employees at major gas station chains and big-box stores, such as Walmart and S-Mart. They paid menacing visits to the Kentucky Club and other bars, restaurants, and shops along Avenidas Juárez and 16 de Septiembre. They hounded just about every one of the Holguins' neighbors: the elderly couple who peddled raspas down the road; the owners of la carnicería, or butcher shop; the corner bodega that sold groceries. They came after the Holguins.

The Holguins remember they began paying the extortion fees sometime in late 2007 or early 2008 after men brandishing guns stopped by their bus company and several other businesses in their vicinity. They let all the proprietors know that if any one of them refused to make the payoffs, all of them would suffer the consequences. They wanted 10,000 pesos (about $500) a week from the Holguins, but the two sides settled on 5,000 pesos, or $250. Others negotiated varying amounts. Even the cart vendors, who barely made 200 pesos ($18) a day, were told they had to pay. Those who refused to abide by the new directives soon saw their relatives abducted and were forced to pay ransoms for their release.

Every week, Luis recalls, he would wrap the cash inside a newspaper and wait for a call from the criminals. They would tell him at which street corner to drop off the package. He or one of their employees usually waited in his car for the masked men to arrive, praying to God each time that all would go smoothly. The brothers kept up the payments for months, but sometime that year another group of gang members—or maybe the same ones; who could tell?—started hitting up bus and car repair shops like the Holguins'. They wanted additional cash.

Alfredo, now in his late forties, first got word of this new racket when a man stopped by their office saying he needed to deliver a message. He handed the bus coordinator on duty a small white slip of paper with a phone number scribbled on it.

"Toma, dile a tu patrón que le llame a este número" ("Here, tell your boss to call this number"), he said.

Shortly after that encounter, one of their bus drivers received a similar missive from a man who climbed off his bus with a swarm of other passengers. The exchange was so quick and the driver was so taken aback that he did not get a good look at the person who had placed the note in his hand.

In the confines of one of the buses, where they discussed all their business and family matters, Alfredo and the other brothers decided to ignore the demands. They were already paying into the neighborhood extortion funds. Who were these men? Why should they have to pay any more? They were scarcely breaking even. But the threats kept coming. They followed Alfredo and his drivers. They called his dispatch office. They called his personal cell phone: voices he didn't recognize, men he didn't know. They likely were members of la Línea or their foot soldiers. But they also could have been part of any number of narco groups now vying for control.

Then one afternoon Alfredo got a frantic call from an employee. He had just driven away when he was told that several SUVs with black-tinted windows were surrounding their offices. Alfredo swerved around and rushed back. He arrived as men clad in black shirts and fatigues, carrying what looked to be AR-15s and AK-47s, were rounding up his workers and shoving them to the ground. They broke a couple of the men's knees and punched others in the face. They grabbed Alfredo and pushed him down, clubbing him with their rifles on his back and neck.

It was their final warning. Next time, they said, he and his brothers would be dead.

TOWARD THE END of the nineteenth century, when the law of the frontier remained, as scholars describe it, "raw, rough, and red with blood," a popular army of five hundred Mexicanos and Tejanos of all classes rose up near the town of San Elizario, the site of la Toma, just outside of El Paso. They were fighting Anglo ranchers and politicians who sought to privatize the salt deposits near the Guadalupe Mountains that Mexican and American residents had used as a major source of salt for years. After they forced a band of about twenty Texas Rangers to surrender, the United States brought in the buffalo soldiers and the mercenaries of a New Mexico sheriff to restore order. The community lost the rights to the communal land, and the San Elizario Salt War of 1877, historian Miguel Antonio Levario indicates, would mark one of the earliest and most significant racial conflicts to define Mexicanos and Tejanos as enemies in the American Southwest. It would also indirectly lay the groundwork for the long history of illicit drug trade in the region as each country increased the enforcement of its border and the political instability enabled crime and corruption to develop alongside the flow of people, goods, and ideas already growing in the frontier.

Not long after the salt war, the first notorious criminal group to reign over the El Paso and Juárez region emerged along 15,000 acres of brush and desert that stretched between the Rio Grande and a dry riverbed in El Paso. The wilds were known as Pirate Island, and according to the Texas Rangers they were the domain of a "bandit gang"—a father and his three sons—who gained control of smuggling and other underground activities in the area after the Rangers shot and killed one of their relatives in the San Elizario Salt War. They were especially difficult to catch because the land on which they operated had been largely formed when violent floods shifted the course of the river, leaving the international boundary between Mexico and the United States uncertain.

Illegal smuggling further evolved in Ciudad Juárez as the United States cracked down on Chinese laborers and the opium many brought as a form of recreation and mental escape. Through the Mexican Revolution, the smuggling routes proved critical to Mexican rebels in need of guns and ammunition from the north to keep their resistance alive, and in its aftermath the informal economy thrived as the conflict had all but decimated the agriculture, cattle, and mining industries across Chihuahua. Trade and commerce had been devastated, and political institutions were in shambles. State lawmakers did not meet once between 1913 and 1920, and not a single governor in the state was able to hold on to power long enough to finish his term between 1920 and 1929. In a short span of eight years, between 1910 and 1917, Juárez had no less than forty-nine municipal presidents or county executives.

The arrival of American Prohibition laws in the 1920s, and the migration of glittering saloons, bars, and casinos south through los años dorados, gave the Mexican border city a fighting chance. But its saving grace also damned it. The same casino owners who contributed substantial funds to local and state treasuries—allowing Juárez to improve its sewers, build schools, and pave roads in those golden years—functioned independently of the government and decided who won local and state races. Whoever controlled Juárez's casinos controlled its political power, paving the path for the organized crime bosses who would one day rule the city.

Through the 1920s, concerns over the use of marijuana and opium rose on both sides of the border with the global eugenics movement, in part because the drugs were often associated with Chinese and Indigenous populations. When Mexico banned the cultivation of marijuana and opium poppies, the United States sought to criminalize the use, selling, and possession of those substances—and their Chinese and Mexican users. But, far from quelling demand, notes researcher Nicole Mottier, attempts at regulation only created lucrative black markets. Trafficking became more profitable and drove the recreational drug trade underground, where its players and the substances they dealt became even more powerful.

Within the decade, Juárez had its first organized crime gang, led by Enrique Fernández, the co-manager of the Mint nightclub, and Ignacia Jasso, a woman known as la Nacha (short for Ignacia). Fernández had cut his teeth counterfeiting and running rum before building his name as the "King of Morphine." He was a well-regarded philanthropist, popular for dressing up as Santa Claus on Christmas and paying for the funerals of Juárenses from families of little means. He likely lined his pockets like all the other casino and bar magnates of the era, but he also funneled his earnings into public projects, like revamping the city's rural schools. Once he dominated the drug trade, he wasted little time wielding his informal political power to install his allies in local office. He also recruited la Nacha, who had lost her first husband, a drug dealer, after he was shot and killed in a brothel. La Nacha started at the bottom. She sold dope to addicts and took the heat for Fernández, who sometimes paid her bail. By 1933, la Nacha was reportedly one of the top drug dealers in a business that had spread far beyond Juárez and El Paso to Parral, Casas Grandes, and Ciudad Chihuahua, cities that had once been the rebel hotspots for Magonistas and Maderistas and Villistas.

Criminals, bandidos, and Indios. In the beginning, the battles that defined Mexicanos as dangerous in the eyes of the Mexican and American governments tended to be over land and resources. The clashes were often ideological, the aggression turned against Native Mexicans who opposed the arrival of Progress; against the intellectuals who fueled la conciencia colectiva and debated capitalism and communism, revolution and retrenchment; against the blue-collar workers who laid the tracks, extracted the copper and silver, powered the cities, and demanded their rights; against the revolucionarios and guerrilleros who shouted "¡Libre fronterizo!" and "¡Tierra y libertad!" In the end, the lofty aims and ideas were washed away in the bloodshed. The business of drugs and war blurred, co-opted, and corrupted las causas.

Revolucionarios turned poppy growers cultivated and harvested small fields in Sonora, Sinaloa, Nayarit, Chihuahua, and Durango. More poppies were grown in India or Burma, where they were converted into opium or morphine. The drugs were delivered to the Green Gang in Shanghai and exported to Los Angeles and finally to Juárez, where Chinese men had moved most of their opium joints as El Paso had been passing fines and ordinances against the places since the early 1880s, when city council members began fielding complaints about the moral evils they posed. The Chinese owners opened the dens inside their homes or in the back rooms of their bars and businesses. Most of the places were a combination of a fumadero, a room where clients could smoke chandu—opium prepared for that purpose—and a picador, where patrons could inject morphine or heroin.

As la Nacha climbed the ranks, Fernández reached the heights of his influence, deploying his charm and charity to elevate his cronies and fix elections. But after the city embarked on a series of reforms and cleanup efforts in 1930, more than one hundred people were ousted from one of the administrations that Fernández had helped handpick. Out of the chaos would arise the Quevedo brothers—Rodrigo, Jesús, and José—who owned the Juárez power company and the city slaughterhouse. Rodrigo Quevedo, a burly man with plump cheeks and dark, slicked-back hair, was the leader of the clan. He had been a Maderista turned Orozquista turned Huertista turned Villista until finally, after multiple defeats in the spring of 1918, he had yielded to Venustiano Carranza and turned Carrancista. After the war, his family had acquired Terrazas agricultural lands that he had used to rebuild the state's cattle industry.

For years, Fernández had not interfered with the Quevedos as they had operated on the same political side. He had even managed the glamorous Tívoli casino with one of their allies. But Juárez saw its first turf war after Fernández fell out with a governor he had helped to take office. To take down Fernández, the governor turned to the Quevedo brothers, who are believed to have set Fernández's Mint ablaze—and then to have turned on the governor. In 1932, when Rodrigo assumed the governorship and his brothers rose to the top of city hall, they declared war on Fernández. Rodrigo obtained even more wealth and property, and the Quevedos began to use their power to protect people involved in the drug trade and ignore their criminal activities.

The organized crime in Ciudad Juárez even then, as scholars like Mottier have found, had structure: Kingpins like Fernández and the Quevedos stood at the top; drug distributors like la Nacha were below them; and under them were gang members with skills and connections but lesser responsibilities and immunities—the Chinese owners of opium dens, the doctors and pharmacists who could prescribe and sell drugs, the pistoleros tasked with murder, and the Juárez madams often described as the boldest in the business. The final and perhaps largest layer encompassed the drug smugglers and drug dealers who took the most risks, were most often arrested, and had neither skills nor connections but kept the whole racket running. They included addicts and felons but also lower-rung city employees and other workers, such as truck drivers, carpenters, street cleaners, and public utility operators. The largest narcotics transactions sometimes took place in Concordia Cemetery in El Paso in the hours before the sun rose.

All across Mexico and Latin America the story would repeat itself. The drug cartels and criminal organizations that arose through the 1980s and 1990s built on earlier lines of trade. As the Cold War gave way to the drug war, the United States retreated from countries such as Guatemala and El Salvador before seeing peace reforms through, moves that partly laid the groundwork for corrupt politicians and criminal groups to exploit their dearth of economic opportunities and overwhelm regional police forces. The United States' homegrown problems further fueled the drug violence south of its border. As the nation attempted to curb its crime rates, it deported young Latinos made gang members on American streets, only to watch homicides soar in Mexico and Central America. And budding criminal organizations there found giant markets in the United States, where American pharmaceutical companies and fly-by-night doctors and pain clinics were beginning to nourish what would become a full-blown national opioid crisis.

With the rise of the narcos in Mexico and beyond, the new fights tended to center on money, individual power, and security. They were about cash flow and portfolio expansion. They were driven by narco-capitalism and American drug demands. They were powered by greed. And here El Paso was, too, and had been since the beginning, at the crossroads of ideas, goods, and people.

AFTER THE ASSAULT, the Holguin brothers paid the higher extortion fees from there on out. But the feuding between the Sinaloa and Juárez Cartels was only growing worse. Joaquín Guzmán, or el Chapo, had the uncanny abilities to co-opt public officials, escape prison, target rival strongholds, and find new ways to bring his drugs to market. He would come out on top, cementing his organization as the most powerful in Mexico and making him the most wanted man in the entire Western Hemisphere. That would not be before El Paso's sister city descended into the depths of darkness. Ciudad Juárez became what it hopes never to be again: the epicenter of the drug war, the murder capital of the world, all while El Paso was pronounced the second-safest city in the United States.

Throughout the Cold War, Mexican and Latin American leaders were so concerned with stopping revolution—under pressure by the United States but also by some of their own people—that they spent years targeting their own citizens. Their armed forces were trained to seek out and eradicate subversive groups and guerrillas using whatever means necessary, including torture and disappearance. The narco wars of the early 2000s in Mexico would reveal just how entrenched criminal bosses truly were within the government, and the narco-state would aggressively turn its powers on Mexicanos, dissidents, journalists, and anyone who dared question the violence.

With the death toll in Juárez and Mexico climbing, Democratic president Barack Obama entered office in 2009 on a bold promise to pass comprehensive immigration reform, including a pathway to citizenship for some 12 million unauthorized immigrants in the United States. But the 2008 housing crash and an economic meltdown would give rise to the conservative Tea Party wave that would oppose his administration at every turn. As he sought Republican support, he stayed true to another part of his platform, continuing plans started under his predecessor, George W. Bush, to build a wall along the U.S.-Mexico border, including thirty-foot slabs of metal separating El Paso and Juárez.

As the wall went up, Juarenses struggled to recognize their city. Women disappearing in the Chihuahuan desert had captured international attention; but the statistical reality would show, as retired research librarian Molly Molloy has captured, that there was no specific surge in the killings of women—Juárez was in a "profound crisis" striking the whole of society. The rolls of the dead and missing were surging. Federal soldiers patrolled the streets with assault rifles. Shootouts could break out at any time. Anyone could be a casualty. The word "fear," Roman Holguin Jr. remembers, fails to capture the deep inner terror that became part of their everyday lives. There had been a time when Juárez had been so alive that many Americans preferred to live there than in El Paso. Now, on some days, he and his brothers felt as though they were wandering through a ghost town. They wondered whether it wasn't just Juárez losing its soul. It seemed like, in forgetting the plight of its sister, El Paso was, too.

As the criminals continued to up their demands for funds, Alfredo and his brothers, tired of the harassment, began to discuss ways to get them to stop. They complained to union bosses. They complained to the Juárez police. They even threatened to organize a march. Not too long after, they found one of the buses in their lot ablaze. Someone had thrown gas on the seats and set it on fire. Months after that, in May 2009, Alfredo's twenty-three-year-old son, Alfredo Holguin Jr., and a friend were out at a bar and restaurant downtown when gunmen entered the venue and riddled their bodies with bullets. They fired on them so many times that they destroyed the young men's faces. Police later classified the case as a robbery, but the

Holguin brothers were convinced the killings had been executions, a response to their attempts to organize against the extortion rackets. Alfredo had barely buried his son when the threatening phone calls picked up again.

That December, Luis Holguin, the youngest of the brothers, was the first to leave. He and his family packed up enough belongings for a long trip and crossed into El Paso. A few days later he called Beto and told him they all needed to flee. The last strange call Luis had received had come with a warning. The criminal group—they never did find out which one—had promised to kill them all. Most of the Holguins left that day with only what they could throw in a couple of suitcases. They caravanned out together in several cars: brothers, wives, in-laws, children, grandchildren. "Don't bother bringing anything; just leave now," Roman remembers their brother insisting.

They were not the only ones fleeing. Like in the bloody years of the revolution, tens of thousands of Mexicanos had begun to head into Texas. As the Zetas officially split from the Gulf Cartel in 2010, they aggressively moved into Juárez and other Mexican cities with brutality as performance art. They beheaded their victims on camera. They left dismembered limbs for police to find. They delivered warnings to their enemies on bloody white banners they hung alongside the bodies of their victims from highway overpasses. But the Mexican military that aimed to put them down inflicted its own form of terror.

Emilio Gutiérrez Soto, a Mexican journalist, and his teenage son escaped Ciudad Chihuahua in 2008 and requested asylum at an El Paso port of entry after a source told Gutiérrez Soto the Mexican military wanted him dead. The journalist had reported on Mexican soldiers who had robbed a group of migrants—and on the threat he had received from the army afterward. To the east of Ciudad Juárez, in the Juárez Valley where Miguel Martinez had walked for miles in the Year of the Hunger, Jorge Luis Reyes and his family made the decision to flee after Mexican soldiers swept through the streets of Guadalupe, a small Mexican farming community along the border with a population of 3,000 people. They ransacked homes in what they said were searches for drugs, guns, and money. But it was not lost on residents that their town was home to Jorge Luis's aunt, Josefina Reyes Salazar, a prominent activist who had rallied against a nuclear waste site and denounced the unsolved slayings of young women in Juárez. Between the attack and when they left in 2011, the strip of desert borderland became known as the Valley of Death. In total, six members of Jorge Luis's family would be killed, including María Magdalena Reyes Salazar, Jorge Luis's mother, who was missing for nineteen days before her body was dumped along the side of a road. He would always remember that at her funeral he had been happy to know where his mother was buried, that he had a place to someday take her flowers. In Mexico, many had been left with absolutely no trace of their relatives.

Of the Holguins, only Alfredo was forced to stay behind. The rest of his family had used their visas to get across the international checkpoints. But Alfredo's was revoked after he had been caught playing a gig at an El Paso restaurant as a teenager during the immigration crackdowns of the 1990s. He had never gotten around to fixing it. As his brothers began looking for lawyers who could help them plead for asylum in the United States, Alfredo crashed at the places of friends and neighbors in Juárez, a vagabond always on the move as criminal group members attempted to find his location. Finally, he scaled the border wall and turned himself in to authorities on the other side. He remained at the Otero County Detention Center in New Mexico for about a month before he was transferred to a smaller detention facility in El Paso.

Over the next few years, most of the Holguins and a couple Mexican activist families settled into life in El Paso, and in 2011, some came together to form Mexicanos en Exilio, an advocacy and support group to raise awareness about their cases. With the help of Carlos Spector, a respected El Paso immigration lawyer, the group joined the lawyers and activists who had been trying to expand the bounds of U.S. asylum through the 1980s and '90s. Much of the nation's asylum and refugee policy had evolved throughout the Cold War, when the United States favored those fleeing communism, and its purview was narrow. Under the Refugee Act of 1980, which established the statutory basis for the process, judges could grant asylum only to people escaping persecution on account of religion, race, nationality, political opinion, or membership in "a particular social group." Now Spector was making a special case for the Holguins and other Mexicanos fleeing the violence in their country in American courts. He was arguing that they should be shielded under U.S. laws because they were fleeing political persecution. Even though the threats themselves were coming from any number of Mexican criminal organizations and their enforcers, those groups were so deeply embedded within the Mexican narco-state that the Holguins were truly victims of their own government.

They were Mexican exiles like Benito Juárez, the namesake of their city, during his earliest efforts to democratize his nation, when he had been thwarted by the conservative dictator Santa Anna and taken up residence in New Orleans, where he had subsisted on the meager wages he made rolling cigars at a small factory; like Francisco Madero, who, while hiding out from Porfirio Díaz in San Antonio, Texas, had begun writing the call to arms that would help spark a revolution.

It was little understood then, but the place where the Holguins had crossed over—linking two communities at opposite ends of the violence, one typically thriving at the expense of the other—was at the center of three border wars, not one: a war against drugs, a war against migrants, and a war against terror on the American homeland.

16

Children of the Uprising

San Gabriel Valley, California
2015

In the summer of 2015, Donald J. Trump descended from the golden escalators of Trump Tower in New York City and announced his bid for the White House, with remarks likening Mexicans to criminals and rapists. Two of the people watching him on television were Blanca and Susan Rubio. They wrote him off. The New York businessman and former reality TV host sounded too much like Governor Pete Wilson, whose vitriol had decimated the Republican Party in California. Democrats in their state were now close to securing supermajorities in both chambers of the legislature, and a whole class of Latino and Asian American lawmakers had ascended to the highest levels of state and local government through the Latino and immigrant rights movements of the 1990s.

Blanca, who remained a school board trustee in Baldwin Park, was now exploring the possibility of her own political bid. Susan's husband, Roger Hernández, a respected former councilman in West Covina and member of the California State Assembly, was terming out and launching a bid for a seat in the U.S. House of Representatives. Blanca and Roger had urged Susan to run for his old seat overseeing the Forty-Eighth District, which encompassed the heavily Latino suburbs of the San Gabriel Valley east of downtown Los Angeles, which the Rubios called home. But Susan had told her sister she was not feeling up for it and encouraged Blanca to go for it instead.

As Blanca crafted her campaign message and platform, she thought through her story: her struggles with English, her family's deportation, and their efforts to stay afloat. This family history had never struck Blanca as remarkable. In southeastern Los Angeles County, many had the same story. But as she spoke it out loud, she realized that it was what deeply bonded her to so many people in her district: immigrants, Latinos, border crossers and dwellers of different ethnicities and nationalities and socioeconomic classes—all part of the fabric of a changing California, of a changing nation. The Rubios might have left the borderland a long time ago, but—like so many of the Latinos she now hoped to represent—she had forever remained in the space between Mexican and American. This was something she no longer wanted to keep hidden. She believed it could be her strength.

In the kitchen of their parents' home a few days later, the Rubio sisters told Estela and Sabino the plan. Blanca had decided she would run for Roger's vacant seat. Sabino did not oppose the idea, but Estela was skeptical about Blanca's prospects. Running for local office was one thing; running for a state seat would be tough—and so very public. Estela was not sure Blanca had a chance.

What would people make of the time their family had been sent back to Ciudad Juárez? she thought. What about all those years they were forced to lay low in the very country they called home?

Estela had not forgotten the anti-Mexican and anti-immigrant fervor that had kept Pete Wilson in the California governor's mansion. If she and Sabino had learned anything over their years coming and going through El Paso, documented and undocumented, it was that it was best for Mexicanos in the United States to keep their heads down. The detention and deportation of a mostly Latino immigrant population had become big business, encompassing private and public prisons and law enforcement agencies at every level of government. The politics of immigration had only grown more toxic, and one simply needed to tune in to coverage of the presidential race to hear the virulence of the past.

The latest iteration of American nativism had been building for some time. In El Paso and along the southern border, migration patterns into the United States had once again changed. For decades, it had mostly been Mexicano workers who headed north—often passing through El Chuco—in search of better jobs and pay. But as American interventions and policies helped fuel drug violence and corruption across Mexico and Central America, more women and children and families like the Holguins were crossing into the United States. By 2011, the Obama administration was also grappling with a record number of children from El Salvador, Honduras, and Guatemala traveling alone over the nation's southern border, aided by sophisticated smuggling networks. Asylum claims and immigration cases were continuing to pile up in overcrowded and underfunded courts, and more Democrats and Republicans had come to agree that the nation's asylum and immigration laws were ill-equipped to address what had become global migration challenges. Still, bipartisan attempts at a broad overhaul of the nation's immigration laws failed in Congress as Tea Party members and immigration hawks stirred fears about a growing Latino population in the United States and decried any pathway to legal status or citizenship for undocumented immigrants as a form of "amnesty." Rising Tea Party stars even turned to state-level immigration crackdowns and Pete Wilson–like rhetoric across the Sun Belt.

Feeling the pressure from both the right and the left, President Obama tapped his vice president, Joe Biden, to tackle the "root causes" of migration from El Salvador, Guatemala, and Honduras, tasking him with spurring economic development and opportunities in the region to prevent people from heading to the United States in the first place. He signed executive orders to provide temporary deportation relief for Dreamers, or young immigrants who had been brought into the country illegally as children, as well as their parents. And he directed his administration to focus its immigration enforcement efforts on targeting smugglers, criminals, and potential terrorists for removal. But as the immigration wars continued, state leaders—often Republicans in Texas—challenged his executive actions on the issue in court, and an ecosystem of anti-immigrant groups and right-wing media personalities, which had been mushrooming for years—on radio stations, late-night television, and later in the far-right reaches of the internet—amplified Americans' worst fears about immigration, terrorism, and economic and cultural decline. Much of their programming flowed on currents of conservative populism, fear of Black racial progress, and resentment over a dwindling white middle class. They maligned Mexicans and Latinos, women, Black people, and members of the LGBTQ community.

Obama's enforcement efforts, meanwhile, disillusioned his supporters on the left. Latino and immigrant rights leaders argued that a wide array of immigrants, most without criminal records, were getting caught in the dragnet. In his first term alone, he had deported more unauthorized immigrants than any president had since Mexican workers had been targeted in the 1950s. As 2014 rolled around, some liberal activists had begun lambasting Obama as "deporter in chief." And despite the aggressive enforcement action, Central American mothers and children continued to arrive at the southern border in higher and higher numbers. The Obama administration then reopened family detention centers and labeled the families "priority enforcement targets": people who American immigration officials believed should be deported or removed from the country as quickly as possible, often ahead of other immigrants.

As Blanca prepared for a heated Democratic primary in the summer of 2016, she positioned herself as Trump's antithesis and believed she might even be able to win over Republicans turned off by his anti-immigrant rhetoric. But Trump emerged as the Republican nominee for president that spring, and it was looking more and more like Estela had been right to worry about the ingrained fear of the Mexican in American society. Trump was presenting himself as the Tea Party heir, and his stunning array of victories across the country showed signs that he was remaking the electorate of the Republican Party itself.

Estela appeared to be right about one more thing as well: The campaign would be hard fought. Weeks into her bid, Blanca learned Susan had been keeping a tightly guarded secret about her marriage. It burst into the open after Susan obtained a temporary restraining order requiring that Roger stay at least one hundred feet from her. Witness testimony in a divorce court hearing and filed witness statements later described her husband as a jealous man who often struck Susan and accused her of cheating, once wrapping a belt around her neck, another time holding a knife above her head. Hernández denied the allegations. Photos in a thick court file captured a hole punched in a wall at their home and Susan's bruised arm.

Political allies, friends of Roger, turned on the sisters, and the publicity around the divorce that ensued threatened to derail Blanca's campaign. Yet, Susan insisted that her sister not drop out of the race. Blanca kept going—without the endorsement of the state Democratic Party and against opponents flush with cash. It became a family affair. Sabino put up signs, Estela made sandwiches and burritos for volunteers, and her two sisters split up the district into three sections and knocked on every door they could.

For Blanca, November 9, 2016, was bittersweet. She won her race—and a few hours later, so did Donald Trump.

Sacramento, California
2016

On the night of the presidential election, Kevin de León, the leader of the California State Senate, called Anthony Rendon, his counterpart in the Assembly, from the balcony of his hotel in downtown Los Angeles. Throughout his campaign, Trump had demeaned immigrants, made promises to build a border wall, and called for a registry of Muslim citizens. Now the two state leaders, who represented immigrant-rich districts in Los Angeles, needed to figure out how to respond.

Beyond that, they believed, their state—and the nation—should be long past a moment like this. It had been the California of the 1870s that had spurred a national wave of anti-Chinese racism so fierce that the United States banned all Chinese laborers from entering the country. It had been the California of the 1990s that had elevated Pete Wilson and inspired the Latino immigrant crackdowns in Arizona, South Carolina, and other states across the Sun Belt through the 2000s.

Since then, their state had become the most populous in the nation. It was home to Hollywood and Silicon Valley, as well as the San Joaquin Valley, one of the most abundant agricultural areas in the world, where 50 percent of the global supply of raisins was produced within a sixty-mile radius of Fresno alone. The state had the sixth-largest economy in the world, behind only the United Kingdom, Germany, Japan, China, and the United States. Immigrant workers—including the very Mexicanos whom Trump maligned, the lawmakers believed—had been crucial to powering every one of those gains with their sweat and their labor. And many had come through El Paso: Nearly 60 percent of the Mexicanos who settled in Los Angeles between 1900 and 1945, as columnist Gustavo Arellano has reported, entered through El Paso ports of entry.

On the phone that night in November, de León and Rendon resolved not to let their state reverse its progress. Borders, immigrant rights, the preservation of a pluralistic and democratic society—these were issues that they were convinced deep-blue California would have to lead on with a fresh progressive vision. The following day, a few minutes past noon, after much back and forth between their staffs, they released a joint statement:

"California was not a part of this nation when its history began, but we are clearly now the keeper of its future," they wrote.

Inside the white dome of the state capitol, the California resistance to the Trump administration had begun. The first day of the legislative session that December, with Trump weeks away from occupying the Oval Office, we watched as state lawmakers rose to loudly denounce Trump in both houses. That same afternoon, in front of a panel of powder-blue curtains and a seal of the state of California, senators and Assembly members, including de León and Rendon, unveiled a series of resolutions that they said would lay the groundwork for protecting more than 2 million immigrants who lived in the state but did not have legal residency. Rendon said legislators planned to follow a similar template on other issues important to California, such as climate, health care, and tech policy. But it was not difficult to see why they had led with immigration: It was often Latino and Asian immigrant workers—los obreros—who lived in the most polluted areas, had the least access to health care, and were most likely to have law enforcement surveil and collect their electronic data.

The issue was also personal for many Californians who saw immigration, whether legal or illegal, and the diversity it brought to the state as a strength. Roughly 10.3 million immigrants, or about 23 percent of the nation's foreign-born population, lived in California, and almost half of all the state's children had at least one immigrant parent. Undocumented immigrants, Rendon told reporters, contributed billions of dollars to California's GDP and paid taxes—"sometimes more than billionaires. Immigrants can be found working in every sector of our economy, technology, health care, agriculture, and construction, to name a few," he said.

The onslaught of bills filed in the following months included proposals that would punish private companies that helped build a border wall; ban state agencies from sharing information for any database based on religion, ethnicity, or national origin; fund a legal defense program for indigent immigrants facing deportation; and require immigration agents to have a warrant or subpoena before entering worksites and businesses. The marquee piece, de León's so-called sanctuary state bill, sought to ensure courthouses and churches remained safe zones for immigrants without legal residency and to drastically limit cooperation between federal immigration agencies and local law enforcement agencies.

Republicans criticized the Democratic rhetoric as grandstanding and a waste of time, and sheriffs in particular were staunch opponents to reducing communication with federal immigration agencies, arguing it would lead to the release of violent criminals from their county jails. Many of the resolutions condemning the president's rhetoric and hardline immigration actions were more symbolic than anything. But for the class of Latino and Asian American lawmakers who had jumped into politics and community organizing through the Proposition 187 era, the memories of Pete Wilson were still fresh. Where you were born, whether you had legal status or not, had often not mattered: White Californians had tended to see and treat Mexicanos and México Americanos and Latinos all the same—as criminals or a threat. Often, some lawmakers told me, it felt illegal to simply be Mexican, Latino, or an immigrant.

But now Latinos were the largest ethnic group in California, and most had been born in the United States. As their share of the electorate had doubled, so had the numbers of Latino and Asian American lawmakers, and many believed they had an obligation to be the voice in office they had wished to have seen in their youth. There was Miguel Santiago, a Los Angeles native and the son of undocumented Mexican immigrants, who defiantly called himself an "anchor baby," a derogatory term referring to the native-born child of a mother without American citizenship. There were Rob Bonta, the first Filipino American to serve in the legislature, and David Chiu, the oldest child of Hakka Taiwanese American parents, who took a lead role in passing bills to ensure immigrant workers were afforded their rights. There was Wendy Carrillo, who was brought to the country as a child, fleeing war and violence in El Salvador. And now there was also Blanca Rubio.

She was not as far left as many of her colleagues: A pro-business, moderate Democrat, she drew funds from charter schools and the finance, insurance, and real estate industries as she built a coalition of Republicans and independents that ultimately swept her to victory. But Rubio did not hesitate to join the Latino legislative leaders who sought to set up the state as a liberal counterweight to Trump. During an emotional day of speeches as lawmakers introduced legislation to protect immigrant rights, I watched as Blanca stood on the Assembly floor and name-checked El Paso and Juárez.

"My sister and I were deported," she said. "Now I am the first Latina to win the district in the San Fernando Valley."

El Paso, Texas
2017

On the Saturday of Donald Trump's inauguration, a small and buoyant crowd of mostly white older Republicans celebrated with cake and donuts at the GOP headquarters in West El Paso. Gold stars and black streamers, Trump T-shirts, and an American flag made of red, white, and blue plastic flowers decked the walls. A few miles south, just a stone's throw away from the border, José Alfredo Holguin and other members of Mexicanos en Exilio joined more than 1,000 people for a protest march that wound from Armijo Park to San Jacinto Plaza in downtown El Paso. Some held American flags and placards that read BUILD BRIDGES NOT WALLS and RESPETO & DIGNIDAD.

"Trump escucha, estamos en la lucha" ("Listen up, Trump, we're in the struggle"), the crowd chanted as they braved rain and intense winds.

Trump's victory had cast a pall over the borderland. Women and young people had rushed to the polls to vote for Democratic presidential nominee Hillary Clinton in hopes of defeating a Republican candidate who bragged about grabbing women's privates and rallied his supporters with chants of "Build the wall!" As the reality of her loss set in, Mexicanos and México Americanos like the Holguins worried about their friends and family and neighbors. They worried about their businesses. They worried about themselves. There was talk that Trump would be bad for trade, that he would place conditions on remittances and charge more for visas. That he would deport so many people that he would crush the economies of countries across Latin America.

Within a week, Trump had signed executive orders to reinstate a controversial Obama-era deportation program, punish so-called sanctuary cities that refused to collaborate with federal immigration agencies, and lay the groundwork for the construction of a border wall that would cost the United States between $12 billion and $15 billion. Almost as soon, he began feuding with Mexican president Enrique Peña Nieto over his refusal to pay for the wall. He froze refugee admissions and banned travelers from certain Muslim-majority countries, spurring mass protests at airports across the country. He announced end dates to temporary programs that allowed Sudanese immigrants to live and work in the United States. Then he did the same for similar programs aiding Nicaraguans, Haitians, Salvadorans, and Hondurans. He rolled back protections for Dreamers and their parents. And as the Holguins had feared when they had marched through the cold streets of El Paso that January, the Trump administration took an almost methodical approach to dismantling the nation's asylum system. Trump and his allies placed greater burdens on asylum seekers to prove their claims. They issued new rules for immigration judges aimed at making claims harder to win. They used memos and legal mechanisms to narrow who could be eligible.

But the policy that would spark public outrage—including from all four living former First Ladies, Pope Francis, and government, civic, and human rights leaders around the world—did not make any headlines. Not at first. Border and immigration officials rolled it out quietly in El Paso, the passageway in the mountains, where Mexicano workers had once been doused with kerosene, where a wall of officers in green had stood watch for criminals and aliens, where victors and victims of "progress" had crossed back and forth for generations, the lines between them blurring with each turn of the compass of time.

In the spring of 2017, writes journalist Caitlin Dickerson, Jeff Self, the Border Patrol chief who had taken over the El Paso sector once overseen by Silvestre Reyes, privately started a regional program that directed his agents to refer all migrant adults they detained for prosecution. The procedure, though couched as a basic administrative change, was rooted in agency strategies that since Reyes's Operation Hold the Line had been testing ways to prevent unauthorized crossings by making them so miserable and arduous that few if any migrants would want to try them. And it was significant: Typically, parents without a criminal history were detained with their children and later released with instructions to appear at a later court date. But the new initiative directed federal officers to jail and arraign parents on a criminal charge of improper entry, requiring immigration officers to separate them from their children because minors cannot be held in federal custody. Likely unbeknownst to him—and certainly unbeknownst to the public, as Dickerson has uncovered—he had been laying the groundwork for what would become the Trump administration's "zero tolerance" policy.

It was not long before public defense lawyers in El Paso, used to representing indigent clients accused of major federal crimes involving drug smuggling, homicide, and assault, began to have migrants assigned to their caseloads who had no criminal history and were begging for information about their children. Four of those parents and a grandmother appeared in a federal courtroom in downtown El Paso in December 2017. Their names were Natividad Zavala-Zavala, Elba Luz Dominguez-Portillo, Jose Francis Yanes-Mancia, Blanca Nieve Vasquez-Hernandez, and Maynor Alonso Claudino Lopez. They sat in blue jumpsuits and shackles as their public defender, Sergio Garcia, urged the dismissal of their cases. Garcia told the judge each one of his clients had left their native country with a child or grandchild seeking to escape violence in Honduras and El Salvador. But now these key material witnesses—the children—were missing.

In failing to bring them into the court or provide any information on where they could be, the defense lawyer argued, the government was infringing on his clients' rights. A prosecutor for the United States argued otherwise. He said each of the people before the judge had been caught attempting to enter through points not designated as ports of entry. In the courtroom, he added, about half a dozen agents in the pews were prepared to testify, some of them summoned with little notice and on their days off. The judge found all five defendants guilty of illegal entry and, before sentencing them, gave each a chance to speak.

"When I arrived here, I had my daughter with me, and up to this day today, I know nothing of her," Dominguez-Portillo told the judge, adding that she and her daughter had been fleeing from the Maras, or MS-13, a Salvadoran gang that can trace its origins to the streets of Los Angeles. "I want to go back with my daughter as soon as possible. That's all."

One story echoed the next. "I only came here to see if I could have a better life for my son," Claudino Lopez said. "The only thing that I want now is to go back to my country with my son as soon as possible."

"I am in the same situation as they are, and I do want to apologize for what we did for coming into this country illegally," Yanes-Mancia said. "I do want to know about the whereabouts of my son."

"Your Honor, I fled the violence in my country. I fled the danger and the violence. I came here with my grandson. I need to be with my grandson," Zavala-Zavala begged. "I need to know where he is. He was taken from me."

SUCH HEARINGS WENT largely unnoticed until the calls for help started pouring into immigration law offices across the country just before Memorial Day 2018. Immigrant detainees, many fleeing gangs and violence and seeking legal asylum in the United States, were filling courtrooms along the southwestern border. Dozens were parents reporting that border enforcement agents had taken away their children. Federal shelters designed to take in "unaccompanied minors," or young immigrants who crossed the border alone—usually teenagers—started to notice a rise in small children who reported having been separated from their families. Child-welfare officials were suddenly scrambling to find beds for babies. In shelters in New York, where ultimately four hundred children landed, staffers with the unaccompanied immigrant minors program at Catholic Charities Community Services repeatedly plugged children's assigned "alien" numbers into an immigrant detainee locator website, varying the last two digits in hopes of drawing a match with their parents.

As family separations multiplied and federal shelters became strained, informal networks of attorneys, immigrant rights advocates, and volunteers sprung into action to reunite adults and children. Early that June, Senator Jeff Merkley of Oregon traveled to a children's detention center in Brownsville, at the southern tip of Texas, to investigate the cases and was denied permission to enter. The incident set off a media firestorm just as I was heading to Washington from Sacramento for a summer stint in the D.C. bureau of the *Los Angeles Times*. Within a day or two of my arrival, we were working the phones, trying to piece together how the policy worked and who was responsible. Few sources were picking up to speak on background, much less on the record. Staffers at one agency would direct us to their counterparts at another agency and so on. Top spokespeople at the Department of Homeland Security tended to "loop in" communications officials from multiple agencies on any given query, none of whom seemed able to answer basic questions: How many parents had been prosecuted? How many children had been separated? Exactly where and at what facilities were the children now?

In the immediate aftermath, we were able to unravel a confusing web of agencies responsible for processing, splitting up, and detaining families. But it has only been years later, in tracing El Paso's origins and its rightful place in our country's history, that I have been able to understand the breathless scope of what we were watching unfold. The part of the law the government was using to prosecute migrant parents, Section 1325, had its roots in the Undesirable Aliens Act of 1929—the law passed just before the Martinezes were repatriated, signed to restrict the future migration of Mexican families like the Rubios. It was the first to criminalize illegal immigration, making it a misdemeanor to cross into the country anywhere besides a port of entry, and it was what James Dupree describes as "the final brick in the wall" of the 1920s quotas and border enforcement apparatus that transformed Mexicanos, and by extension all Latinos, into forever outsiders in the United States—an alien caste.

The secret El Paso experiment ran for about five months, between July and November, resulting in the separations of at least 188 children from their families. Lomi Kriel, a reporter for the *Houston Chronicle*, was the first to expose some of those cases that fall, and immigration lawyers have since told me that they suspected even then that the American government was splitting the families apart not by incompetence or chance but as a matter of policy, a form of deterrence, to discourage others from coming north. Similar proposals had been floated during the Obama presidency, and the Trump administration had considered the very idea earlier that year. But top Trump officials initially denied there was any such official strategy in place.

By early May, with Trump fuming over stalled efforts to build his border wall and a spike in illegal immigration—the number of families with children attempting to illegally cross the border had climbed in mid-April to the highest level it had been since 2016—Trump officials relaunched and expanded the child separation policy across the southwestern border. Trump officials came to describe the El Paso initiative as a "pilot," pointing to data that showed illegal border crossings in the sector had dropped 64 percent. But as federal officials struggled to house minors, they opened an emergency detention center in Tornillo, just outside the border city, to temporarily hold young migrants attempting to enter the United States alone. The photographs of boys in sneakers, T-shirts, and basketball shorts walking beside beige tents against stark white and brown desert sand further rattled the nation. After the images came the sound. On June 18, 2018, Ginger Thompson, a journalist and Army brat who went to high school in El Paso and began her journalism career there as an intern, obtained an audio of ten children who had been separated from their parents, screaming "Mami" and "Papá" from the halls of a Texas facility. Many of them were crying so hard, she wrote in releasing the recording, they could "barely breathe."

"Well, we have an orchestra here," a Border Patrol agent was heard joking. "What's missing is a conductor."

As the cries were heard around the world, Trump administration officials at first defended their actions as a deterrent against "illegal aliens," drug smugglers, gang members, and other criminals from Honduras, El Salvador, and Guatemala. Trump stirred up another whirlwind of criticism when he claimed that migrants who enter illegally "infest our country." But with the 2018 midterm elections coming up in November, congressional Republicans worried about the political backlash brewing at home. They pressured Trump into a retreat: The president, who initially claimed he could not end the child separations with an executive order, signed an executive order to effectively do just that. In all, investigations would later find, at least 5,500 children had been separated since July 2017. Hundreds of children would remain without their parents years later.

San Gabriel Valley, California
2018

The images of crying children seared through the Rubio sisters' minds. They could have been those young immigrants had they been born only a few decades later. Susan saw the cases as another sordid chapter in American history. They became part of her motivation for launching her campaign for the California State Senate that year as Trump began screening footage of nameless, faceless immigrants traveling in caravans and denounced the "invasion" at the southwestern border.

After the destruction of Susan's marriage, it had taken her a while to find her voice. But the #MeToo movement that shook the California Capitol and the nation emboldened her. More than 140 women—Susan and Blanca among them—signed an open letter denouncing a pervasive culture of sexual harassment in politics. The flood of other women's stories deeply touched Susan, and in a 2017 op-ed in *The Sacramento Bee*, she wrote: "I had an image of what a battered victim would look like, but somewhere along the way the image transformed into my reflection. Victims are everywhere. Look and you will find us."

Susan won, and at her swearing-in ceremony in December 2018, Senate leader Toni Atkins of San Diego heaped praise upon Sabino and Estela Rubio, "the only parents in California history who can say they have had two daughters in the Legislature."

That same month Blanca, perhaps feeling the embers of the borderland where she was born and raised, made national news when she told *The Sacramento Bee* they were now Trump's nightmare. "We are those bad Mexicans that he talks about," she said. "We were undocumented, and then we fought hard, we got an education, and now we're sitting here."

PART THREE

Borders and Bridges

Even the journey of Christ took place in the desert. That's where he meets his demons. That's where he meets his God. And he can't meet one without the other. And that's the border. And that's the desert.

—Benjamin Alire Sáenz

17

Pink and White Crosses

HERE IS WHAT I remember from the place in my hometown where twenty-three people were massacred: high school dates, taking metal shopping carts for a ride through empty parking lots, filming our pranks on an old camcorder, watching the city lights and cars passing by as we waited for our parents or debated what to do next—with the night and with our lives.

We were bored kids back then, in the early 2000s. Good students with a mischievous streak. We called ourselves Mexicanos and México Americanos and Hispanics and Latinos. Afro-Latinos and Blaxicans. Gringos and gabachos and coconuts if we looked Mexican but acted white. Fresas and juniors if we had a little money. Mexas and Frontchis if we came in from Ciudad Juárez or looked like it—and our parents drove cars with license plates marked with decals that read "Front" for Frontera and "Chi" for Chihuahua. Chucas and chucos if we knew our history. Chicanos and Chicanas if we had love for our patria and claimed our rights.

Many of us were underestimated, even as we dreamed of going away to college and moving to bigger cities and living the better lives that our parents—some immigrants, some here for generations—had wanted for us. Not old enough to drink, and even after we were, we would wander through the collection of parking lots, stores, and chain restaurants off of Interstate 10 that descended into chaos on that sweltering August morning. The Cinemark theater, Cielo Vista Mall, Olive Garden, and Walmart, not quite suburbia, no skyscraper-lined metropolis either. This was before the city built a swankier shopping district next door, attracted a music festival and a baseball stadium, and renovated the downtown San Jacinto Plaza, which had once featured live alligators.

Nearly four years after the mass shooting, in July 2023, friends and family members of the victims packed into a federal courtroom for the killer's sentencing. It was an exercise not unlike mass. People sat in uncomfortable pews and spoke in hushed whispers and waited in reverence. It was a ritual to punish the guilty but also to remember.

Over the next couple of days, the people of El Chuco shared their memory—with the killer and the nation—of the lives he took and the city they shaped. Some sobbed when they first saw him enter in shackles, a navy blue jumpsuit, and thin-rimmed glasses. Most news accounts of the testimony say he bobbed his head and swiveled in his chair, showing little remorse. At least two witnesses accused him of smiling and rolling his eyes as they spoke, though some saw him hold back tears as the testimonies condemning his racist crimes went on.

On the stand, Genesis Davila, sixteen, remembered the first crackling round of shots that sounded like fireworks, the screams of people, the blaring of a fire alarm, and the voice of an adult yelling at her and the other girls on her soccer team to "just run." Before that, they had been having fun. She had helped unload the aguas frescas from her dad's truck and set up their outside stand at the Walmart. They had been collecting a ton of donations for their out-of-state tournament. She had greeted her coach Guillermo "Memo" García with a hug. It would be their last.

"We are all grieving his loss, but why was it us in pain and not you?" she asked.

Kaitlyn Melendez remembered she was nine when she lost her grandfather David Johnson as he shielded her and her grandmother Kathleen from the gunfire. The young girl said she had thought of the mass shooting drills she had practiced in school as they walked out past the dead and injured.

Back in her bed that night, she lay awake for hours, unable to sleep. Kathleen felt that the shooter had robbed her of herself, saying that since the massacre she was often deeply depressed and struggled with uncontrollable emotions. But she told the young man that he had not taken from her the memories of her husband nor "the light and joy he brought to his family."

Raymond Attaguile, David's brother-in-law, told the killer he had fired and missed.

"You hit the whitest man in El Paso—NASCAR-loving, bass-fishing, golf-loving, Dallas Cowboy–loving person—man—in El Paso," he mocked. "You hit the white man that you were not able to see in the mirror."

The city's origins and history ran deep in the Remembering. The people of El Chuco spoke of the bicultural and transnational veins that ran through their community, of the worlds within worlds that existed in la frontera. They were speaking out for fronterizos and Mexicans and Mexican Americans but also for immigrants and Latinos, the journeys of their loved ones tracing those of people who had passed through the Pass for over one hundred years, as well as the roots of families who had lived in the borderland long before the U.S.-Mexico border had been drawn.

Gloria Irma Márquez, who had been huddled in the small bank branch inside the store when she was killed, had followed the paths of Mexicanos into the city from Sinaloa and had been hoping to reunite with the daughter she had been separated from for thirteen years. After years of struggling with American immigration laws, her Mexican daughter had finally been granted a visa to attend her mother's funeral. Raul Flores and his wife, Maria, who died near the checkout aisles, had met in Juárez as young adults and raised their family in the San Gabriel Valley of Southern California. They had moved back two decades earlier to a spacious, brightly lit home in El Paso.

As a longtime ironworker, Luis Alfonso Juarez—at ninety, the oldest victim of the massacre—had scraped together a pedacito (small piece) of the American Dream, his family first told *The Washington Post*. He had been a traquero who worked on the railroads. He had been a construction worker who helped erect buildings across El Paso and Los Angeles. He had earned his citizenship and bought a home. Together with Martha, his wife of seventy years, he had raised a large family, including seven children and many grandchildren, great-grandchildren, and great-great-grandchildren.

In the federal courtroom, Luis Alfonso's daughter, Meg Juarez, remembered both her parents had been shot but only her mother had survived. She denigrated the defendant and other "ignorant white supremacists" for contributing hate to society and decrying an "invasion of Hispanics" when in reality, she said, Hispanics like her father contributed more to the United States and its economy than they ever would.

"Let me tell you something: Native Americans and Mexicans were already here in Texas when your American settler homies rolled up," she testified. "Think about that when you say it is your country that you're defending."

LATINOS, WHETHER WE call ourselves Latino, Hispanic, or Latinx, now total 62.1 million people, or nearly 19 percent of the American population, making us the second-largest racial or ethnic group in the United States, according to the U.S. Census. We have gone from roughly 6.5 percent of the population in 1980, when the federal government first officially started counting us, to about 19 percent in 2020 and are projected to make up almost 30 percent of Americans by 2060. More than 60 percent of us can trace our roots to Mexico, and more than two-thirds of us were born in the United States, as American as American can be. But in the immigration battles that have rocked and divided El Paso and the nation, it has often been Latinos—and Mexicans and Mexican Americans specifically—born, raised, or racialized in this country who have become the scapegoats. With our numbers underrepresented in the ranks of government, in boardrooms and newsrooms and Hollywood, as scholars say, we remain relegated to a liminal space in American society, a perpetual in-between place, neither here nor there, the contributions of our workers and our families forgotten and relegated to the margins.

Inside and outside the courtroom, the specter of Donald J. Trump and the debate over his role in an attack that had been one of the deadliest against Latinos in the United States persisted. In his online screed promoting the

Great Replacement, the shooter had said his views on race predated the president's rise and that attempts to blame Trump for what he did would be "fake news." Trump was, after all, only the latest politician to espouse the fear of the Mexican that had been embedded in the nation's identity since El Paso and Juárez had been split in two. Nonetheless, the man had tended to praise Trump's staunch immigration policies online, tweeting #BuildtheWall, and some witnesses denounced him as a white nationalist and a racist and a coward and a Trump follower.

Others could not shake the disturbing notion that many right-wing politicians and pundits in the media had been sounding more and more like the man who had shot and taken their loved ones. Through the 2022 midterm cycle, Trump and his acolytes continued to spread the Big Lie that the 2020 presidential election had been stolen from him and that Democrats were trying to bring more immigrants into the United States to change its demographics and gain a political edge. At his campaign rallies, Trump whipped up fears of "open borders and horrible elections" and aired promos for a far-right-wing documentary that denounced "voter trafficking," likening the work of what appeared to be Latino voter outreach groups to the "Mexican mafia" and referring to people delivering mail-in ballots into drop boxes as "mules."

By the time of the El Paso shooter's sentencing, as the 2024 presidential primaries began in earnest, many Republicans holding prominent positions in Congress, in statehouses, and in town and city governments—or who aspired to be, running in electoral races up and down the ballot, in states near and far from la frontera—were emulating Trump's xenophobic rhetoric. The word "invasion" to describe the arrival of migrants at the 2,000-mile line dividing Mexico and the United States had become a staple in campaign ads, national news interviews, floor speeches, and state and federal legislation.

The refrain across MAGA U.S.A. went like this: The border is in trouble, in crisis, a dystopian nightmare that haunts Americans and American dreams. The border is lawless, wide open, so disorderly that people are flooding in. No, not people: rapists and terrorists and child predators and fentanyl traffickers. Aliens and criminals and illegals. Immigrants let in by "radical

Democrats" and leftists on their way to steal jobs—and votes. Every state had cause for grievance and concern, they warned, because just about every state was seeing its communities change.

For many fronterizos, as for many of the witnesses who took the stand that July, the real Big Lie was that there was or had ever been such a clear-cut demarcation between Black and white, between the blessed and the bad, between "us" and "them." En la frontera, realities could be much more gray—or Brown: Borders could not exist without bridges; divided cities could not thrive without connection. Industry, trade, history, blood, culture, land, and ideas bound people, as did conflict and pain.

Perhaps no clearer symbol of these truths could there be than the shooting. The defendant had come after Mexicans and Hispanics only to slaughter victims of all different races, ethnicities, and nationalities, the young and old, Democrats and Republicans, people who had been on competing sides of the national immigration debate. And when the borderland mourned, it mourned as one.

Thomas Hoffmann remembered he was eating breakfast with his family when they caught the news of the tragedy on television. A picture of a man lying in a pool of blood captured his attention, he said, because he was dressed like his German father, Alexander Gerhard Hoffmann, whom they would later learn had been slain near the front entrance. Hoffmann had served in the German air force and had once been stationed at Fort Bliss. He had met his wife at a discotheque in Juárez during the last flashes of its golden years.

Nearly 4,000 fronterizos lined the streets in Central El Paso to pay their last respects to Margie Reckard, the Baltimore native with strong Nebraska ties who had wrestled with Parkinson's and moved to the city in 2016. In the courtroom, Harry Dean Reckard, her son, called himself "a proud Republican" who had voted for Trump and likely would again. He remembered that his father had been an alcoholic who had put his family through a rough life and that he knew what it was like "not to feel loved." He added that he had been feeling anger over the nation's immigration problems, too. But he shamed the young man for the actions that took his mother.

"I don't ever recall hearing Trump tell people to go out and kill Mexicans. I don't know where you got that from, man," Reckard said. "Yes, there is a problem we have in the United States with the borders, but it is not for us to deal with, man. That's for people in law enforcement to deal with."

At Horizon High School in the days after the massacre, relatives released doves into the air and a student choir sang in honor of Javier Amir Rodriguez, the high school sophomore who was its youngest victim. In court almost four years later, his father, Francisco Javier Rodriguez, wore a white T-shirt imprinted with his son's face on the front and his name memorialized in angel's wings on the back. He demanded the killer look at his son and remembered seeing a cap and gown draped over an empty chair at his graduation as other students walked the stage to receive their diplomas. The irony was, he said, his son had wanted to become a Border Patrol agent.

MONTHS AFTER THE shooting, I and my childhood friend Andrea—whose father had been in the Walmart parking lot at the time and was able to escape unharmed—would finally embrace and cry about the memory of those hot August nights. We had ducked into a beach-themed dive bar in the Lower Valley to catch up during the holidays. She told me she would always remember that day through her father's eyes.

18

Feliz Viaje

Santa María Nebaj, El Quiché, Guatemala
2019

He left his hamlet deep in the western highlands of Guatemala just before dawn and without much time to say goodbye. Kaxh Mura'l, a thin father of three, had been part of a tight-knit circle of Indigenous activists spread across the Ixil Maya region in the Sierra de los Cuchumatanes. The mountains in the northwestern department, or Guatemalan state, of El Quiché were rich in water and mineral resources, such as barite, a colorless crystal essential to oil and gas drilling fluids and other industrial products, and Kaxh had long been among youth leaders organizing opposition to mining and hydroelectric projects tearing up the countryside. But as momentum for their causes had grown, so had an authoritarian backlash. First came the random assaults, then the assassinations.

Trouble for Kaxh started heating up in 2018 after a friend, Jacinto David Mendoza Toma, only twenty-one, had staggered into an area hospital so badly beaten that he could not utter a word. Mendoza, a university student, had been an active member of Paraíso Desigual, a collective dedicated to shedding light on inequality in Guatemala, and only two weeks earlier his name and photo had appeared on a website accusing dozens of activists of "spreading disinformation" against a powerful politico. Kaxh and other friends rushed to collect funds in hopes of covering the cost of a helicopter ride to another medical facility. But they could not gather the money together in time. Mendoza died days later, one of twenty-six human rights and climate activists killed that year.

The death toll was still mounting when, on a cool May afternoon, some 150 people, mostly students and young adults, crowded into a large banquet hall in the town of Santa María Nebaj, in the Guatemalan department of El Quiché, for a municipal candidate forum. Kaxh, a member of the human rights organization that was hosting the event, was supposed to be there solely as a spectator. Group leaders had even specifically asked him to refrain from participating because he had been working as an organizer for one of the political parties represented. But he could not help himself. He knew one of the candidates on the panel had a history of downplaying or outright denying the Cold War–era attacks that a United Nations truth commission had long ago found to be a genocide against Ixil Maya communities like his own.

So, when it was time for the audience to drop questions into a box for the speakers to answer, he took a slip of paper and wrote down a query asking about the man's beliefs on the crimes. It was drawn from the pile, and a thick tension fell over the room as the aspiring officeholder argued that the massacres against the Ixil people—massacres that so many in the audience or their families had lived through—had not amounted to a genocide but were the kind of casualties that happened in any brutal war. Mayan council leaders and others in the room forcefully pushed back against the candidate's claims. Kaxh's question had been anonymous, but he jumped into the fray as the exchange devolved into a shouting match until calm was restored.

Afterward, Kaxh went out to dinner nearby with some friends. It was dusk by that time. The shops, small businesses, and stands selling snacks and cold drinks had shut down for the day, and the bustle on the streets had largely died down. He did not make it too far away from the restaurant when he noticed a towering man in a button-up shirt and slacks following close behind him. Kaxh recognized him as one of the right-wing agitators known to badger genocide survivors. He inched closer toward Kaxh, wrapped an arm around the young activist, and casually began pressing him on his recent politicking as the man walked them to the edge of a desolate road known as Feliz Viaje, or Happy Journey.

"You need to stop with these chingaderas," Kaxh recalled him saying. "You need to stop with this fuckery."

"My problem was not with you. I have nothing personal against you," Kaxh replied as he resisted.

He did not want to go any farther down that isolated path. He was not sure he would return. Luckily, as he tried to push away, his cell phone rang. It was one of his friends. Kaxh, with as much coolness as he could muster, quickly gave his whereabouts and mentioned who he was with. It seemed to startle his assailant. He let Kaxh go home that night but not without a warning, the metal touch of a gun in his waistband.

Back in the safety of his house, Kaxh called a few friends to tell them about the incident. His initial impulse was to lay low for a while. But when he woke up the next morning, his nerves were still rattled. He had already been beaten up in the streets over his activism, and he did not want to end up like Mendoza. Finally, he called La's La B'oxh, an older human rights activist he had known for years, and told him about the clash over the genocide.

"I am leaving town. I am heading north," Kaxh told him. "Maybe next month."

La's had been listening intently. He had been considering heading north, too. In fact, secretly, he had been planning his exit for weeks.

"You can head north with me," he told Kaxh. "But we're not leaving next month. We're leaving the day after next."

NEBAJ SITS IN the mist-shrouded countryside of central Guatemala, a municipality home to roughly 72,700 people, where cars, motos, and red tuk tuk taxis rumble down narrow Spanish colonial–style streets and women tend to dress in the distinctive red skirt and brocaded blouse, or huipil, symbolic of Ixil identity. True to its Ixil namesake, which translates to "lugar de nacimiento del agua," or "the birthplace of water," its surrounding forests and caves are riddled with rivers and waterfalls. To its east lies San Juan Cotzal and to its northeast Chajul. Together, the three make up the Ixil region in El Quiché, an insular region that forms the heart of the Ixil community and where la cultura se mantiene viva (their culture survives).

In the Ixil region, most families subsist on the corn, beans, and squash in their fields and have for generations. But, as in Mexico, Indigenous communities like the Ixil began to see the theft of their land as the Spanish maimed and colonized their way through Guatemala in search of gold and silver, bringing God, war, and sickness. The land grabs ramped up again amid the Western imperialism and eugenics movements in the late nineteenth and early twentieth centuries when the Guatemalan state, under military dictatorship, aided the spread of American and European coffee plantations.

The land. The land. The land. In Mexico, the land grabs happened in a country where the majority of the population was mestizo. In Guatemala, the new world order came to a country where most people were Indigenous, meaning land and wealth were concentrated among an even smaller few. Through often nefarious means, scholar Giovanni Batz has uncovered, state officials persuaded the Ixil Maya and other Native groups to sign over their fertile communal lands. When they refused, the state sometimes forged documents or bribed city and other government officials to acquire them. The state then essentially handed over the fertile terrains to military officials, Europeans, and non-Indigenous or mestizo Guatemaltecos, known as Ladinos. Indigenous groups like the Ixil, displaced all across the western highlands, were forced to live on fincas, or small ranches in territories that used to be their own. Many had to migrate every harvest season to other plantations on the coasts, where they worked to be able to afford their rent back home. The farm labor paid so little that families struggled to get by, and it was so arduous that death and illness became commonplace, the ordinary costs of "progress."

Not all the Ixil went quietly, their history of resistance, as chronicled by their elders and descendants, dating as far back as the Spanish conquest. As disaffection with the nation's oligarchy spread across Guatemalan society, many joined the underground networks of Indigenous and Ladino rural workers and labor unions that began to unify the working class—la clase obrera. A significant target of the people's frustration became the United Fruit Company, an American firm that had acquired so much land in the highlands it began allowing huge tracts of it to lie fallow, even as many campesinos believed they could cultivate those territories to improve their livelihoods.

The land. The land. The land. Revolution over the uneven distribution of the land swept through Guatemala in 1944, as it had through Mexico in 1910, as it had through Cuba and Nicaragua and Bolivia and El Salvador in the years in between. As impoverished campesinos began to reclaim their rights, Ixil activists joined the grassroots leftist movements that in March 1951 propelled Jacobo Árbenz Guzmán into the presidency. But, like the wars for independence across Latin America before them, the aims of the revolutions would largely come short of benefiting most Latin Americans other than Spanish-descended elites. Three years after Árbenz was elected, the Central Intelligence Agency helped take him down before he could see his signature promise through: a "New Deal-style economic program," according to historian Aviva Chomsky, to empower workers and campesinos and overhaul the oppressive plantation system.

The United States believed support of authoritarian rule was necessary for the sake of national security. American businesses like the United Fruit Company, Chomsky adds, had long discovered that it was better to support authoritarian regimes because "too much democracy" allowed workers, campesinos, and the government to challenge their dominance. Though Árbenz identified as a reformer and not a communist, the United States used the communist support behind him to make him a target as the Second Red Scare tore through America and President Dwight D. Eisenhower launched the first major Cold War interventions in Latin America. Left-wing guerrilla groups quickly rose up against the propped-up right-wing military leaders, and civil war broke out. Abductions, mutilations, and slayings of dissidents, whether they took up arms or not, became everyday occurrences.

Over thirty-six years, from 1960 to 1996, according to the United Nations truth commission, the death toll rose to more than 200,000 people and the number of disappearances totaled about 45,000. The bloodiest period came under General Efraín Ríos Montt, who assumed control of the nation in May 1982 in another CIA-backed coup, this one authorized by President Ronald Reagan. In a scorched-earth policy to eliminate the armed leftist rebels, General Ríos Montt dispatched death squads into Indigenous communities and dropped bombs from the sky over their lands. The hardest-hit victims were the Ixil Maya of El Quiché, where Kaxh and La's were born thirteen years apart. Between 1981 and 1983, some 70 to 90 percent of Ixil villages were demolished and an estimated 60 percent of Ixil families would be forced to hide out in the mountains.

As the ancestral elders in Nebaj and the surrounding Ixil region tell it, their towns were able to maintain their Indigenous mayoral councils for some time after the fall of Árbenz, but as the U.S.-backed coup gave rise to a string of authoritarian and military rulers in Guatemala, it was usually those same leaders who became the first targets of the random kidnappings and assassinations that army patrols began to carry out, especially in Ixil communities where residents continued to fight finqueros for their lands. Toward the end of the 1970s, the military attacks in the Ixil highlands ramped up even further. The Guerrilla Army of the Poor (Ejército Guerrillero de los Pobres, or EGP) had formed in the Ixcán lowlands of El Quiché in 1972 and moved into the Ixil region to build support. At first, it found little among Ixil communities, who were among the most conservative of contemporary Mayan societies. But more began to change their minds as the disappearances and crimes escalated and military soldiers ambushed villages to forcibly recruit young Ixil men into their armies. At the sight of their uniforms in the distance, young men, not looking to become cannon fodder, also began to flee into the Cuchumatanes to hide out. In time, officers were wiping out entire villages of women and children left behind and accusing Indigenous leaders of colluding with the enemy. Right-wing paramilitary death squads, which worked independently of the Guatemalan government, operated in the nation with impunity. They were funded by wealthy planters and largely comprised military officers, who were directed by military leadership and provided with military intelligence, as historians such as Greg Grandin have documented.

La's must have been four or five when his family began to escape into the sierra. His father, Ma'xh Cha'v, a carpenter and merchant peddling clothes, wares, and building material, was an Ixil leader and activist long involved in the Indigenous movements that had sought to forge community consciousness—la conciencia colectiva—and solidarity with Ladinos and different Indigenous groups. He spoke Ixil, K'iche', and Spanish, allowing him to rely on a web of sources to keep tabs on military forces and warn villagers of incoming attacks. Every time they received word that soldiers were near, they climbed into the Cuchumatanes, taking refuge inside rocky crags or under the shade of soaring fir trees in small shacks that his father learned to build out of pine branches and twine. Sometimes they left with only what they could carry. Other times they were able to pack clothes and a bit of food. When they needed to buy more time in hiding, his father would risk leaving their shelter to sell their old garments on the roadside or in neighboring villages, at times walking three or four hours to the nearest market.

Soldiers stormed in so many times, pillaging their village and hacking away at their milpa harvests with machetes, that residents stopped rebuilding their cabins and settled into small huts with straw roofs. When General Ríos Montt took control of Guatemala, the whispers spread that he was convinced the Ixil had been providing aid to the rebels and believed the people of all three Ixil Mayan towns—Nebaj, Cotzal, and Chajul—should be exterminated. La's's father received information that the soldiers would be landing in their region by helicopter. He had no idea from which direction they would be coming in or which direction his family should head to best avoid them. All they could do was pick a path and rush into the sierra. La's and his sister, To', scrambled ahead of their parents, La's holding a plump chicken under his arm. He was six, his little sister three. As they waded farther into the forest, their parents scooped each of them up and ran faster and faster. They missed the military by moments. The soldiers raped women and children. They bludgeoned and beat and hung many of their friends and neighbors.

La's and his family wandered within the confines of the Cuchumatanes for six months, the longest and hardest stretch in the wilderness they had ever endured. They foraged for food and walked for days. At times they came across the charred remains of towns and sick and elderly people beaten and injured. From mountain crevices, they watched as homes were engulfed in flames with whole families inside. The soldiers slaughtered thousands, dumping their bodies in unmarked graves.

And yet, when they were safe in the sierra, far away from the brutality and chaos, La's, who was still only a child, found levity in playing with his sister. Toward their final weeks in hiding, he recalls, they came across a soaring resplendent quetzal—a bird with iridescent green feathers, a red underbelly, and a long tail—which is emblazoned on Guatemala's flag and coat of arms and is said to have served as the spirit guide to a Mayan prince who battled Spanish conquistadors. Another time they crossed paths with a troop of monkeys. He and To' ran around that day, imitating their sounds and climbing trees.

After the massacres under General Ríos Montt, the government turned over most of the Ixil territories to coffee growers and private landowners. La's's grandfather and father lost their plots and, after years of life on the run, his family was captured. Soldiers executed his father and tore La's and To' away from their mother. The two were taken to the grounds of a Catholic church in Chajul that the Guatemalan army had converted into a military installation. They joined more than one hundred orphaned and displaced children kept in the crowded facilities. When a group of Catholic nuns and priests in Nebaj learned of the abuses at the base, they petitioned the military to let them take charge of the boys and girls in their custody. They eventually managed to move the children to an orphanage that they set up at their parish in Nebaj. It was there that La's and his sister were reunited with their mother, Kat Matóm, though it was not a joyful occasion. La's and To' did not recognize her and they did not want to leave their new home. La's especially had become certain that both of his parents were dead. For a year, Matóm visited her children at the Catholic parish, where they went to school and received counseling from nuns, teachers, and psychologists until they finally agreed to return home with her.

Foreign activists, international human rights organizations, and leftist priests began to arrive in the Ixil region, bolstering the efforts by Indigenous communities to push the government to investigate the war crimes. They wanted the remains of their loved ones exhumed and properly buried. They wanted the 1982 Ixil genocide recognized in their nation's history. Every step was a challenge. Forensic teams needed permission to excavate the land in search of bodies. They needed to find ways to identify the dead. They needed to collect records to account for the victims and amass evidence of the massacres.

La's was seventeen or eighteen when he and his friends founded a group to support children and teens who had become orphans in the armed conflict. As campaigns for human rights gained momentum in Guatemala, they came to consolidate their group with those of other war survivors, widows, and parents who had lost children. Across Latin America, and in Argentina, Chile, and Guatemala in particular, a much larger movement was building to acknowledge and remember the crimes and human rights violations that right-wing regimes, often with American funding, training, and support, had committed. Memoria histórica—historical memory—was needed, its proponents believed, to ensure such periods of dictatorship, war, and political repression would never be repeated and that the victims would not be forgotten.

In Guatemala, the quest for memoria histórica took shape alongside efforts to strengthen the rule of law, weed out government corruption, and end violence against Indigenous communities. Ixil leaders and young activists like La's rejoiced when, in December 1996, la Unidad Revolucionaria Nacional Guatemalteca and the Álvaro Arzú administration officially ended the conflict with the signing of a series of peace accords. The leaders who signed them envisioned a pluralistic, democratic society where the army no longer acted without repercussions and infractions against human rights were prosecuted and punished. But the presidencies that followed made little effort to carry out those social contracts, and as the United States retreated from the region, the ground was set for unscrupulous politicians and narco-traffickers to exploit the growing poverty and instability.

There would be no enforcement of laws against the persecutions of activists. Schools would not teach the history of the war—not its origins, not its impact, not the lessons that Ixil leaders had hoped would prevent such massacres from ever happening again. New justice and reconciliation and truth and democracy commissions and institutions established to memorialize the lost, dead, and taken would go underfunded and struggle to survive. What the peace accords did accomplish, almost immediately, journalist Paolina Albani notes, was the ushering in of a new era: extractive capitalism. Electricity was privatized. Huge multinational corporations and hydroelectric firms stepped into Ixil territories to ramp up mining, water, and oil projects, promising economic development, and Indigenous communities were once again forced to defend their lands.

As the social justice and climate movements intensified, so did the authoritarian backlash. A crop of right-wing leaders now denied the 1982 genocide had ever happened. Ladino leaders labeled Ixil leaders and activists who opposed the intrusions on their lands dangerous guerrilleros and criminals. They called them Indios. The movements to recognize and memorialize the massacres perpetrated against Ixil communities were further complicated by the fact that many Ixil officers had been complicit in the horrors—they were former members of las Patrullas de Autodefensa Civil, civilian police forces who patrolled their communities for the military, either because they were coerced or because they wanted to protect their families. It also did not help that an international media firestorm and debate was sparked after David Stoll, an anthropologist, claimed that Rigoberta Mençhú, a prominent K'iche' activist from El Quiché and Nobel Peace Prize laureate, had provided testimony from the war inconsistent with the testimonies of her relatives and neighbors and accused some anthropologists and historians of ignoring the distortions to fit their own political and ideological narratives. (She defended the veracity of her central claim: Her people were dead.)

Nevertheless, in 2001, a group of activists filed a lawsuit against General Ríos Montt, seeking to bring a head of state to trial for genocide for the first time. After overseeing the deadliest period of the war, the military leader had been elected to Guatemala's congress multiple times and had even served as its president. Constitutional appeals were filed on his behalf, seeking his immunity as a member of Congress, and the case was still stalled in the courts when the American Dream arrived in Guatemala in the 2000s. Men fed up with the rise of drug traffickers and gangs and lack of upward mobility had begun tracing the paths of Mexicanos north, to the United States, passing through cities like Brownsville and McAllen, like El Paso. With the earnings they made in construction and in fields, nurseries, restaurants, and factories across the United States, they built tall, cavernous homes for their families out of wood, cinder block, and colorful ceramic tile. Entire villages seemed to grow out of the side of the sierra, along the roads and down gorges.

As the years passed, more and more children began leaving alone. Soon, more mothers and children followed.

ONE YEAR BEFORE President Biden made his way to Guatemala to address the "root causes" of migration, General Ríos Montt went to trial on charges of genocide and crimes against humanity for the 1982 series of massacres he had enabled against the Ixil communities, particularly those in El Quiché. Hundreds of Ixil Maya leaders, activists, and genocide survivors packed into an auditorium in Guatemala for the proceedings. La's traveled down to the capital from Nebaj on a bus with other survivors. Every morning over the next nine days, he and other survivors and Mayan spiritual guides rose before dawn to take in the energy of the sun's first rays and make a special offering for their ancestors killed in war. They burned lime, herbs, and incense. His mother, Kat Matóm, had died years earlier, and this would be his first major human rights battle waged without her. But the ceremonies made him feel that he was accompanied by his family, by the many.

On the day it was finally La's's turn to testify, a guide prepared a special tea for him. He lingered awhile longer by the altar, inhaling the sweet fumes of their offerings, imagining a day with his father. He had never been one of those activists who could articulate his pain well or hold forth on the microphone, delivering fiery remarks. He often lost his train of thought. Others in the movement had criticized him for coming off too strong or not strong enough. But when the time came, he looked up at the room filled with Ixil activists and townspeople in the stands. His voice broke as he recalled the painful reunion with his mother years after military forces had pillaged his village.

"My sister and I, we didn't think we even had a living mother," he said, pausing to compose himself as Ixil women in the audience wiped tears from their eyes.

In the stands sat a younger generation of Ixil Mayans, including Kaxh, whom Indigenous authorities had invited so that they, too, could witness history and carry on their fight for justice. Kaxh, a short, skinny kid in his mid-twenties, had been helping to escort La's and the other witnesses to and from the courtroom as right-wing agitators like the man who would later confront him screamed into microphones outside. He had been raised in Salquil Grande, a tiny community northwest of Nebaj, which had been constructed as a military "model village," or development project (most of them never saw true development), and where the Guatemalan government had forced Ixil citizens to live after the civil war. Kaxh's entire family was marked by the conflict, as were the families of most of his classmates. His mother had lost a son only to find out many years later that he had survived.

In the Ixil region, the government, in a vestige of the era of colonial conquest, imposes Spanish names on people. (Kaxh is registered as Gaspar Cobo Corio, and La's as Francisco Chávez Raymundo.) In school, children like Kaxh had been versed in Spanish history but not their own ancient story in this land—"the names of kings and queens but not the rivers running through Ixil land that serve as our water supply," as he would later explain it to me. But Kaxh had been among the first graduating class of the Ixil University, which was founded by a nongovernmental organization and activists to teach Ixil culture, history, and farming. One of his tutors remembers that Kaxh stood out even then for his outspokenness.

Kaxh went on to become a subsistence farmer and an activist. He would spread the word about the ecological crisis brewing as multinational companies encroached on their region, traveling the winding roads of the Cuchumatanes by motorcycle, passing forests and ferreterias (hardware stores) and construction businesses; piles of concrete blocks and plastic drums; mining projects tearing into the sierra; tienditas selling rows and rows of snacks and wooden stands with palm leaf straw hats, woven baskets, giant bowls of fruits and vegetables, and pink, blue, and yellow candy balls of maize. Salquil Grande was successful in pushing back against a major hydroelectric project through demonstrations. But by the spring of 2019, only five months before Kaxh and La's would decide to flee, thousands of activists blocked major roads to demand justice for Indigenous communities as the nation sat on the verge of a constitutional crisis.

The two had no big illusions about el Norte. Kaxh had watched many of his friends leave but had not felt the pull himself, believing the true fight was at home. La's especially knew the American Dream was not all it seemed.

When he had been a younger man, as the genocide case dragged on and his family fell into poverty, he had tried his hand at working in the mango fields in Florida. He had spent almost two years in a cramped apartment looking for work in a time of bad harvests and had come back with little to show for it.

But La's had been through a turbulent few years after the trial. He had been arrested twice in 2014 for violence against his spouse and accused of stiffing donors, all allegations he denied. He was also the target of mounting violence. Men had held a gun to his head three times, once or twice running off with records from his activist organization. Unlike Kaxh, he had tried to trust the new processes to protect human rights defenders, filing complaints with the police and the public ministry. When he had to hire security guards to follow him around, he decided he had had enough.

The night before his departure, Kaxh tucked in his three children, Xhep Sin, Xhun Xhu'l, and Ma'l, for the last time. The next morning, he bid his wife, El, goodbye, and met La's at the central bus station in Nebaj in the amber light. They were prepared to trace a well-worn path to the Mexican border town of Tapachula, up through Oaxaca, Puebla, and Mexico City, up through roads where transnational currents of migration had flowed since Chinese and Mexican traqueros had helped build the earliest railroads, until finally, if fate and fortune favored them, reaching the United States.

19

El Paso, U.S.A.

EL PASO, TEXAS
2019

THE SUN WAS setting in El Paso on a cold, windy day in February, when Beto O'Rourke, a native son and former U.S. congressman, led thousands of protesters bundled in jackets and coats on a march along the U.S.-Mexico border. More than a dozen people clutched two massive white banners that dragged at their feet and read NO MORE LIES and NO BORDER WALL. Other demonstrators carried American flags and held signs declaring THE BORDER MAKES AMERICA GREAT. The people chanted, "El Paso united will never be divided."

O'Rourke, a Democrat, had rocketed to political stardom when he challenged Senator Ted Cruz, a Republican, for his seat. He ultimately lost the race but came so unexpectedly close that he helped bring a windfall of momentum to his party's candidates down the ballot in the Republican-controlled state. Now he was weighing a presidential bid, and he was one of the few Democrats going head-to-head with President Donald J. Trump.

The protesters made their way past the metal slabs of the border fence, silhouetted against mountains crossed by Mexicanos and Americanos for generations, to a park about a mile away, near the El Paso County Coliseum, where Trump was set to arrive for his first major reelection campaign rally of the year. A crowd of Trump supporters waited outside. Some wore fire-engine red "Make America Great Again" hats and waved American and Trump flags. A few hurled insults. Two multitudes with two competing visions of the borderland many called home.

The coliseum, a large, redbrick concert venue with a sloping roof and framed posters of upcoming concerts and performance acts, was situated a few miles east from el Segundo Barrio, where Mexicano journalists had once churned out broadsides in the name of democracy, and less than a mile from el Chamizal, the tract of land more than two-thirds the size of Central Park in New York City where the United States and Mexico had disputed their international boundary for more than one hundred years. As night fell, inside the building, a theatrical male voice flooded the speakers: "Please welcome, the president of the United States, Donald J. Trump."

Thousands of arms went up, hands clutching cell phones, as if prepared to catch the tantalizing first glimpses of one of the many Latino pop stars who had trod this stage. Long, bright red banners dangled from the ceiling and clung against black drapes, declaring FINISH THE WALL in white letters. Within moments, Trump emerged from behind the curtain, clapping to cheers and screams and his signature walkout song, "God Bless the U.S.A."

After the avalanche of criticism over the separation of migrant families in El Paso and along the border, the Trump administration did not stop approaching the issue of immigration as spectacle, or the use of the U.S.-Mexico border as the backdrop. It doubled down. Days after ending the "zero tolerance" policy, Trump hosted an event with a group he called "Angel Families," people who had lost loved ones in homicides and drunk-driving crashes that reportedly involved undocumented immigrants. That August, as his administration placed higher burdens on people applying for visas and called for the termination of what hardliners termed "chain migration," or immigration preferences for family members of legal residents, Trump's wife, First Lady Melania Trump, sponsored the citizenship of her Slovenian-born parents in a private though well-covered ceremony in Manhattan. By the fall, as the number of migrants reaching the southern border had not stopped but climbed, Trump fired up his base at campaign rallies, warning that the United States was under attack by caravans of immigrants heading north. "You look at what is marching up, that is an invasion!" he cried at one event. "That is an invasion!"

Many of the questions Trump was tackling over American citizenship and identity—over who should and should not be allowed into the nation—were rooted in real, complex, and long-standing challenges. Plenty of Democrats and Republicans had come to agree that the nation's asylum and immigration laws were not designed to address what had become harder-to-solve problems, including drug wars and poverty, the expansion of smuggling networks, and climate changes that were causing more severe weather calamities and the displacement of entire communities. Many Americans had long believed that any crime committed by a person not lawfully in the country was one too many, and in surveys by the Pew Research Center from 2010 to 2018, a plurality of American voters had reported that they wanted compromise from lawmakers: equal priority given to forging legal pathways to citizenship for undocumented immigrants in the country, as well as border security and stronger law enforcement measures.

But Trump and his allies often stoked racism and xenophobia, pitting immigrants against native-born Americans and documented immigrants against the undocumented as they sought to sort people into the good and the bad—the wanted and unwanted, the desirable and undesirable—as white nativists had since the nation first forged its borders. They also often ignored the facts. Though there is little comprehensive data on the crimes committed by undocumented immigrants, multiple studies have concluded through the years that, overall, immigrants have not committed crimes disproportionate to their population numbers and have almost always been arrested at lower rates than natives. More recent statistics have shown that crime in the United States has dropped while illegal immigration has increased.

Likewise, most caravans of people making their way north from Central America or farther south—usually a few thousand immigrants trekking on foot—disband before heading too far. And even as the foreign-born population of the United States has at times reached record heights in recent years, the immigrant share of the population has remained below the record 14.8 percent in 1890, according to Pew. In other words, the numbers have not reached the levels of an "invasion," nor have illegal migration and smuggling ever qualified as such under international law, as legal scholar Ilya Somin has written, "either today or at the time of the founding of the United States."

Nonetheless, Trump political appointees pursued policies that democracy experts and voting rights activists warned would make immigrants less likely to respond to the 2020 census, leading to an undercount of Black and Latino voters and thus a diminishing of their political power. Trump blasted migration from El Salvador, Haiti, and African nations, referring to them as "shithole countries," and later proposed ending birthright citizenship in a stunning contradiction of the way the Fourteenth Amendment to the U.S. Constitution has long been interpreted. In a theatrical show of force, he deployed nearly 6,000 active-duty troops to the U.S.-Mexico border. Their most visible accomplishment: stringing concertina wire in cities like El Paso. A few months later, in January 2019, his administration implemented its "Remain in Mexico" program, forcing migrants and refugees to wait across the border while their asylum cases went through U.S. courts.

Then, of course, there was the wall. To many residents on both sides of the U.S.-Mexico border, Trump's wall was a symbol of his racism and fear of "the other." It was often referenced as a joke, a laughing matter: Pues que no sabe el Trumpetas que ya hay una ahí? Does he not know we already have a wall? A tall one built under the Obama administration that stretches so deeply into American territory that in some areas it cuts into people's backyards, forcing them to use metal gates to cross it on their own property? Y que gasto de dinero. And what a waste of money: Aquí en la frontera, it was well-known that illicit drugs and guns were more likely to be smuggled right through ports of entry by citizens of the United States. Immigrants without legal U.S. status were just as likely to fly in and overstay their visas as they were to ford the river.

But to Trump, journalists Julie Hirschfeld Davis and Michael D. Shear observe, the wall was an obsession, a potent symbol of his political brand. He wanted it "flat, black, and beautiful." He wanted it electrified, with steel bollards and spiky tips. He wanted it hot and sharp to pierce the flesh and keep it free of bird droppings. Privately, as the journalists reported, he had even talked about digging a trench alongside it, and filling it with snakes or alligators. The wall would spark lots of tweets, ongoing tensions with Mexico, and an emergency government shutdown that would deprive 800,000 federal workers of their wages.

Onstage in El Paso, Trump hyped up the crowd, proclaiming that "walls work" and "save tremendous numbers of lives." He denounced illegal immigration, "far-left radicals," and Democrats, whom he claimed wanted to "pave the way for socialism" and release "criminal illegal aliens" into the country.

"You heard, right? Today we started a big, beautiful wall right on the Rio Grande," he said, bobbing his head, crowned with a wispy, dark-blond helmet, and wearing his typical blue suit and red tie, a tiny American flag pin clipped to his lapel. "We need the wall, and it has to be built, and we want to build it fast," he said. "We're doing whatever we have to do. The wall is being built. It'll continue." In fact, the building projects underway in the border region merely sought to upgrade or replace small portions of old fencing that had long stood in place.

The boom of the president's rally carried into the night, over to the sporting center at the park, where O'Rourke was making the counterargument that every major border city—from El Paso to San Diego—had been deemed safer than major American cities deep in the heart of the nation.

"We are not safe because of walls but in spite of walls!" O'Rourke shouted, his sleeves rolled up and a microphone in hand as his slim frame bounced about a makeshift platform set up against the batting cages of a baseball field. A fourth-generation Irish American born Robert Francis O'Rourke, he wove fluent Spanish into his remarks and was backed by a mariachi band, his voice rising and falling and cracking at times as the audience chanted, "Beto! Beto! Beto!"

As his fame would continue to grow that year, political reporters in Washington would snicker at the thought of Robert becoming Beto. But in El Paso, where lines and categories and borders—physical and cultural and racial and ethnic—have long been crossed and defied, mixed, blurred, and blended, O'Rourke supporters told me often he was beloved because there was no question he was of and for la frontera.

"Here, in the largest binational community in the Western Hemisphere," he said that night, "two and a half million people, two countries speaking two languages with two cultures and two histories, who come together, are joined—not separated—by the Rio Grande river, forming something far greater and more powerful than the sum of people or the sum of our parts."

Our city had been here before and would be here again, the so-called Ellis Island of the Southwest, our national symbol of all we fear and all we could be. This time, in this chapter of history, the stage was set. The crew: thousands of troops deployed to the dividing line between Mexico and the United States. The melody: the pouring of cement; the jackhammering of metal; the uncoiling and stringing of sharp razor wire—the sort used in prison camps and on battlefields, the kind named after an instrument, the concertina, a free-reed musical contraption that bends and bellows like an accordion—chiming all along the border fence, at ports of entry, and on the banks of the Rio Grande in Texas. The cast: migrants and agents locked in a cruel and desperate game of cat and mouse. The audience: you and me and the nation.

SINCE THE EARLIEST days of the Trump presidency, immigration lawyers, immigrant rights leaders, and church groups in El Paso had been rushing to respond to the crush of people arriving at its doors. When they learned border officials were leaving hundreds of people stranded downtown after processing them at international checkpoints, volunteers organized to bring them food, water, and clothes and set up a system to help immigrants buy bus tickets to reunite with their families in Texas and across the country. Local nonprofits at times even helped by chartering buses to Dallas, Denver, and Albuquerque.

As the Remain in Mexico program went into full swing, immigrant help groups redoubled their efforts to support people in overcrowded shelters and tent cities springing up across Ciudad Juárez as thwarted asylum seekers and migrants awaited responses to their applications. On the other side of the border, Mexico, like the United States, had been departing from some of its long-standing traditions on asylum. Mexican president Andrés Manuel López Obrador, caving to some of Trump's demands, had stepped up measures to prevent migrants from entering some border towns and to stop young migrants traveling alone from reaching the United States at all.

Parents and children continued to arrive in El Paso from Guatemala, El Salvador, and Honduras in large numbers as O'Rourke prepared to launch his presidential bid from his hometown. Border agents estimated they were apprehending as many as 570 migrants a day in the city's metro area and, citing a lack of space at processing facilities, set up a large white military tent under the gray beams of the bridge that many fronterizos still knew as the Santa Fe. People were granted access to portable toilets, water, and food. But hundreds of people were forced to wait outside behind chain-link fences—sometimes for hours, even days—spurring some local priests and activists to disparage the camp as a stunt to derail O'Rourke's political prospects. By the time the former congressman held his first campaign rally that March, crowds of migrants remained corralled in the pens, sleeping on the desert ground, with only tinfoil blankets for cover.

More than 6,000 people gathered to wait for O'Rourke on the same downtown street where la Santa had once lived, where Sacred Heart Church had become a shelter for migrant families at the center of the humanitarian crisis. Congresswoman Veronica Escobar warmed up the audience, calling El Paso the "capital of the border" and the "new Ellis Island." Once onstage, O'Rourke promised to focus on security without fear, and as the *El Paso Times* described it, bring "his vision for bridging divides." He acknowledged the city's legacy of struggles for civil rights and workers' rights, led by Mexicanos, México Americanos, Chicanos, and Black leaders like Dr. Lawrence Nixon and Thelma White, who he said had not only secured voting rights in Texas but had "ensured that El Paso would be among the first cities of the former Confederacy to desegregate our public places and integrate our education."

Federal agencies cleared out the "holding pen" under the Santa Fe soon after. But all through the following months, the tensions at the border continued to escalate as migrants continued to come.

Through the ongoing political saga, Kaxh and La's trekked up, relying on the network of human rights activists and journalists they had known back home for support. In Guatemala, they took ruteras like the ones the Holguins used to run through the streets of Ciudad Juárez, but these old buses—some bought at a bargain in Mexico and driven down—were souped-up and repainted white with stripes of green or blue or red and adorned with bright, flashing lights, their names scrawled in bold, cursive letters on their backs. The vehicles blew off huge plumes of black smoke as they passed through the mining and exploitation sites that cracked and ate the earth. In Tapachula, Mexico, just north of the Guatemalan border, they stalled out for a few days just when Mexican authorities began ramping up their efforts to apprehend the hundreds of migrants arriving from all over the world. Finally, somewhere in central Mexico—likely in the state of Querétaro, outside of Mexico City—they purchased tickets to Ciudad Juárez solely by chance: It was the cheapest in comparison to all the other Mexican border town destinations.

When they arrived in the borderlands, they were crouching in the back seat of a car and had no view of El Paso. They knew neither its name nor its history—only that they hoped to cross into the city with the help of coyotes, or smugglers, to plead asylum once on the other side. But their handlers held them in a Juárez warehouse with an open roof and little food for days. When it became clear that no one was coming to retrieve them, they slipped out unnoticed by the sole guard keeping watch on a hot day in July. Kaxh reached out to an American filmmaker he had met in Guatemala for help, and she worked with a veteran border journalist to find them shelter and connect them with the circle of volunteers and activists long active in El Paso, including Carlos Spector, the Holguins' human rights lawyer and cofounder of Mexicanos en Exilio. Spector moved quickly to get them into the Remain in Mexico program and, in time, helped them find a place to stay with a friend in Juárez.

As they waited in limbo, they became two of more than 25,000 migrants stranded at the border. Taxicabs at the foot of the Sante Fe continued to shuttle those marooned to shelters in colonias tucked into the Sierra de Juárez mountains, where the fliers of missing girls and women were still adhered to lampposts. Immigration lawyers and volunteers kept coming to provide aid as the crisis showed few signs of abating. National and international journalists swept in to capture the crush of misery only to move on to the next story. Mark Lambie, a photographer for the *El Paso Times* and one of the many local reporters frustrated by the portrayals of his home as a war zone and the one-dimensional coverage of migrants merely as victims, not people, started documenting immigrant families in shelters and makeshift camps, attempting to capture their children's joy amid the trauma. Only a couple of months after wrapping up the yearlong project that spring, he was called to an assignment he would never forget. There had been a shooting at the Walmart.

THAT DAY, THE life drained from the arteries that connected El Paso and Ciudad Juárez. Streets emptied. Shops, restaurants, and pharmacies shut down. News of the massacre reverberated across the two cities at the heart of two clashing visions of the United States and among expat and Latino communities far beyond them. Kaxh was shaken by the realization that the United States was not as free or secure as he had always imagined—that, as in Guatemala, people could persecute and kill others solely on the base of their race or identity.

The Holguin brothers watched the scenes unfolding on their television screens with horror and sadness. The Martinezes' grandson Raúl Reyes and his wife, Margarita, felt the energy shift as they drove in from Houston for a visit. In Los Angeles, the Rubio sisters' text groups with El Paso friends and relatives in California and Texas lit up with grief and love. And on the bench in a downtown El Paso courtroom, Judge Linda Chew, Herlinda and Antonio Chew's granddaughter, arraigned the killer. Before she had become a judge, she had been inspired by Herlinda to become an immigration lawyer. She had risen in prominence during the national border battles of the past that decades later remained a part of the present.

20

Oasis in the Desert

WASHINGTON, D.C.
2023

"I WAS POOR," MY father, Mauricio, a scientist, begins his telling as he swirls a glass of red wine at the kitchen table in my home in Washington. I roll my eyes. He is not taking this seriously.

"¡Ay, por Dios! No eras pobre" ("Oh, for God's sake! You were not poor"), I exclaim.

"I was poor," he insists again, in English this time, waving away my rebuke, lost in thought.

I may not know much about our past, but if there is anything I do know, it is that he was not poor. As evidence, take this as the rough sketch that up until this moment I have heard about my father—some from him, some from others.

My father grew up in one of the wealthiest families in Puerto Vallarta, Jalisco, back when it was just a small, secluded beach town off the Pacific Coast, without thundering nightclubs or multimillion-dollar resorts. His father, Don Pepe, came from a long line of artisans and clockmakers. He owned a chain of jewelry stores, including one he had opened in a busy downtown square about the time that Richard Burton and Ava Gardner arrived to film *The Night of the Iguana*. The timing was impeccable. It placed him at ground level for Vallarta's boom as tourists flocked in to its pristine beaches and lush jungles. My father's mother, Victoria, the vivacious matriarch of the family, ran their administrative tasks and their large adobe-and-brick home wedged in a mixed-use building in what was then the heart of Vallarta. It had an open-air, hacienda-style courtyard with a towering palm tree in the middle, and it sat across the mile-long esplanade named el Malecón. Day and night, visitors and locals walked its length beside the ocean. It led to Playa de los Muertos. The Beach of the Dead.

When my father was fifteen, he traded his tropical paradise for the mountain pass that had once been known as an oasis in the desert. He joined his older brother, my uncle Beto, in Ciudad Juárez, where he enrolled in the Escuela Superior de Agricultura Hermanos Escobar (the Escobar Brothers Agricultural College), then the second-oldest and most expensive high school and university system in Mexico. My father rolled around in a sleek yellow car. He wore crisp button-ups, aviator sunglasses, and flashy silver watches and chains. When he permed his wavy black hair, some said he looked like a young and handsome Michael Jackson. He was a fresa before we called them fresas. A rich boy. Un junior. El consentido: the spoiled one. The youngest boy out of six children, and so his mother's favorite—he swears it.

They called him la Liga. The Rubber Band. Because he was long, brown, and lanky.

"I am telling you I was poor because everyone thought I was poor. All my friends, all my coworkers here in the United States," he says with a hint of frustration. He is taking this seriously. I am not listening.

In his half-musing, half-jesting way, as many Mexicanos do—even or especially when recollecting the most tragic of events or saddest of memories—he was trying to tell me something serious about the pass through the Pass, about an experience he had struggled to understand and had often buried: that when he crossed that line between Mexico and the United States, he became a Brown man in America, a worker without a face or a history, expected to be here for a little while and then gone.

In the immediate aftershocks of the shooting, as the pain continued to ripple through El Paso and Ciudad Juárez, fronterizos experienced an outpouring of community support and solidarity. Our pride in who we were and the place where we were from swelled. Hundreds of people on both sides of a borderland where bridges run like veins rushed to donate blood. The El Paso police station was flooded with food and water contributions for officers and first responders. Mexican and American charities and funeral homes covered the costs of burials. For weeks and months, people continued to gather at various memorials to light candles, leave flowers, and whisper prayers.

El Paso was so close-knit that I had lived in other places for years and still considered it home. It was that connectedness that, whenever I came back, made me feel as though I had never been gone. But the truth was that as I went in search of the Chews and the Martinezes, the Holguins, the Rubios, and the Mura'ls, their stories the very pieces that made El Paso what it was, I kept coming face-to-face with how little I knew about my family and their journey. Peering into our city's past, its ghosts and its silences, the time had come to finally look into my own.

So, now that I am listening, my father and I, we return to the origins. I want to know about his crossing, to know our story to better know El Paso. For a time—after my parents' divorce, through my early angsty teenage years—we had seen each other less. I had mostly heard his story in bits and pieces. I ask to hear it again, from the beginning and in full, and here is what I learn.

Mauricio, like Kaxh and Alfredo—maybe even like Ylario—did not intend to follow the routes of other Latinos into El Paso and beyond. The plan after finishing up his studies in Juárez had been for him to return. His father, Don Pepe, a conservative turned liberal, had always been civic-minded. He had helped found the first chamber of commerce in Vallarta and had been among the local leaders promoting its economic growth and stability. He had instilled in his children the desire to do the same—to work toward a greater good. To that end, my father had grand ambitions of moving out to the fertile lands his family owned in the rural outskirts of the city. He wanted to bring the future of agriculture home.

Those lands had been in his family's hands for generations. His maternal grandfather, Adolfo, had worked as a foreman for a Spanish hacendado, who owned ranches and farms from the Pacific Ocean all the way to the Gulf of Mexico. Adolfo was a short man with dark brown skin, which could have relegated him to the bottom rungs of the unspoken caste system that had persisted in his country despite the aims of two wars. But he had prominent Spanish ancestry and a big personality, and he could read and write. He came to buy some of his patrón's territories to become a patrón himself. Adolfo protected his ownership of the lands through the revolution by funneling support to whatever group of federales or leftist rebel faction controlled the area at any given time; and through the Cristero War by backing the staunch conservative Catholics who fought the redistribution of private property; and through the Mexican government's creation of communal ejidos by consigning them down to his children, though he ended up having to forfeit much of them then.

My father's prospects for cultivating the land appeared bright. Ever since the revolution—Emiliano Zapata's rallying cry, "La tierra es de quien la trabaja," etched in the national consciousness—farmers and campesinos had been seen as vital to Mexico and its prosperity. Several Mexican presidents had even been agricultural engineers. In my father's youth, jobs in farming and agronomy became even more valued as the Bracero Program had ended and the tens of thousands of Mexicano workers left without jobs and land helped usher in support for the green revolution. The latest period of fierce technological change since the last, it aimed to increase the types and quantities of crops in Mexican fields to alleviate rising hunger. In short, it promised opportunity, land, labor, and of course, progress. As my father left Vallarta, many Mexican farmers were experimenting with new varieties of beans and corn and with the development of chemical fertilizers and pesticides. Their strides were looking to be replicated in other parts of Latin America and around the world. My father's strengths lay in biology, math, and chemistry, and the green revolution offered exciting prospects in all.

But in la frontera, as in Mexico and much of Latin America, social unrest and economic pressures had been mounting. The authoritarian regimes that had clinched power in the wake of U.S.-backed Cold War interventions had already begun deploying the repressive powers of their states against their citizens. As civil wars enveloped Guatemala and El Salvador, revolution erupted in Nicaragua, and Chile and Argentina were fighting dirty wars. In these shady armed conflicts, national militaries amplified the public perception of the threat of violence to justify their use of even greater violence.

The onslaught of state force had allowed right-wing leaders to subdue their people, dismantle political, social, and land reforms, and privatize their country's resources and industries. It also thrust many nations into debt. As they grappled with restoring political stability, many sought loans from foreign banks and governments to spur economic development. The deals tended to come with strings attached: unfavorable trade policies and budget-tightening measures that led to severe cuts to education and social services. The austerity in turn increased poverty.

As inflation and unemployment rose across Latin America, so did disappearances, torture, and executions. Death squads roamed. In Chile, General Augusto Pinochet drew international notoriety as his administration censored newspapers and magazines, outlawed political parties, and subjected labor unions to staunch regulations. In Argentina, Jorge Rafael Videla, who established his country's ruling military junta, cast a dragnet to suppress leftist guerrillas that widened to ensnare lawyers, students, journalists, and union leaders accused of holding ties to radical organizations. Congress was suspended, strikes criminalized, and political parties also abolished.

The Dirty War in Mexico had received far less attention. Domestic anticommunist sentiments had helped suppress leftist activity, and because the Institutional Revolutionary Party (Partido Revolucionario Institucional, or PRI) had controlled Mexican politics for decades, the government could go further to cover up human rights violations against students, campesinos, and Indigenous groups. But, as an independent commission would find years later, at least 1,000 people would disappear between 1965 and 1990. Hundreds would be extrajudicially executed and discarded in "death flights," their bodies tossed into the Pacific Ocean from planes. Much of the state-led violence had been concentrated in Guerrero, the Pacific Coast state below my father's native Jalisco, where the repression would become so entrenched that during the drug war in 2014, forty-three students from Ayotzinapa were abducted in a case implicating organized crime and government authorities; and in Mexico City, where dissidents from Guatemala, Chile, and other countries in Latin America had been arriving in search of refuge. The most infamous of the attacks, the Tlatelolco massacre, had occurred there ten years before my father headed to Ciudad Juárez: Only two weeks before the 1968 Olympics, Mexican police unleashed rounds of fire into la Plaza de las Tres Culturas, killing hundreds of leftist students who had gathered in peaceful protest to demand greater democracy.

Less known is that Juárez itself, where the embers of rebellion had burned since los magonistas whispered in the alleys of the borderland, had also become a hot spot of both guerrilla activity and civil protest. In flashes of déjà vu, all through the 1960s and 1970s, a wide breadth of revolutionary and leftist groups—and counter groups—met throughout the city to debate the government's human rights abuses and the democratization of education. Neo-Zapatistas. Castro-Guevaristas. Maoístas. Marxistas. Some pushed for nonviolent forms of dissent. Others for armed resistance. And the intellectual project of Western democracy continued.

Since his high school days at Hermanos Escobar, my father had participated in some of the student marches in favor of opening up their campus to more students from rural and impoverished areas. As President Ronald Reagan took office and escalated the war on drugs and the Cold War interventions his freshman year, the student movements picked up even greater steam. Mexico had been among Latin American nations borrowing heavily from the World Bank and the International Monetary Fund, which hit the country hard when the global economy entered into a recession. In February 1982, the peso plummeted by 30 percent. The nation defaulted on its debt about six months later—a total of some $80 billion. Other countries would follow. Sixteen, including Mexico, were from Latin America. They would hurl the region deeper into economic decline and send the next major waves of Mexicano and Latino workers to el Norte. It would become known as la Década Perdida, the Lost Decade.

When my father returned to school from a break that spring of 1982, the movement hit home. He learned that the tuition had doubled without notice. He had acted big to fit in at a place that had launched some of his country's top politicians. But outside of Vallarta, at a school as costly as Hermanos Escobar, in a metropolitan city as large as Juárez, he and Beto were not affluent. They were squarely middle-class, and such a hike was exorbitant.

Mauricio and his friends joined the students organizing against the federal budget cuts that were raising the price tag on their education. They spent afternoons in between classes boteando, or collecting money on city corners and at traffic lights to cover the printing of pamphlets, bulletins, placards, and other expenses for upcoming demonstrations. Their efforts culminated in May 1982 when about 1,500 students walked out of their classes and went on strike for three weeks, setting up blockades on the street named Hermanos Escobar. A group of student leaders briefly held the school's director hostage, occupied buildings on campus, and commandeered twelve buses that they used to take students to Ciudad Chihuahua for a march. Eight hundred federal troops surrounded Hermanos Escobar in response, and the movement expanded to encompass twenty-five other schools.

My father, who preferred the insular worlds of math and science over politics, was not involved in the more aggressive actions. But he and his friends took part in the strike and the peaceful demonstrations over those several weeks, dashing off whenever police arrived to round up and arrest students. He and his friends also drove his car down to Chihuahua for the main demonstration. Out there, he was lying on the ground with his head on his backpack in a plaza filled with students when he heard a couple of his classmates yelling at him to come take a look at a nearby statue.

"Mauricio! Come here!" they called.

"Your relative is out here," one joked.

He walked over and squinted at the plaque. Don Antonio Deza y Ulloa. He had never heard of this man but doubted he was an ancestor. His family came from Jalisco, not Chihuahua.

Years later, he would go digging through our family history and discover that he may be in fact a far, far distant ancestor. At this point in his story my stomach drops—that former town official in Santa Eulalia had been right: Don Antonio Deza y Ulloa and I were related.

The Spaniards ravaged and proselytized for their wealth. Mexicanos buried it in the earth during wars to hide it—my mother's grandfather in the golden hills of Chihuahua from Villistas, my father's grandfather in the lush countryside outside of Vallarta from revolutionary government forces. And in that turbulent spring of 1982, my grandfather, Don Pepe, began to lose it all. The peso drop, coupled with a bad business investment a few months earlier, financially ruined him.

When Mauricio came home from school for the holidays that winter, Don Pepe sat his six children down at the kitchen table and warned them some financial hardships were coming. The family would have to limit their spending. They would have to start closing down stores. They would have to sell much of the land they had owned since before the Cristero War. My father was seventeen and confessed with some shame that in his short and privileged existence his first reaction upon hearing the news was the petty regret that he would not, after all, be getting a new car for his birthday. He would quickly learn this would be the least of his troubles in the free fall.

Ciudad Chihuahua, Chihuahua
2022

For my mother, El Paso had always been exactly as its namesake: a mountain pass. Laura had been born in El Chuco and raised in Juárez, in a borderland where Mexicanos like to say the line dividing Mexico and the United States crossed them, not the other way around. Life tended to ebb and flow between the sister cities with ease, and when the Martinez family finally moved north for good in her late teens, it was in some ways like going from one side of town to the other.

Let me tell you a little bit about my mother. For her sporadic changes of mind and heart and location, Laura has been described, depending on the narrator, as "free" or "wild." A vaga. And maybe she is, a little. She still likes to blast Los Ángeles Azules from car speakers and revels in the open road. The odd jobs she has taken on—artist, fashion designer, teacher's aide, administrative assistant, nursing assistant, prison guard, long-haul truck driver—have been as fickle and short-lived as her hair color, which has gone from brown to black, to red, to pumpkin, to a mesh between dirty and metallic blond, to brown again. As kids, my younger sister, Bianca, and I shifted in and out of El Paso with her, following the trails of nomadic Chihuahuenses and Spanish wanderers and pachucas, of Mexicanas en Exilio. First, it was my father's new job that led us to the onion fields of El Centro in Southern California, and then it was the divorce that returned us to El Paso. My mother's second marriage, to a U.S. Marine, again pulled us to the Golden State, first Camp Pendleton and later Fallbrook. That did not work out either. And so we arrived once more in El Paso, only the three of us. I guess I learned a thing or two about uprooting and upheaval, about passing through the Pass: To keep moving forward, one has to stop looking back.

But in Ciudad Chihuahua, after my futile search for Victoria in Santa Eulalia, we are feeling nostalgic. We wander past the ghosts in the same colonial plaza where I would later learn my father had lain with hundreds of other students in May of 1982. Night is falling, and a large white moon is hanging in the sky. Rarámuri women in flower-patterned dresses and flowing skirts are enjoying pistachio ice cream cones next to small stands selling handwoven dresses, baskets, bracelets, and colorful dolls. Families and children and a few tourists are sitting on the steps of a baroque cathedral and a nearby kiosk in the garden.

We are talking about the legend of el Curro, the Spaniard who appears to the inebriated in Victoria's hometown, of the sacrifices we make for wealth and its tenuousness. My mother had the privilege of being born in El Paso because her mother had been living with an older sister during her pregnancy. But, unlike my father, she *had* grown up poor. Her childhood barrio—el barrio Obrera—had been lined with humble shops, secondhand markets, and brick-and-adobe tenements. Neighbors sold homemade shoes and clothes out of their homes and tacos and enchiladas out of baskets and carts. Ruteras rumbled past, spewing smoke. But she had another form of privilege, too. She had fair skin. Some called her "güera" (blondie).

Her father, Arturo, had been one of the many obreros from which her barrio took its name, a bracero and construction worker in the United States. He was an orphan who made his way up to Juárez from his native state of Puebla as a boy. My mother's mother, Alicia, came from a middle-class family, the descendant of Chihuahuan hacendados who had lost or sold most of their ranches through multiple wars.

My mother met my father at a dance hosted by my father's school the year he arrived in Ciudad Juárez. Like him, she was fifteen. The event was meant for Juárez's high society, a chance for wealthy Mexicanas to find a match among wealthy Mexicanos. My mother happened to get invited because her sister's boyfriend, a radio journalist, had a couple of extra tickets. When my father caught sight of my mother, a curvy güerita with a mess of long, wavy brown hair, he asked her to dance. She turned him down at first, but all the other boys broke into claps and chants of "¡Que bailen, que bailen!" ("Let them dance, let them dance!") until she relented. They ended up dancing all night.

My mother recalls she was embarrassed at first to have my father pick her up in such an impoverished neighborhood as barrio Obrera was in those days. But the two kept on dating even after she and her family moved to El Paso two years later. As my father watched his family's fortunes fall, my mother saw her family's rise in the American economy that immigrant workers had chased for generations, whether through Chuco Town or Ellis Island. Her father had saved enough over his years working in the United States to start an auto parts and mechanic business that he eventually moved to El Paso. He then went on to open up a supermarket, butcher shop, and a gas station in Juárez. Tired of commuting back and forth, he built my grandmother Alicia a large white brick home in the Lower Valley to persuade her to move. By the time they headed over the border, they had established legal residency. Even after she and her family left Juárez, my mother spent most of her days on the southern side of the border, working in a bank, going on dates with my father, and visiting friends.

For my parents, the American Dream and the upward mobility it promised was not something they initially set out to pursue. After the protests at Hermanos Escobar, the students won some important concessions, including a reduction in tuition. My father was able to graduate in 1984. He had not given up on his desire to return home, and he asked my mother to come with him. She enrolled as a student at the University of Texas at El Paso, then had to contend with aspects of the U.S.-Mexico divide she hadn't anticipated: Though she had been a straight A student on one side, often helping my father with his homework, she was having trouble learning English and feeling lost on campus on the other side.

My mother ended up dropping out and marrying my father. The two moved to the last remaining plot of land the Ulloa family had managed to hold on to outside of Vallarta. It was a small ranch, where they planted tobacco, beans, and corn for three years. But by then the energy behind the green revolution had dissipated, and Mexico and nations around the world were dealing with its unintended consequences. Although the movement had increased food production and helped feed quickly growing populations, overuse and mismanagement of fertilizers and pesticides had polluted waters, poisoned workers, and decimated insects and wildlife. It also widened the gap between the rich and the poor in many countries as it was mainly large landowners and commercial farmers who were able to access the irrigation and resources needed to adopt its new technologies.

In Mexico, the situation became even more dire for small farmers working their own private land. As the economy turned, their lines of credit dried up, and unlike campesinos on ejidos, they did not benefit from government subsidies. When my father's tractor broke down, they discovered that the cost of fixing it would have been greater than the profits they had made toiling in the fields since they started. They decided to cut their losses and return to Vallarta. My father went to work in a bank and then got a job with the county helping manage ejidos. My mother painted portraits of Vallarta beaches and landscapes that she sold in a stand on el Malecón. And still my father would not give up on the idea that he could revitalize his family's land. They decided to head north again, to pass through the Pass.

By the time I was born, my parents were living in a small, one-bedroom apartment in El Paso. My mother was back in school, pursuing the career in marketing she had left behind. My father was working as a mechanic for my mother's father. He spent his days fixing cars at the shop and his nights learning English at a community college. Luckily for him, numbers and equations did not need translation.

Over the next several years, my mother came just a few credits shy of obtaining her bachelor's degree, and my father earned his master's degree in horticulture and his doctorate in agronomy at New Mexico State University in Las Cruces, about an hour west of El Paso. Soon after he graduated, we moved to El Centro, where he took on work as an assistant scientist for a seed company. Their plan had continued to be that they would return to Vallarta, that my father would take all of his studies and apply them to the fields in Mexico. But as the years wore on, he began to see the value in American institutions. He came to the conclusion that perhaps the best way he could make a difference for farmers on both sides of the U.S.-Mexico border was through his research. He became an American citizen and fell for the American Dream as James Truslow Adams had defined it when he first popularized the term in 1931: "Not a dream of motor cars and high wages merely, but a dream of social order in which each man and each woman shall be able to attain to the fullest stature of which they are innately capable, and be recognized by others for what they are, regardless of the fortuitous circumstances of birth or position."

After my parents grew apart and went their separate ways, my mother finally did complete a degree in computer and information technology. My father went to work for the U.S. Department of Agriculture. He was a big believer in its large divisions of independent research, which demanded their scientists follow strict ethical rules to prevent politics or corporate influence from interfering with their findings. He preached the importance of speaking English and continued to believe that American racism could be overcome through hard work regardless of his own constant reminders that he was a Brown man in America—experiences he did not like to talk about. My mother, on the other hand, remained committed to a liberal democracy in the spirit of the Juárez that had raised her. She taught us Spanish and Mexican art and history over school breaks. She called my father a secret Republican. He argued that his disillusionment with the politics of the leftist student movements of his youth and his experiences working in both Mexican and American fields had transformed him into more of an independent.

For a long time after their divorce—I was eight at the time—I was angry at them. My mother and I had our fights. Bitter ones. She slammed the door in my face so hard the windowpanes shook. Through my preteens, I reproached her for everything. I wanted clothes and shoes and other things she could not afford. I wanted her to be normal—whatever that was. To give me a curfew. To stop moving us around. It would be years before I realized she had given me more than I could possibly need: her love, her adventurous spirit, and her strength. A deep pride in the borderland where we were from.

El Paso was a refuge. In the rural California of the late 1990s, the fear of the Mexican could bubble up at any time. A teacher once tried to hold my sister back a grade because she spoke Spanish in class. A white girl at my junior high school once uninvited me from her birthday party after her mother found out I was Mexican American. Mexicans, she was informed, were all thieves and criminals. In rural California, the girls tended to be white and wealthy or cool and pretty cholas, with little room for any girl who wasn't those things. In El Paso, there were cholas and cholos and also frontchis and fresas and Mexas. There were nerdy Latinos and punk Latinos and later emo Latinos. There were Latinos who were rich and Latinos who were poor. Latinos who were all shades of black, brown, and beige. Latinos from different ancestries and religions. My hometown afforded me the privilege to be all parts of myself—as much Mexican as American, as much from here as from there. Before the shooting, I realized when reminiscing with my mother, I had not ever really felt compelled to go searching because I had not ever really felt that something was missing.

21

The Forgetting

BLANCA AND SUSAN saw themselves as carbon copies of each other, but in many ways, like El Paso and Ciudad Juárez, the sister cities of their youth, they were complementary opposites. Blanca was outgoing and blunt, quicker to attract a circle of friends at any party or political fundraiser. Susan, a year younger, tended to be more reserved and meticulously organized.

For the Rubios, El Paso had been, as its namesake declared, a pass to opportunity and a better life. Their roots had been firmly replanted in California, where they shuttled back and forth with other state lawmakers between Los Angeles and Sacramento. The sisters bought a two-story house with walls of pearl-white stucco in a quiet suburb northwest of the state capitol. By early 2020 their youngest sister, Sylvia, was running for another Assembly seat, and Blanca was watching her children, Nadia and Aiden, grow up at ease among the kind of powerful people who had intimidated her as a girl.

As the sisters worked to build their name, Kaxh Mura'l waited on the Mexican side of the border for American courts to determine his fate. José Alfredo Holguin waited for the same on the American side. Alfredo would never know Kaxh, and Kaxh would never know Alfredo. But the two were now fighting the same fight for political asylum in the United States on either end of a line that, for them—unlike for me or for the Rubios or for many other fronterizos—was stark and immovable. Alfredo, who had been transfixed in the in-betweenness for many more years than Kaxh, often told his brothers and his friends that he felt stateless: ni de aquí, ni de allá (neither from here nor from there).

Kaxh was still living in Ciudad Juárez, with La's La B'oxh, in the home that their lawyer, Carlos Spector, had brought them to when they had escaped from the smugglers at the warehouse. Their hosts, an engineer and his wife, were letting the two men stay in the old bedrooms where their children had grown up before they headed off to college. The arrangement was supposed to be temporary, but as their cases faced delay after delay, they lodged there for weeks, then months. If they had outstayed their welcome, Kaxh was grateful to the family for not mentioning it. He kept a routine that helped him pass the time and stay sane.

Nearly every morning he rose with the sun, took a quick shower, and pulled on his blue maquiladora uniform. After a light breakfast, he caught a rutera to the unofficial job he had taken with an immigrant rights organization. He had studied accounting at his university back in Guatemala and was helping them keep their books. By early afternoon, with the desert heat rising, he grabbed lunch and took another bus to a maquiladora at the edge of the border where workers assembled cardboard boxes that were shipped to the United States and around the world. He worked there from four in the afternoon to four in the morning. He had started out sweeping the floors because his bosses had initially believed he was too short to operate an air-powered machine that sliced through the corrugated cardboard. It was hard and heavy labor. The last worker who had taken it on had been rushed to the hospital with swollen hands and shoulders. But Kaxh proved to be stronger than he looked.

At the end of his shift, under the darkness of dawn, he climbed into yet another rutera and headed back home, through streets where the Holguins' buses had shuttled workers in and out, past maquiladoras where young women like Claudia had been snatched and killed. Another Latino dreaming the American Dream. Another obrero making American products at the U.S.-Mexico dividing line. Call Carmelita! Call la Santa! Watch her ride in on her fluorescent white horse. To touch each hurting part that no longer feels human. To heal the festering wound between the hearts of two nations. A custom cut made for American packaging. A Taking and Splitting that Americans were perpetually forgetting.

Some activists back in Guatemala, upset with Kaxh for leaving, cast him as just another young man searching for fame and fortune in el Norte. A mayor of Juárez once called exiled Mexicanos in El Paso like Alfredo cowards and opportunists even though the Mexican city official lived in the Texas city himself and made his way to work with bodyguards. Despite their legal claims to asylum, some saw Kaxh and Alfredo as criminals for migrating across international boundaries with little but a plea for help. Like Kaxh, Alfredo had developed his own routine to cope with the frustration and monotony of the days. Unlike Kaxh, Alfredo could drive to the edge of la frontera and see his homeland, even if he could not step foot on the other side. One could not tell which position was worse to be in.

Alfredo was a burly man with a thin gray mustache and the lyricism of a poet. From El Paso, he had watched city officials build a towering red sculpture of an X in honor of Ciudad Juárez with some bitterness. He saw it as a move to gloss over the hollow of destruction that the drug war had caused— a hole without a bottom that he said would always be a part of his life and that of a generation of Juarenses. Alfredo carried the sadness of the murder of his son everywhere. He felt as though he were missing a hand. He kept looking down, expecting to get it back.

But he tried to keep going. He continued to run their bus transportation company through intermediaries. He continued his activist work with Carlos and their group, Mexicanos en Exilio. He got back into writing songs, and he and his brother, Roman, began attending an evangelical church. They found comfort in the community. They even formed a band with a couple of friends and performed at church events and restaurants.

Speaking to an oral historian in May 2013, Alfredo said that his days had grown calmer. But he longed to be a revolucionario on the other side, raising hell against the Mexican government that had failed to keep its citizens safe, he said, like the men whose names lined the childhood streets and schools of the Juárez where he had grown up. Pancho Villa. Emiliano Zapata. Francisco Madero. To that, his interviewer reminded him that the seeds of the revolution had been planted by Mexicanos in the city where he was exiled.

El Paso, Texas
2020

In late July, in the heat of multiple crises and almost one year to the day that a self-proclaimed white supremacist arrived in my hometown with a racist bloody mission, I returned to El Paso. Over the next few days, a photographer, Erin Clark, and I set out to capture a snapshot of the city a year after one of the deadliest attacks on Latinos in modern American history. We would find we were already in the midst of another forgetting.

In Texas, as the COVID-19 pandemic spread around the world, Governor Greg Abbott declined to implement statewide measures to fight the disease, leaving it up to cities, counties, and schools to individually decide what to do instead. Within months, El Paso became a state epicenter within a national epicenter for the health crisis. Hospitals swelled with coronavirus patients, and the city, much like the rest of the border region, tallied coronavirus deaths far ahead of other major urban counties in the state.

EL PASO STRONG murals and billboards dotted the boulevards and businesses. But inside coffee shops, restaurants, and stores and on the Paso del Norte bridge, where Carmelita had once led dozens of women in revolt in the middle of another epidemic, many fronterizos told us they wanted to move on from the pain of the shooting, the migrant family separations, the harsh anti-immigrant rhetoric. Many already had. Like other sordid chapters in the history of our city and our nation, parents and grandparents—who had uprooted and upheaved and endured and sacrificed so much for their children to get ahead—were grappling with its impact the way they always had: by looking away, by sweeping it into the silence, by leaving it in the past. *Work hard. Keep your head down. Don't look back.*

In Ciudad Juárez, Kaxh felt a deep sense of dread, fearful not only that he would never reach el Norte but that he would never be able to go back home again. The Trump administration had used his national emergency powers, as well as the aggressive travel restrictions recommended by public health experts, to effectively enact the immigration crackdown at the U.S.-Mexico border that he had always wanted. Federal officials began to instantly deport or turn away virtually all refugees and asylum seekers. They moved slowly to release people from detention centers, and they shut down immigration courts.

Kaxh worried about losing the work that had given him some semblance of normalcy in the limbo, and soon he and La's were rushing to find a new home. Their host family had taken in their elderly relatives and were concerned the two could bring home the virus from the factory where they worked. In El Paso, Alfredo, president of Mexicanos en Exilio, moved the group's meetings online. He hoped to continue to foster the relationships that had helped carry him through some of the toughest moments of his life. But as the pandemic put their demonstrations and activities on pause, Roman could see his brother retreating back into himself.

Like Kaxh and Alfredo, people were fretting about their jobs, businesses, and families. They were scrambling to take care of their loved ones and patients, planning funerals, and mourning the losses of relationships to sickness or closed borders. Only Americans could cross back and forth because of Trump's immigration restrictions. Mexicanos were not entirely upset about that. They did not want their paisanos contracting the illness in El Paso and bringing it back.

The solid front against racism and white supremacist violence that had emerged in the wake of the mass shooting had also started to crack. In May, the country had watched a police officer press his knee on George Floyd's neck for more than nine minutes, killing him while he lay facedown and in handcuffs on a street corner in Minneapolis, Minnesota. It had been only the latest high-profile slaying to take the lives of unarmed Black people in months. In February, three white men in trucks had chased down Ahmaud Arbery, twenty-five, while he had been out jogging in a subdivision in southeastern Georgia. One shot and killed him with a Remington shotgun. In March, police had slain Breonna Taylor, twenty-six, a Black emergency-room technician, in a spray of bullets after they forced their way into her apartment.

The summer of demonstrations that followed was dividing fronterizos.

As some protests turned violent, Trump denounced their participants as thugs and criminals, threatened to send active-duty troops to cities and states, and escalated his show of force in Washington. Scholars such as Guadalupe Correa-Cabrera warned that his militarized efforts, like those he had deployed against migrants in El Paso and along the southern border, resembled those of authoritarian regimes in Latin American countries like Chile and Argentina. These actions, they said, were not solely about reining in social justice activists or cracking down on immigration. At their core was a threat to the nation's very democracy.

But Trump's rhetoric cut deep in many American cities like El Paso, where anti-Black racism had never been entirely eradicated and a slice of Mexicanos and México Americanos had always wanted to officially belong in the white American mainstream. To be Black in America, after all, had meant death, violence, or loss of land, freedom, and property. Some fronterizos participated in Black and Brown demonstrations of solidarity or sought to balance their calls against police misconduct with tributes to the officers who had responded to the El Paso massacre. But others did not see their struggles reflected in the Black Lives Matter movement in a place where Latino, Black, Asian, and Indigenous communities had often been pitted against one another and where border and law enforcement jobs had become some of the few steady and respected paths for Latinos to move up. Some were turned off by the images of violence and burning cities they saw on television, others by the destruction of city landmarks—unfamiliar with the history of civil disobedience in the United States, the legacy of Black and Latino civil rights movements forgotten in other forgettings. And still others were grappling with old tensions over how Spanish and Native histories were told: Even the airport where we had landed had once been at the center of this contentious debate. A towering, gleaming statue of Oñate erected at its entrance had spurred fiery discussion about whether it celebrated the city's Spanish heritage and hybrid culture or a despot who had massacred about eight hundred villagers in the Acoma Pueblo in New Mexico.

One night, Erin and I stopped at the thirty-foot golden obelisk built at the edge of the Walmart parking lot in memory of the twenty-three victims killed in the shooting. A couple of young employees stowing away shopping carts told us that they had been among the workers lauded for their bravery the day of the massacre. But now they were facing threats from customers who refused to follow store policy to mask up. Not too far from where we stood, the makeshift memorial of flowers and white crosses that had sprung up after the tragedy had been moved to a nearby park. When I had gone by there earlier, the few mementos left—faded banners, rosaries, wooden stars—baked in the sun.

Sitting at a wooden kitchen table in her home a few days later, Stephanie Melendez, whose father, David Johnson, was killed at the Walmart trying to protect her daughter and mother, told us she felt trapped in the thick of a fog as the rest of the world went on. Her daughter, Kaitlyn, ten, did not want to talk about what happened or much at all. She could not go into stores or crowded places. Isolated at home, away from work, school, and friends, as El Paso tried to tame the pandemic, coping had become even more difficult.

"As the time went on, it's like reality set in," Stephanie said. "The grief got worse."

Across town, on a scorching afternoon, Gilbert Anchondo showed off photos of his son on a wall full of frames in an office decked with treasured possessions: toy car models, band posters, trophies, sports team banners, a set of drums, and Hollywood memorabilia; a bell that he rang before each workday in hopes that Andre and Jordan "get their wings." Andre, his son, and Andre's wife, Jordan, had been slain as they held on to their two-month-old son, Paul.

Born in El Paso and raised in Juárez, Gilbert had moved to El Paso when he was fourteen. He had competed in bodybuilding contests, married, and opened an auto body shop forty years earlier that now housed shiny custom cars and Harley-Davidson motorcycles. Andre had overcome some trouble with drugs. He had been entrepreneurial like his father and had opened his own granite business only blocks away. Now, Gilbert told us, his life had become like a puzzle tossed into the air.

"I'm trying to assemble a new picture," he said.

Even before his son's death, he had been caught in that space in between the remembering and the forgetting. A heavyset man with clear-rimmed eyeglasses, he had stopped crossing the border bridges back into Mexico after he put down roots in the United States. He did not want to talk politics. The Anchondos had caused a national stir when, at a hospital only days after the massacre, they had posed with the man who many—including other survivors—believe provided fuel for the attack. In the photo, President Trump smiled, giving a thumbs-up, as Melania Trump held the infant Paul. Anchondo told us he did not vote but had agreed to the presidential visit because he had been trying to show respect for his adopted country. His younger son, Tito, said it was what he thought his brother Andre—"a full-on Trump supporter"—would have done.

Back on the boulevards stretching in and out of the Paso del Norte bridge, Erin and I walked past struggling discount and trinket shops, over the parched Rio Grande, into a nearly desolate Avenida Juárez. If there was a single landmark on the street to gauge how dire the state of the world had become, it was the World Famous Kentucky Club, one of the first establishments to greet travelers near the foot of the international thoroughfare. The ancient dive bar had opened its doors in the Mexican city's años dorados.

Inside, neon lights cast green and red hues over old mahogany chairs and portraits of Mexican celebrities. Legend had it that one of its bartenders had invented the margarita in the 1940s (though it was likely actually the place next door that had been called Tommy's). Elizabeth Taylor and Marilyn Monroe were said to have been among its patrons shortly after their divorcios al vapor. The place had been a central witness to the tussles between Mexico and the United States over immigration, national security, and trade—an oasis within an oasis in the harsh desert sun—through constant border closures after 9/11, through the violent years of the drug war that swept Ciudad Juárez, through a humanitarian crisis that left thousands of migrants stranded not far from its doors. But the coronavirus outbreak proved too much. It forced the Kentucky Club, like most of the bars and restaurants along Avenida Juárez, to temporarily close just before it turned one hundred years old.

We wandered through the two sister cities, witnesses to a century of wars on migrants, on drugs, on terror. One hundred years of border and identity battles. One hundred years of competing visions for their futures. I wondered whether to keep moving forward, whether it was better to remember or to forget, whether it was better to keep and preserve or to break down and let go—and whether that answer was, as usual, not an even split, not black or white but gray, something or somewhere in between.

As Trump officials had virtually shut down the country's borders, many Central Americans headed back to their native countries, fed up with the racism, from the Americans and the Mexicans. No belief in the great mestizaje had lessened Mexican animosity toward poor and Brown Central American migrants, and especially not poor and Brown Indigenous Central Americans like Kaxh, who endured constant racial slurs and harassment. But many other Latinos stayed.

Near the cathedral, on a busier market street, we stumbled across a group of Cuban and Mexican men hauling crates of melons from the back of a truck. For decades, the United States had welcomed Cubans as political refugees. But after Obama ended the protections, stranded Cubanos started working in restaurants, bars, and markets around the bridge and around downtown Juárez. Like Kaxh, they were now required to wait in Mexico while they petitioned American courts for asylum.

"We are here against our will," Manuel Gonzalez, thirty-five, who had two daughters and a wife in Cuba, told us.

"Like hostages," another added.

Jose Angel Garcia, thirty-one, had arrived alone at the Juárez side of the bridge once known as the Santa Fe with just enough money to bribe Mexican police to leave him alone. He found a job serving drinks at the Mariachi Bar right next to the Kentucky Club. The pandemic had only added to the uncertainty of his fate.

"I just wish I could get my papers to start planning my future," he said.

The border was a sweltering, strange, hard place. In Cuba, guns did not flow in from the United States; drugs did not move out. Women did not disappear in the desert. There was time for dominoes and soccer games. All there was to do in Juárez was work, the men said, and it was not always a sure thing you'd get paid. Police harassed migrants for bribes; cartel members threatened their lives.

Garcia, who like my father had been trained as an agricultural engineer, blasted Trump for stoking racism against Black people, Latinos, and immigrants.

"What measures did he take when the African American man was killed? It's racist," Garcia said, pointing to Trump's response to the George Floyd protests. "And why did they kill the African American man? Because of racism. They killed him in cold blood."

Even so, Garcia felt the pull north. He dreamed as he waited, and he waited as he dreamed.

"From me, no one will take the American Dream," he said.

22

The New Ellis Island

WHEN THE FIRST rays of sunshine cast shadows over the Franklin Mountains, the cool desert air carries the faint scent of sagebrush. Families rouse to life in the sprawl of homes and cookie-cutter subdivisions. The low hum of cars, trucks, and SUVs begins on the interstate that was once an old camino to gold in California. The processions of commuters start to assemble on international bridges.

El Paso is church on Sundays and high school football games on Friday nights. It is carne asadas in big backyards with squat stone walls, runs to Chico's Tacos and panaderias, confetti eggs and children running wild at Ascarate Park on Easter. It is Power 102.1 and retro Rock en Español. It is Mexican and American flags decked on the backs of lowriders that its pachucos made popular. It is the morning caravans of students on their way to Catholic and public schools. It is young Tiguas in Ysleta learning to make adobe blocks out of sun, sand, and water. It is tamales in the winter and the call of mourning doves in the spring, Texas-sized margaritas at Carlos & Mickey's, and slow dancing to oldies blasting from jukeboxes in dive bars on Mesa Street. It is the dust and wind that rustles through pines and cottonwoods like a giant feathered serpent, bridging earth and sky, the material and the divine.

El Paso could tell the United States a lot about itself. The city, so integral to its founding, had been a green valley that native Chihuahuenses knew as an oasis in the desert, a far western outpost that cowboys and debauchers shot into infamy as a netherworld of lawlessness. To the Chinese, it had been a beacon of hope, and to Mexicanos a refuge, a stop on the road to the American Dream. But as the months wore on in that fall of 2020, the city—the crossroads always at a crossroads—receded from the national consciousness as it had so many times before. It disappeared into the fog.

All across the country, the forgetting was repeating itself. As we continued to crisscross the nation in the middle of a presidential election, a pandemic, an economic slump, a national reckoning with race and racism—and the backlash—Americans were reconsidering their heroes and their myths and what they evoked about the nation's identity. But the debates were occurring in a haze of crises, often on alternate planes without shared facts or realities.

For years, Mexican Americans and Latinos had been, overall, reliable Democrats. After Trump's maligning of Mexicans, after the massacre in El Paso, the party had been expecting the growing electorate to turn Republican-controlled states like Texas and Arizona deep shades of blue. Instead, election results and polls were showing that a far greater number than expected were becoming independents or drifting right. Some Latino voters were espousing the same kind of racial animus and concerns as white voters that immigration was increasing crime and damaging American identity. Some were drawn specifically to Donald Trump, whom they trusted more on the economy despite their distaste for his anti-immigrant rhetoric and policies. Many more were frustrated with the Democrats, whom they saw as too left leaning or not left leaning enough, too focused on high-minded debates on race and gender over the needs of workers and the middle class, too willing to make sweeping promises to fix the nation's immigration system that they did not keep.

Some political strategists and researchers argued the largest group of voters of color in the United States was undergoing a massive political realignment. They offered theories and explanations to explain the rightward shift.

They tended to do with the failings of the Democratic Party, the evangelization and Americanization of a generation of Latinos—the majority now born in the United States and far removed from their roots—and the erosion of trust in American institutions and norms that was blanketing all segments of the U.S. population. Others contended the changes would not last beyond Trump, whose showmanship and cultlike ability to pull people in was unlike any other political figure in modern American history.

But as I interviewed Latinos across the country, I realized that what we were truly watching unfold was another crisis—one of belonging—and at its heart was a story of neglect. Many were rejecting both parties altogether, disillusioned with a political system that they believed granted them little to no power. Mexican Americans did not know our history as a people in the United States, or even their own personal histories. Many Latinos felt invisible or were struggling to find their place in an American society that tended to see our large multinational, multiracial, and multiethnic group as a blank-faced monolith when it saw us at all.

The Chinese. The Irish and the Germans and the Italians. The eastern and southern Europeans. The Mexicans. This story of neglect had repeated itself in the American story over and over again. The waves of immigrants who helped build the United States through the nineteenth and twentieth centuries—laying railroad tracks, building bridges, and working in mines, mills, and factories—all arrived with little means and were smeared with accusations of criminality. Their influences and contributions were often overlooked and forgotten. It all had me thinking about another name that had been bestowed on El Paso through more recent decades, perhaps its most debated: the New Ellis Island.

Like that processing station in New York Harbor, El Paso had long served as a portal into the United States, a revolving door in and out of the American Southwest. When historians and politicians summoned the powerful myth to describe the city, they sought to mark its place as a gateway to new beginnings and the American promise, to cement the labor and contributions of immigrants—the majority Mexican or Latino—into our American ethos. But Chicano scholars had long countered that we could also not ignore the stark differences. Unlike in that northeastern seaport, the current through el paso por las montañas was not so much a steady stream to opportunity and assimilation but an ebb and flow blending worlds. Its travelers were drawn in and tossed out with the whims of each decade, and they tended to be described not as symbols of hard work and prosperity but as aliens and criminals, destined to be watched, bound, and shackled.

This told us a lot about ourselves, too.

Ciudad Juárez–El Paso
2020

Kaxh Mura'l was exhausted. Other businesses had shuttered or laid off workers because of the pandemic, but the maquila where he continued to put in grueling hours assembling cardboard boxes had kept on humming through the winter. He was grateful for the paycheck and the new lodgings it afforded. He and La's La B'oxh were now living in downtown Juárez, in an apartment building that rented out a few of its rooms to migrants as tens of thousands of people from around the world waited at the edges of El Paso's bridges.

On a night in November, Kaxh had been on the verge of falling asleep when his phone began buzzing with notifications. Messages flooded in from unknown numbers. The senders told him to watch his back and threatened to take his life. He would have ignored them except that one note deeply startled him. It included a photo of his Indigenous name scrawled on a scrap of white paper surrounded by brass bullets. The image was especially ominous because most of his friends and acquaintances in Juárez knew him only by his Spanish name, Gaspar.

Though Kaxh could not be sure who was targeting him, he had an idea. Mexican gang members often exploited the migrants who had taken shelter in tents along the border or earned meager wages peddling fruits, spices, and tourist goods in local markets. Giant white banners scrawled with death threats directed at the newcomers appeared at times, hanging from lampposts or highway bridges in the neighborhoods in which they clustered, recalling the bloodiest years of the drug war. Some of his fellow maquiladora workers had been followed. A few had been beaten. Kaxh and La's themselves had already been robbed.

Kaxh woke up La's and handed him his phone. La's scrolled through the chain of missives in shock. As they debated whether to flee, La's called their lawyer, Carlos Spector. He told them to head to a nearby hotel while he tried to connect with American immigration officials. They stuffed what they could in a couple of backpacks, and once again they were on the run for their lives. Outside, they searched for a safe place to hail a cab, fearing someone might be watching them. Kaxh kept expecting an assailant to jump out of the shadows, maybe members of la Maña, maybe some of the same men who had pursued him back in Guatemala.

At the hotel, they lay low for a few days until Carlos came to retrieve them. He had mixed news. They would be allowed to cross the border into El Paso, but they would be immediately placed in immigration detention. It was likely they would remain locked up for months as their cases moved through the court process, and there was always a chance they would be deported. But the men believed their asylum cases were strong. They decided they had no other choice. They had to go.

That night, more than a year since they had arrived in the borderland, they walked over the Paso del Norte bridge as they had done twice before. This time they were not turned back. At the gates of the New Ellis Island, they were questioned, stripped of their belongings, and taken into custody. Immigration officials loaded the migrants onto a bus and moved them to a large detention center in Las Cruces, New Mexico. Years earlier, José Alfredo Holguin had once been held in the same place as he had sought refuge.

Kaxh and La's were confined to bunk beds they shared with other men in jumpsuits. They were allowed only a few hours of communal time each day. As they ate lunch and dinner in the cafeteria of their new dwelling, Kaxh watched the news on the television screens. The presidential election had occurred only days earlier, and ballots were still being counted. Within a week, Joe Biden, the former vice president and senator from Delaware, was declared the winner. All Kaxh really knew about him was that Biden was not Donald Trump, and for him and many of the other men in detention with him that was enough to bring some relief.

As he continued to languish in detention, Alfredo was confined to his bed. He fell ill with Covid not long after Thanksgiving. He lost his sense of smell and his energy. He thrashed in his sleep. He struggled to breathe. The Holguins tried to take care of him at home, but soon they had to rush him to a hospital, where he died, just days before Christmas, without ever seeing a resolution to his asylum claim. He was fifty-nine.

At his funeral, his friends and relatives recalled his charisma and optimism, his resilience and unwavering solidarity with other families who, like his own, had been torn up by the drug war, and with other immigrants who, like him, were suspended in a condition of statelessness in the United States. Alfredo had learned a lot about pain as part of Mexicanos en Exilio, he had once written. He had learned that his suffering was not unique, nor the most immense. He had learned that his group of asylum seekers had not been the first to feel its torment, nor would they be the last. For those reasons, he explained, he had continued to plead his asylum case. He was fighting not for himself, he believed, but for their common cause.

The death of his brother hit Roman the hardest. He and Alfredo had grown closer than ever before in El Paso. The two had resumed attending church on Sundays after some Covid restrictions were lifted and enjoyed taking long weekend drives through their far west side neighborhood, where the streets were quiet and the modest, single-family homes neatly landscaped with stones and gravel. It was with Roman that Alfredo could shake off the veneer of strength and self-assurance that he projected before others. It was to Roman that Alfredo could admit that he still felt broken.

Ciudad Juárez–El Paso
2021

Two weeks after rioters attacked the U.S. Capitol, Joseph R. Biden took the oath of office and, in ways both symbolic and substantive, immediately sought to make good on his pledges to bring forth a "new day" and a more humanitarian approach to immigration. He overturned a ban on travelers from some Muslim-majority countries, stopped border wall construction, and fully reinstated the program protecting Dreamers from deportation. He sent legislation to Congress aimed at clearing visa backlogs, improving the family-based immigration system, and providing pathways to citizenship for roughly 11 million undocumented immigrants in the United States. He rolled back Trump administration orders for harsher immigration enforcement in the country's interior. He even mandated federal agencies to stop using the word "alien" to refer to immigrants.

Migrants on both sides of la frontera held out hope that they would be welcomed into the United States. Yet, a new wave of challenges was quietly building. Hurricanes in the late fall and early winter had added to the devastation in El Salvador, Honduras, and Guatemala, which had already been heavily battered by the pandemic. The natural disasters left half a million people without homes and ready to make the perilous trip north to the United States. Soon, immigration officials were racing to process and shelter tens of thousands of minors who had once again begun arriving at the southern border alone. A few Texas Democrats decried the conditions in which children were being detained, with many sleeping on the floors of freezing border enforcement facilities known as "hieleras," or iceboxes, with nothing but tinfoil blankets. Republicans started their pilgrimages to border cities like El Paso to denounce Biden policies with the desert and iron walls of the border fence as their backdrop. And the new day on immigration was turning out a lot like yesterday.

When Kaxh and La's were released from immigration detention in January, the Biden administration had begun to unwind the Trump protocols requiring asylum seekers to wait out their cases in Mexico. But federal immigration officials were struggling to rebuild an asylum system that had been hollowed out under the Trump administration. The president continued to keep refugee numbers down and to expel most migrants under the public health rule that Trump had invoked during the coronavirus pandemic.

Kaxh and La's first stayed in Las Cruces for a few weeks with a friend and professor whom Kaxh had met back when he was a skinny teenage activist riding his moped through the highland roads of Guatemala. They then made their way back to El Paso, where they took on odd jobs as gardeners and day laborers and rented out a small apartment in a cinder block building with a mural of la Virgencita on one of its outer walls. It was located just a few feet from the border wall, in a neighborhood where some of the Martinez grandchildren had gone to school. Kaxh tried to keep up with his family back home as much as he could. His wife, El, had given birth to his fourth child, Tx'umil, months after his departure, and the thought of his children growing up without their father often moved him to tears.

By May, a sort of cruel dissonance had begun to envelop the line that cut through Mexico and the United States. More people were arriving after making their way through a treacherous rainforest between Panama and Colombia known as the Darién Gap. Some were allowed to cross while others were immediately turned back or flown from congested border processing centers in South Texas to others in El Paso or San Diego, where they were then released on the Mexican side of the border. To immigrants caught in the choke hold—and to many Americans watching the images of people crowding at the nation's gates from their screens at home—the process looked and felt haphazard and chaotic.

With the numbers of migrants climbing to record levels, Republicans like Texas governor Greg Abbott seized upon the widespread public discontent to ratchet up the rhetoric. "Homes are being invaded," he said in an echo of the El Paso shooter's violent internet screed as he unveiled plans in 2021 to finish Trump's border wall in the Rio Grande Valley. That year, immigration apprehensions would hit levels not seen in twenty years, and more than 1.5 million people would cross the southern border for the first time. The common refrain from Republican elected officials and candidates running in 2022 midterm races up and down the ballot, in districts and states near and far from the border, went something like what Senator Marsha Blackburn would later remark in Tennessee: "Under this administration, every town is a border town, and every state is a border state."

But it was not until April 2022 that the issue began to concern the broader American public. That month Abbott organized charter buses to shuttle migrants out of El Paso into blue cities like Washington, D.C., and New York.

Governor Ron DeSantis of Florida would one-up him and fly migrants to Martha's Vineyard, Massachusetts. As Democratic mayors and governors grappled with housing the new arrivals in overcrowded camps, hotels, and shelters, they would join the chorus of lawmakers demanding that the Biden administration do more to address the challenges at the southern border. By the time Trump had vacated the White House, more Americans favored increasing immigration for the first time in six decades of Gallup polling. As Biden's term wore on, attitudes started to swing in the other direction. More Republicans and independents would cite the issue as a top concern. The fear of the outsider—as it had throughout El Paso's history—was taking hold.

On a hot spring day at a Juárez shelter along the border fence, not too far from la Casa de Adobe, where revolucionarios had congregated in the desert brush, several Guatemalan families told me they had turned themselves in at the El Paso port of entry to request asylum only for immigration officials to drive them back to Juárez. They were dropped off near the city's downtown plaza as the streets emptied and the skies grew dark, and a few went in search of a church in hopes that they would be taken in for the night. To one of those migrants, a young coffee farmer from Guatemala, the New Ellis Island had become "the place where dreams end and a sadness strikes."

On the other side, Kaxh and La's were volunteering at Sacred Heart Church. Later that morning, under the foreign brightness, far from the lush green paradise they called home, they joined immigrant rights advocates and lawyers at the exit of the Paso del Norte International Bridge. The group applauded new migrants arriving. The two Guatemalan activists offered guidance and helped haul their luggage into shuttles to Annunciation House, another shelter, at times joining in cheers of "Welcome to the United States!" It was the kind of welcome they would have wanted for themselves.

Ciudad Juárez–El Paso
2023

In the third year of Biden's term, I am back home again. Immigration officials are setting up rings of concertina wire along the banks of the Rio

Grande. The evening news on my aunt Alicia's old television set is filled with grainy images of shadow people congregating under the glowing yellow floodlights of the border wall. It is early May, and Biden is set to lift the health rule known as Title 42 that has shut down the border to most migrants and asylum seekers since the coronavirus first spread around the world. Immigration officials are preparing for a rush of humanity. Migrants are gathering at different gateways along the Mexican side of the river in anticipation. They carry luggage and backpacks and blankets that many do not realize they will be forced to discard into garbage piles when they cross.

The next day, a light breeze is blowing, and the sun is an hour or so from setting. I walk past the brick tenement en El Segundo where la Santa lived. Migrants are sleeping on the sidewalks that surround Sacred Heart Church. Bottles of shampoo and conditioner, sticks of deodorant, and cans of mushrooms, collard greens, and Chef Boyardee pasta sit on the windowsills. Worn blankets—soft and velvety quilts, plain sheets, Red Cross throws—and black plastic bags stuffed with clothes hang from the fences. Members of the Red Cross in red vests walk through the crowds. People are sitting on old garb spread out on top of greasy pizza boxes for some semblance of comfort. The streets looked like this when I was last in town for Christmas. But now that public sentiment has started to turn against the newcomers, fronterizos are no longer allowed to stop by and drop off donations. Police officers have started issuing citations to those giving out water bottles.

On Father Rahm Avenue, named for a Catholic priest who once ministered at Sacred Heart, a small group of people gathers before activists holding crosses. These are painted black and in memory of each of the eight migrants killed only a few days earlier when a thirty-four-year-old man, likely driving under the influence, slammed his Range Rover into a crowd of people waiting at a bus stop in Brownsville, Texas. Ángel Galindo, twenty-five, from Venezuela, tells me that he and some of the other young men around us scaled the wall with their bare hands. No ladder, he says, only a deep fear in his insides. On the other side, they turned themselves in.

He is in a black sweatshirt and khakis. He has crossed Costa Rica and Panama. He has seen much of Chile and Brazil. He has sold caramel candies on the streets. He has trimmed hair as a barber. He has done some plumbing and painted homes. He has taken out the trash for businesses. Before El Paso, the last city he spent any real time in—six months—was Foz do Iguaçu, or Foz, a Brazilian city on the border of Iguaçu Falls, the lush and flowing cataratas de Brazil that he tells me I need to visit someday.

"Nothing as beautiful as South America," he says. But the city he is dying to get to, risking his life for, his dream city, he says, is la ciudad del sueño Americano (the city of the American Dream). Kansas City. He is a longtime fan of their baseball team.

On May 10—roughly one hundred and twelve years since Francisco Madero, Pancho Villa, and Pascual Orozco took Ciudad Juárez, forcing old Porfirio to renounce his dictatorship—El Paso and Ciudad Juárez are once more on edge. Some restaurants and businesses on Avenida Juárez are shutting down early in case the hordes of migrants flood in. Title 42 is due to expire the next day, and Title 8 will begin. Under the new law, no longer will people be summarily deported, but they will face steep criminal penalties if they attempt to cross anywhere along the 1,800-mile line other than international checkpoints.

As I make my way to the Paso del Norte International Bridge, it is almost seven p.m. and the raging masses have not arrived. I bump into Galindo again. He is in a bright white tank top, white shades, black skinny jeans, and white sneakers. He has been sleeping on one of the cardboard boxes on the ground outside of the church, selling cigarettes and begging for coins in hopes of taking the next bus to Denver. We say our goodbyes and wish each other well before I cross into the other side. I duck into el Kentucky.

The neon lights are glowing and a modern corrido is blasting from a jukebox. Pancho Villa's ghost sits in a dark corner. A few moments later, my aunt Bertha joins me and we order a couple of beers as I wait for Ivan Pierre Aguirre, a friend and local photographer, to join us so we can head to the border fence where people are waiting for passage. As we chat, time splits, and I find myself reminiscing about another time, same place. My mother and my sister were there, as were other members of my family: my aunts Bertha and Alicia and my uncles Roberto and Fernando. It was a hot summer afternoon, and the light peeked in from the windows. We drank tequila until we were tipsy and then wandered together outside through a makeshift market, our feet kicking up dirt. On our way home much later that day, we crammed into a small car, my sister and I sitting on the others' laps to make us all fit, and we belted out rancheras and boleros as we wound back over the bridge. Just another ordinary crossing.

Once Ivan arrives, he and I head out into the night. There is a cold front coming in, bringing wind gusts of nineteen miles per hour. We drive to the spot along the border fence that journalists now know as Puerta 32, or Door 32, and park near the brush. Along the chain-link fences, there is a constant flow of Ford trucks and green military jeeps and long white vans. Migrant families are standing up along the bank against the towering iron bars. The dust swirls white against the tungsten floodlights, humming and oscillating in waves. Sand spirits engulfing the borderland. Old Villa's ghost is in the dunes, I am sure of it. I search for Teresa's iridescent horse in the darkness.

El Paso is alive. It breathes and heaves with human life. Your poor and huddled masses. Your staunch conservatives. Your rebels and living saints. Your Border Patrol officers and your paisanos. And you and me. The confines of our worlds negotiated and renegotiated, outside forces making and unmaking lines and aliens and criminals of some of us. The process often neither fair nor the one-sided affair that the United States projects it to be.

El Paso is Urrea and Madero. It is the Chews, the Rubios, the Martinezes, and the Holguins. It is the Rodríguezes and the Garcías and the Anchondos and the Márquezes. The O'Rourkes and the Reckards. The Ulloas. It is Ángel Galindo making his way to Kansas City. It is Kaxh Mura'l passing out pantry meals to other newcomers from Guatemala and El Salvador and Colombia and Venezuela. El Paso is its people and its passersby. It is its borders and bridges.

We climb out of Ivan's truck and follow the line of people walking along the banks and into the brush. Many have their heads wrapped in blankets and shirts and sweatshirts or shaded with hoodies to shield their faces from the sand. They look like they've been exploring deserts in faraway lands. Another line of people is coming back in the other direction, fed up with the waiting or headed to nearby convenience stores to buy more food and water. A couple of young men come through with a battered umbrella. A man asks for Tylenol, anything to cure a blistering headache. He scrunches his face and rubs his temples. He couldn't take the dust storm, he tells us. He is going back downtown to try another day instead.

We cross with the people jumping the banks, over the same river where my grandfather and my grandmother's father and grandfather had crossed. We cross where Miguel Martinez, feeling the desperate pangs of hunger, had crossed with Juan in his arms. We cross where Estela Rubio had crossed before she took a train to Los Angeles with her children, and I finally understood what she had meant about making sure not to soak her ankles. I wondered if they, too, had smelled the stench of the foul water against the discarded plywood or whether it was cleaner then. One slip in the wrong direction now and one could stumble into the barbed wire protruding off the side of a chain-link fence that American immigration officials only recently installed.

On the other side, people wait in the open against the border fence with no protection from the whipping sand and wind. The dirt gets into our noses, mouths, and eyes, and adds another scratchy layer of skin. It hurts our throats. It makes it hard to breathe. Families with children huddle around in blankets in the dust storm. The global outrage over children in cages, over children in hieleras (freezers), has long dissipated. Few news outlets have said much about the children now sleeping in the dirt.

There is a nervous energy in the waves of sand. Many people who had been out here for days are leaving in frustration, and yet many also continue arriving with hope and with optimism. Back in the brush, a father and son tug two small pieces of rolling luggage filled with food and clothes. The father, Andres, has on loafers and a gray pullover. His son is wearing black basketball sweats. They tell me they flew in from Colombia.

"What made you decide to make the journey?" I ask.

"Para encontrar nuevos rumbos" ("To find new horizons"), he tells me.

El Paso is the city not on a hill but at the foot of the mountains that reminds us of our promise—the place that reminds us there is no invasion between neighbors who inhabit the same third space. There are some who seek to stir fear in the hearts of Americans by claiming that every city and state is now El Paso. Perhaps that has never been truer, and there has never been less of a reason to be afraid. We are, all of us, grating against each other and creating a new lifeblood.

EPILOGUE

A New Day

On the day Donald Trump returned to power, he issued ten executive orders and proclamations sweeping across nearly every aspect of the American immigration system. Many of the decisions resonated with those from his first term. He sought to cut legal and illegal entry into the United States, resume the construction of a border wall, and claw back at the demographic trends changing the face of the nation by limiting who could call themselves an American citizen. Some of his legal arguments were novel. They opened the way for more severe criminal punishment, the deployment of the military, and invocations of the centuries-old Insurrection Act and Alien Enemies Act to repel, detain, and deport migrants and asylum seekers. The foundations for all his actions had been laid long before, decade by decade, in El Paso.

When I set out to write about my hometown, I was not too sure what I would find. All I knew is that I wanted to capture a fuller picture of a desert city that had been treated as a fringe character in our nation's history because of the makeup of its people and its physical place at its southern edge, even though it had long been at the center of some of its most seminal events: its formation, its debates over Western democracy, its racial violence, and its activism and resistencia. We are in a much different era than when I started searching for our roots. The "Trump Resistance" was at its peak in the months after the El Paso shooting and through a summer of social justice protests in 2020. It has since waned as independents and moderates have lost political battles against Trump, Democrats have grown more divided, and attitudes toward immigration have shifted as a whole across the nation.

As I wrote the final chapters of this book, federal officials were targeting immigrant rights organizations and lawyers and rounding up students on visas for their support of the pro-Palestinian movement on college campuses. Hundreds of deportees were sent to a prison in El Salvador without due process over claims that they were all members of transnational gangs, though some of their lawyers and family members came forward to refute the claims. Many scholars were no longer arguing whether the United States could still call itself a representative or pluralistic democracy but whether its swing toward autocracy would be permanent. Latino civil rights leaders were contending with election results that showed a massive disconnect between their organizations and the Latino blue-collar workers they claimed to represent—and some worried many of the victims of bigotry had become the bigots.

For this moment, El Paso offers its lessons, too.

To be sure, the city is only one of dozens of crossroads between the United States and Mexico and surely not the only one Americans should know. If fronterizos had their way, Americans would study and understand each and every one. But the mountain pass has been a pivotal gateway into the land that would become our nation since its founding. It is the place of the Taking and the Splitting and the place where one can see the evolution of our immigration and border policy most clearly. It is also now one of the many American cities serving as the backdrop to an immigration fight that at its crux, scholars say, is truly about the preservation of U.S. democracy.

For many of the families I interviewed, the crossing has been worth it. Sabino and Estela Rubio saw their daughters reach heights they never dreamed possible for themselves. But the Rubios are also contending with the messy world of politics. When Susan and Blanca's youngest sister, Sylvia, ran for office, it set up a clash with another prominent political family in their working-class corner of Los Angeles. The family feud captured attention in a district where Susan had already lost political allies after denouncing her husband's domestic abuse. Susan, as reported in the *Los Angeles Times*, was later questioned in a federal corruption probe dating to her time on the Baldwin Park City Council; Baldwin Park city officials were said to be taking bribes for permits to operate marijuana businesses, and the newspaper found an unnamed public official matching her description was accused of taking cash for a 2018 campaign bid. Susan, who has denied wrongdoing and was not the target of the investigation, was never named in the case and no charges came from the allegations detailed in an embattled city attorney's plea deal. The sisters went on to lead their districts through devastating wildfires in early 2025, and Susan has continued to make strengthening her state's domestic violence laws one of her top legislative priorities.

Their state of California has learned some lessons in resistance—mainly that it is complicated. As my colleague Melanie Mason and I uncovered for the *Los Angeles Times*, many of the proposals to protect and improve the lives of immigrants during the Trump administration did not go into effect. Some have since been scaled back or thrown out entirely. The legacy of former Senate leader Kevin de León, who went on to become a Los Angeles City Council member, was tarnished in November 2022 after a leaked audio captured him bemoaning the lack of political power of Latinos in Los Angeles as compared with that of its Black community. He also mostly stood silent as three other Latino political leaders made racist comments against Black people, Oaxacans, Jews, Armenians, and others. De León apologized for some of his behavior but refused to step down from office and was defeated in 2024. The incident reverberated in El Paso and across the Southwest, renewing conversations among Latino community leaders and activists about the need to tackle the issues of racism and colorism within our communities.

Raúl and Margarita Reyes were able to retire in early 2021 to a small home on a quiet street just west of the city's center, a feat he attributes to the sacrifices his grandparents made for the Martinez clan. Most of the Chew grandchildren have also retired from their successful immigration and judicial careers. They have continued to dig into their past by means of Herlinda and Antonio Wong Chew's letters, photographs, and archival records.

But others are only beginning their struggle in a foreign place. After trying to make ends meet in El Paso for months, Kaxh Mura'l moved to South Florida in search of new jobs in construction and the citrus fields. He has since been one of the main subjects of the 2024 documentary *Borderland: The Line Within* by filmmakers Paco de Onís and Pamela Yates. He dreams of earning enough to one day return to his hometown of Nebaj in Guatemala and continue educating the next generation of activists. On a cool night in May 2023, Kaxh's brother, Kulaxh, drove me and a couple of Guatemalan journalists, Paola and José, out of Nebaj and deep into the countryside through winding, bumpy roads along the Cuchumatane Mountains. We ate boxbol, a traditional Maya Ixil dish of corn dough wrapped in squash leaves and boiled, with the Mura'l family. Kaxh's wife, El, told us of the time Kaxh returned home beaten and of her family's struggles to make ends meet since he had been gone. Kaxh had been sending remittances as he could, but he could not work for a time while he was undocumented. At his home in South Florida later that summer, Kaxh acknowledged that his activism did not help him feed his family, but he said he continued to engage in social justice work because it helped sustain his spirit and he hoped that in time it could help stir people's hearts and minds—la conciencia colectiva.

Roman Holguin also continues to hope to tap into that activism network as he works to keep his older brother's legacy alive. But he has since diverged some from José Alfredo's views. Whereas José Alfredo and Roman once together thoroughly opposed Donald Trump while Alfredo was alive, Roman now has mixed feelings about the president. He does not agree with all of his immigration policies. But through his new evangelical church, Roman has come to meet many Trump supporters, some of whom have helped him through his grief, and, he said, he has come to agree with their belief that Trump will "clean" the nation of evil.

As for me and my family, El Paso remains the place we call home, no matter where some of us may be living now. I wasn't the first kid to dream of leaving their hometown, and I won't be the last, but this work has given me a newfound appreciation for the place that made me and our nation. It will forever be the crossing that always draws me back because it is filled with people with whom I can always pick up right where we left off.

El Paso should hold the same special place in the nation's story as Ellis Island. Yet its rich Mexican and Mexican American history would all have been lost had it not been for fronterizo and Chicano historians and allies who have cared enough to preserve it even when the field of border research was still nascent and primary sources were lacking. After all, most impoverished immigrants like my grandfather didn't stow away their heirlooms or personal records.

Just before the one-year anniversary of the El Paso shooting, as the coronavirus pandemic continued to cause devastation around the world, one of those historians, Irma Montelongo, walked with me through a park in downtown El Paso, not too far from the Santa Fe Bridge and the hotel where Mexican dictator Porfirio Díaz and American president William Taft met for breakfast. A professor at the University of Texas at El Paso, Irma told me her great-grandmother had lived in a humble brick complex nearby and would often tell her of her life during the Mexican Revolution. It's why she chose to become a historian.

Montelongo, like so many other borderland scholars, wanted the city to have a memory. She wanted people to see the through line of discrimination from then to now: the hateful rhetoric against Latinos and anyone who is not white; the cruel treatment of migrant families; a pandemic that was striking Black, Latino, and immigrant homes especially hard.

This book will be part of that memory.

ACKNOWLEDGMENTS

THIS BOOK COULD not exist without the historians, librarians, and community leaders on both sides of the U.S.-Mexico border who have worked to recover the untold histories of the place where I am from. In the United States, the story of the American Southwest has tended to prioritize federal, Anglo-American, and institutional narratives. It has rarely been told by the people of and from the border, and it has been a hard one to tell. Indigenous, Mexicano, and Mexicano Americano stories have often been passed down through oral traditions not always valued in academia. Families ravaged by forced displacements and deportations—or fearful of government agencies—have tended to lose records and archives, or to not keep them at all.

In El Paso and along the border, the people whose work made this book possible include historians Mario T. Gárcia, Oscar J. Martinez, Yolanda Chávez Leyva, David Dorado Romo, Julian Lim, Trinidad "Trini" Gonzales, Rick Quezada, Monica Muñoz Martinez, Bob Chessey, and, of course, Raúl Reyes, who for years has been toiling to put together a fuller picture of Mexican Americans in Texas, like his abuelitos Victoria and Miguel Martinez. Yolanda and David took time to sit with me for interviews and pointed me to rich oral history repositories. Yolanda impressed on me an important lesson, as she has for so many of her students (including Raúl), that as historians and journalists we do not have to be a voice for the voiceless. Our community already has a voice. What we need to learn is how to listen.

Raúl and his wife, Margarita, welcomed me into their home and even had me over for a carne asada as they sought to reunite the Martinez clan. Judge Linda Yee Chew and Justice David Wellington Chew helped provide me with invaluable primary sources to tell the stories of their grandparents Herlinda and Antonio Chew. The Holguin brothers—Alberto, Roman, and Luis—sat with me for interviews in Juárez and El Paso, as did El, Kulaxh, and other loved ones of Kaxh Mura'l, at his old home en el departamento de Quiché in Guatemala. Ixil Maya leaders Feliciana Herrera Ceto, Miguel Ceto, Juan Velasco, and Francisco Marroquín shared with me their memories of living through the years of genocide and civil war in Guatemala or their aftermath. Historian Giovanni Batz, Guatemalan journalist Paolina Albani, and filmmaker Pamela Yates aided me in delving into that history.

Over four years, through a heated 2022 midterm and two presidential elections, I wrote on the road, in hotel rooms, coffee shops, and airports, at Trump rallies. Historians Julian Lim, Mae Ngai, Evelyn Hu-DeHart, Kelly Lytle Hernández, Erika Lee, Anna Louise Fahy, and Alexandra Minna Stern added rigor to my research and writing on the page. Journalists Marcela García, Marcela Valdes, Elizabeth Williamson, Stephanie Elizondo Griest, and Efrain Hernandez Jr. offered crucial writing advice, feedback on drafts, and boosted my morale during the most difficult of times. And helping me dig through worn books and archives were Claudia M. Ramirez, a library archivist at the El Paso Public Library; Claudia A. Rivers, the head of special collections at the University of Texas at El Paso library; Dani Thurber at the Library of Congress; and Barbara Rust, Jenny McMillen Sweeney, and all the other archivists at the National Archives in Fort Worth, Texas, and the National Archives in Washington, D.C.

In Ciudad Juárez, historian Daniel Leonardo García Salinas showed me around la Casa de Adobe, a museum replica of one of the squat adobe houses where Madero's revolucionarios camped out as they argued and debated over when to start la batalla de Juárez. It stood on brushland now only steps away from the thirty-foot steel bollards of the U.S.-Mexico border fence and had been established by El Paso and Juárez historians who, like Leonardo, had been working to resurrect a rich regional history often overlooked or forgotten, both by Mexico and the United States. José Roberto Fernández Muñoz took me on a walking tour of the streets of Juárez and the interior of the Museo de la Revolución en la Frontera (MUREF). César Martínez, a historian at el Museo de Arqueología e Historia de El Chamizal, led me to a life-size model of the large pit-house structures of adobe where the Mogollon Natives of Casas Grandes once lived. It is a place where you can crouch through the openings in the cliff dwelling, feel the coolness of the walls on a hot desert day, and consider: When did the border begin? What are its points of origin?

Farther south along the border, Trini directed me to critical primary and secondary sources, reports, and archival material. In Chihuahua, Chihuahua historian Juan Luis Longoria Granados educated me on the history of Nación N'dee/N'nee/Ndé; and in Mexico City, historian Rolando Guzmán walked me through the grounds of el Castillo de Chapultepec and was on hand years later to answer all my outstanding questions. In Texas, I have had great journalists to learn from, including Cecilia Ballí, Alfredo Corchado, and Angela Kocherga, along with my first journalism teacher, Pat Monroe at Burges High.

This work also would not have been possible without my editor at Dutton, John Parsley, or editors at *The Boston Globe*, Brian McGrory and Jim Puzzanghera. Brian and Jim offered me unyielding support as I covered the aftermath of the El Paso mass shooting, the pandemic and social unrest through the summer of 2020, and the siege at the U.S. Capitol on January 6, 2021. At *The New York Times*, I have followed in the steps of incredible Latino journalists and editors, including Jennifer Medina and Manny Fernandez, and have had the ongoing encouragement of David M. Halbfinger, Carolyn Ryan, and Marc Lacey.

The fact-checkers and researchers who made this book stronger include Chris Cameron, Eliza Fawcett, Nicol Roman, Bess Lovejoy, Autumn Baccellia, and Vianey Alderete Contreras. And the people who helped make me stronger along the way have been my friends and family: my mother, Laura, who first imparted on me her love of stories and history and was always up to take a trip with me; my dad and stepmom, Mauricio and Rebecca; my sisters, Bianca and Jade; my grandmother Alicia and my aunts Alica, Bertha, and Nora; my partner, Zack, and our dog, Rodolfo, mis hombres olvidados pero amados por siempre.

WORKS CITED

Prologue

BOOKS AND JOURNALS

Julian Lim, *Porous Borders: Multiracial Migrations and the Law in the U.S.-Mexico Borderlands* (University of North Carolina Press, 2017); W. H. Timmons, *El Paso: A Borderlands History* (Texas Western Press, 1990); Richard McSherry, *Essays and Lectures* (Kelly, Piet & Company, 1869); Clayton Anderson, *The Conquest of Texas* (University of Oklahoma Press, 2005); James Creelman, "President Díaz: Hero of the Americas," *Pearson's Magazine*, March 1908; María Isabel Sen Venero, *Historia de Chihuahua* (Centro Librero La Prensa, 1999).

INTERVIEWS

Julian Lim, historian at Johns Hopkins University, virtual interview by Jazmine Ulloa, January 17, 2023; Rolando Guzmán, historian at Castillo de Chapultepec in Mexico City, virtual interview by Jazmine Ulloa, August 25, 2022; David Dorado Romo, historian on El Paso history and borderland studies, interview by Jazmine Ulloa, El Paso, TX, July 14, 2022; Yolanda Chávez Leyva, professor of history and director of the Center for Inter-American and Border Studies (CIBS), interview by Jazmine Ulloa, El Paso, TX, March 8, 2021; Juan Luis Longoria Granados, historian and representative member of the Nación N'dee/N'nee/Ndé, interview by Jazmine Ulloa, August 5, 2022; César Martínez Berrouth, historian at Museo de

Arqueología e Historia de El Chamizal, virtual interview by Jazmine Ulloa, May 10, 2023.

News Articles and Other Media

Ryan Quint, "Mexican-American War 170th: The Storming of Chapultepec," *Emerging Civil War*, September 13, 2017, https://emergingcivilwar.com/2017/09/13/mexican-american-war-170th-the-storming-of-chapultepec/; Christopher Minster, "The Battle of Chapultepec in the Mexican-American War," ThoughtCo., August 24, 2018, thoughtco.com/the-battle-of-chapultepec-2136193; "Treaty of Guadalupe Hidalgo (1848)," National Archives, accessed July 16, 2023, https://www.archives.gov/milestone-documents/treaty-of-guadalupe-hidalgo.

PART ONE: REBELLION AND RESISTANCE

Chapter 1: Amazing Grace

The journey and rampage of the El Paso shooter was reconstructed using police and court records; interviews with witnesses, survivors, and the family members of victims; news clippings and videos of the bloody scenes; notes and recollections from my time covering the aftermath; and a trip to the killer's home in an upscale suburb of Dallas, TX.

Interviews

Adria Gonzalez, El Paso shooting survivor, interview by Jazmine Ulloa, El Paso, TX, July 27, 2020; Stephanie Melendez, El Paso shooting survivor, interview by Jazmine Ulloa, El Paso, TX, July 28, 2020; Gilbert Anchondo, family member of El Paso shooting victim, interview by Jazmine Ulloa, El Paso, TX, July 27, 2020; Tito Anchondo, family member of El Paso shooting victim, interview by Jazmine Ulloa, El Paso, TX, July 27, 2020; Armando Vela, photographer, *El Diario de El Paso*, interview by Jazmine Ulloa, El Paso, TX, July 25, 2020; Mark Lambie, photographer, *El Paso Times*, interview by Jazmine Ulloa, El Paso, TX, July 25, 2020.

News Articles and Videos

Simon Romero, Manny Fernandez, and Mariel Padilla, "Day at a Shopping Center in Texas Turns Deadly," *New York Times*, August 3, 2019, https://www.nytimes.com/2019/08/03/us/el-paso-walmart-shooting.html; Alfredo Corchado, Lavendrick Smith, and Loyd Brumfield, "'So Many Bodies,'" *Dallas Morning News*,

August 4, 2019; Simon Romero, Manny Fernandez, and Mariel Padilla, "20 Are Killed in Shooting in El Paso," *New York Times*, August 4, 2019, https://www.nytimes.com/2019/08/03/us/el-paso-shooting-walmart.html; Molly Hennessy-Fiske and Jeffrey Fleishman, "20 Killed in El Paso Shooting. At Least 26 Others Are Wounded in Massacre at Shopping Center. Suspect to Be Charged with Hate Crime," *Los Angeles Times*, August 4, 2019, https://www.latimes.com/world-nation/story/2019-08-03/el-paso-texas-reports-of-shooting; Dakin Andone, Hollie Silverman, and Nicole Chavez, "20 People Killed in El Paso Shooting, Texas Governor Says," CNN Wire, August 4, 2019, https://www.cnn.com/2019/08/03/us/el-paso-shooting; Molly Smith and Aaron Montes, "Families Reunite, Wait for News after Shooting," *El Paso Times*, August 4, 2019; Rosa Flores and Chelsea J. Carter, "Family and Friends Gather to Wait for News of Missing Loved Ones in the El Paso Shooting," CNN, August 4, 2019, https://www.cnn.com/2019/08/04/us/el-paso-reunification-center-scene; Nellie Bowles, "'Replacement Theory,' a Racist, Sexist Doctrine, Spreads in Far-Right Circles," *New York Times*, March 18, 2019, https://www.nytimes.com/2019/03/18/technology/replacement-theory.html; "Video Shows Victims Lying in Walmart Parking Lot," CNN, August 3, 2019, https://www.cnn.com/videos/us/2019/08/03/el-paso-texas-shooting-outside-graphic-walmart-vpx.cnn; "Video Shows Man Hiding as Shots Ring Out Inside Walmart," CNN, August 4, 2019, https://www.cnn.com/videos/us/2019/08/04/el-paso-texas-shots-fired-inside-walmart-bts-nr-vpx.cnn; "El Paso Shooting: Several Killed as Gunman Opens Fire in Texas Walmart," *Telegraph*, August 3, 2019, https://www.youtube.com/watch?v=15vNhuHp8t4; "El Paso, Texas, Shooting: Witness Videos Capture Terrifying Scene," *NBC News*, August 3, 2019, https://www.youtube.com/watch?v=E1UTfMCjwGA.

Court Records

El Paso Police Department, Complaint Affidavit, August 3, 2019, No. EP-20-CR-389-DCG, U.S. District Court for the Western District of Texas, El Paso Division, Indictment, February 6, 2020; No. EP-20-CR-389-DCG, U.S. District Court for the Western District of Texas, El Paso Division, Plea Hearing, February 8, 2023; No. EP-20-CR-389-DCG, U.S. District Court for the Western District of Texas, El Paso Division, Sentencing, July 6–7, 2023.

Chapter 2: The Most Dangerous Girl in Mexico

The rich Chinese history of El Paso was one often left untold. But prominent Chinese American scholars and community leaders like the Chew family have worked for years to capture and preserve it. This chapter was written based on interviews with members of the Chew family and historians in Chinese American and Mexican American studies and border history as well as a review of more than a dozen books, journals, and news articles.

Books and Journals

Mexican Revolution, La Santa, and Battle of Tomóchi: Friedrich Katz, *The Life and Times of Pancho Villa* (Stanford University Press, 1998); David Dorado Romo, *Ringside Seat to a Revolution: An Underground Cultural History of El Paso and Juárez, 1893–1923* (Cinco Puntos Press, 2005); Paul J. Vanderwood, *The Power of God Against the Guns of Government: Religious Upheaval in Mexico at the Turn of the Nineteenth Century* (Stanford University Press, 1998); John Womack, *Zapata and the Mexican Revolution* (Vintage Books, 1970); James S. Griffith, *Folk Saints of the Borderlands: Victims, Bandits, and Healers* (Rio Nuevo Publishers, 2003); Alexandra Minna Stern, *Eugenic Nation: Faults and Frontiers of Better Breeding in Modern America* (University of California Press, 2005); Francisco R. Almada, *La rebelión de Tomochi* (Sociedad Chihuahuense de Estudios Históricos, 1938); Liliana Illades Aguilar, *La rebelión de Tomochi* (Instituto Nacional de Antropología e Historia, 1993).

El Paso History: Oscar J. Martínez, *Border Boom Town: Ciudad Juárez Since 1848* (University of Texas Press, 1978); Julian Lim, *Porous Borders: Multiracial Migrations and the Law in the U.S.-Mexico Borderlands* (University of North Carolina Press, 2017); W. H. Timmons, *El Paso: A Borderlands History* (Texas Western Press, 1990); "Locomotive 'Dumfounding': E.P. Celebrated Coming of Rails, Southern Pacific Officials Honored with Salute, Speeches, Banquet, Grand Ball," *El Paso Herald-Post*, April 28, 1956.

Chinese American History: Evelyn Hu-DeHart, "Immigrants to a Developing Society: The Chinese in Northern Mexico, 1875–1932," *Journal of Arizona History* 21, no. 3 (1980); Anna Louise Fahy, "Chinese Borderland Community Development: A Case Study of El Paso, 1881–1909" (master's thesis, University of Texas at El Paso, 2001); Irwin A. Tang, ed., *Asian Texans: Our Histories and Our Lives* (The It Works, 2008); Nancy Ellen Farrar, *The Chinese in El Paso*, Southwestern Studies Monograph no. 33 (Texas Western Press, 1972); Marvin Charles Bendele Jr., "Food, Space, and Mobility: The Railroad, Chili Stands, and Chophouses in San Antonio and El Paso, 1870–1905" (master's thesis, University of Texas at San Antonio, 2003); Edward Staski, *Beneath the Border City*, vol. 2: *The Overseas Chinese in El Paso*, Occasional Paper no. 2 (New Mexico State University, 1985).

Interviews

Josephine Wong, Grace Got, and Herlinda Leong, interview by Richard Estrada, July 28, 1978, interview no. 257, transcript, Institute of Oral History, University of Texas at El Paso, El Paso, TX, https://scholarworks.utep.edu/interviews/257/; Linda Lee Chew, David Chew, Chew family members, interview by Jazmine Ulloa, El Paso, TX, June 9, 2023; Anna Louise Fahy, retired lecturer and adjunct professor at El Paso Community College, phone interview by Jazmine Ulloa, January 30, 2021; Evelyn Hu-DeHart, professor of history and American studies at Brown University, interview by Jazmine Ulloa, January 20, 2023; Julian Lim, historian at Johns Hopkins University, interview by Jazmine Ulloa, January 17, 2023; Daniel Leonardo García Salinas, Ciudad Juárez historian, interview by Jazmine Ulloa, Ciudad Juárez August 21, 2022; Rolando Guzmán, historian at Castillo de Chapultepec in Mexico City, interview by Jazmine Ulloa, August 25, 2022.

News Articles and Videos

El Paso Times Editorial Board, "Editorial: El Paso's Black History," *El Paso Times*, February 4, 2017, https://www.elpasotimes.com/story/opinion/editorials/2017/02/04/editorial-el-pasos-black-history/97499756/; Lakshmi Gandhi, "A History of Indentured Labor Gives 'Coolie' Its Sting," *Code Switch*, NPR, November 25, 2013, https://www.npr.org/sections/codeswitch/2013/11/25/247166284/a-history-of-indentured-labor-gives-coolie-its-sting; Olivia B. Waxman and Paulina Cachero, "11 Moments From Asian American History That You Should Know," *Time*, April 30, 2021, https://time.com/5956943/aapi-history-milestones/; El Paso Community College, "History of El Paso," EPCC Library Research Guides, accessed May 8, 2023, https://epcc.libguides.com/c.php?g=754275&p=5406009.

Chapter 3: Revolt in the Borderland

Depending on the teller's perspective, El Paso and Juárez sit either at the center of American and Mexican history or at the margins. For this reason, it was important to craft this chapter with the help of sources who have viewed the border from the north, the south, and within. A lot has also been written about los magonistas. But their legacy doesn't give itself up easily: Buried in myth, contradiction, and debate, they are seen as far-left extremists by some and a force for the working class and collective good by others. This chapter seeks to unravel their stories and the seeds they planted for the Mexican Revolution through interviews with members of the Reyes family and academics in Mexican and Mexican American studies and border history; a review of books, journals, and news articles; and dives through materials and archives at the University of Berkeley, the MUREF, the Library of Congress, the National Archives, and the National Archives at Fort Worth, TX.

Books and Journals

Kelly Lytle Hernández, *Bad Mexicans: Race, Empire, and Revolution in the Borderlands* (W. W. Norton, 2022); Kelly Lytle Hernández, *City of Inmates: Conquest, Rebellion, and the Rise of Human Caging in Los Angeles 1771–1965* (University of North Carolina Press, February 2017); Charles H. Harris III and Louis R. Sadler, *The Secret War in El Paso: Mexican Revolutionary Intrigue, 1906–1920* (University of New Mexico Press, 2009); Friedrich Katz, *The Life and Times of Pancho Villa* (Stanford University Press, 1998); David Dorado Romo, *Ringside Seat to a Revolution: An Underground Cultural History of El Paso and Juárez, 1893–1923* (Cinco Puntos Press, 2005); John Womack, *Zapata and the Mexican Revolution* (Vintage Books, 1970); Paul J. Vanderwood, *The Power of God Against the Guns of Government: Religious Upheaval in Mexico at the Turn of the Nineteenth Century* (Stanford University Press, 1998); Mario T. García, *Desert Immigrants: The Mexicans of El Paso, 1880–1920* (Yale University Press, 1981); Julian Lim, *Porous Borders: Multiracial Migrations and the Law in the U.S.-Mexico Borderlands* (University of North Carolina Press, 2017); Irwin A. Tang, ed., *Asian Texans: Our Histories and Our Lives* (The It Works, 2008); Anna Louise Fahy, "Chinese Borderland Community Development: A Case Study of El Paso, 1881–1909" (master's thesis, University of Texas at El Paso, 2001); Juan Gómez-Quiñones, *Sembradores: Ricardo Flores Magón y el Partido Liberal Mexicano* (Chicano Studies Research Center, 1973); Justin Akers Chacón, *Radicals in the Barrio: Magonistas, Socialists, Wobblies, and Communists in the Mexican American Working Class* (Haymarket Books, 2018); Oscar J. Martínez, *Border Boom Town: Ciudad Juárez Since 1848* (University of Texas Press, 1978); Ricardo Flores Magón, *Dreams of Freedom: A Ricardo Flores Magón Reader*, ed. Chaz Bufe and Mitchell Cowen Verter (AK Press, 2005); Alan Knight, *The Mexican Revolution, vol. 1, Porfirians, Liberals, and Peasants* (University of Nebraska Press, 1990).

Interviews

Chester Chope, interview by Wilma Cleveland, July 26, 1968, interview no. 27, transcript, Institute of Oral History, University of Texas at El Paso, El Paso, TX; Margarita Reyes and Raúl Reyes, Martinez family members, interview by Jazmine Ulloa, El Paso, TX, May 12, 2023; Kelly Lytle Hernández, professor of history and holder of the Thomas E. Lifka Endowed Chair, UCLA, Zoom interview by

Jazmine Ulloa, December 20, 2022; Roberto Fernández, historian at Museo de la Revolución en la Frontera (MUREF), interview by Jazmine Ulloa, El Paso, TX, May 10, 2023; Daniel Leonardo García Salinas, Ciudad Juárez historian, interview by Jazmine Ulloa, August 21, 2022; César Martínez Berrouth, historian at Museo de Arqueología e Historia de El Chamizal, interview by Jazmine Ulloa, El Paso, TX, May 10, 2023; Miguel Ángel Berumen, historian and iconographic investigator in Mexican culture, interview by Jazmine Ulloa, May 10, 2023; José Roberto Fernández Muñoz, historian at MUREF, Ciudad Juárez, interview by Jazmine Ulloa, Ciudad Juárez, May 10, 2023; David Dorado Romo, historian on El Paso history and borderland studies, interview by Jazmine Ulloa, El Paso, TX, July 14, 2022; Yolanda Chávez Leyva, professor of history and director of the Center for Inter-American and Border Studies (CIBS), interview by Jazmine Ulloa, El Paso, TX, March 8, 2021.

News Articles and Videos

James Creelman, "President Díaz: Hero of the Americas," *Pearson's Magazine*, March 1908; Jose Maria Herrera, "Lauro Aguirre: Mexican Dissident and Revolutionary Journalist," TSHA: Texas State Historical Association, October 18, 2016, updated February 3, 2017, accessed May 9, 2025, https://www.tshaonline.org/handbook/entries/aguirre-lauro; Lauren Villagran, "Before Flint, Before East Chicago, There Was Smeltertown," Natural Resources Defense Council, November 29, 2016, https://www.nrdc.org/stories/flint-east-chicago-there-was-smeltertown; Ruta Magón, "El Paso, Texas: Goodman House. 7 3rd St.," Archivo Magón, accessed May 9, 2025, https://archivomagon.net/en/ruta-magon/el-paso-texas-7-3rd-st/.

Library Materials and Archival Records

Enrique Creel, Letter to Ministro Don Ramón Corral, October 6, 1906, Silvestre Terrazas Papers, Box 26, Folder 7A, Online Archive of California, University of California, Berkeley; Ramón Corral, Letter to Chihuahua governor Enrique Creel, October 2, 1906, Silvestre Terrazas Papers, Box 26, Folder 7A, Online Archive of California, University of California, Berkeley; Lauro Aguirre, Letter to Sr. Antonio J. Villarreal, June 29, 1906, Silvestre Terrazas Papers, Box 27, Folder 13A, Online Archive of California, University of California, Berkeley; U.S. District Courts, Western District of Texas, El Paso Criminal Case Files, Cases of Magonistas, RG 21, Box 49, 1354–1377, National Archives and Records Administration, Fort Worth, TX.

Chapter 4: Pancho Villa's Teen Soldier

Hilario, Ylario, or Elario Martinez. Victoria Martinez's father spelled his name many ways and his family is not sure which one is correct, but this book uses the name as listed on his border crossing cards and his death certificate. It traces the young man's recruitment into the Mexican Revolution and the Mexican men at its center through interviews with his relatives and historians; seminal works on Pancho Villa and the Mexican Revolution in both English and Spanish; mining journals; and visits to some of the most prominent revolutionary sites in San Juanito Escobedo and Guadalajara, Jalisco, and Santa Eulalia and Ciudad Juárez, Chihuahua.

Books and Journals

Pancho Villa: Friedrich Katz, *The Life and Times of Pancho Villa* (Stanford University Press, 1998); Martín Luis Guzmán, *Memoirs of Pancho Villa*, trans. Virginia H. Taylor (University of Texas Press, 1965); Paco Ignacio Taibo II, *Pancho Villa: A Revolutionary Life*, trans. Todd Chretien (Seven Stories Press, 2024); Kelly Lytle Hernández, *Bad Mexicans: Race, Empire, and Revolution in the Borderlands* (W. W. Norton, 2022); Liliana Illades Aguilar, *La rebelión de Tomochi* (Instituto Nacional de Antropología e Historia, 1993); María Isabel Sen Venero, *Historia de Chihuahua* (Centro Librero La Prensa, 1999); Paul J. Vanderwood and Frank N. Samponaro, *Border Fury: A Picture Postcard Record of Mexico's Revolution and U.S. War Preparedness, 1910–1917* (University of New Mexico Press, 1988).

El Paso: Mario T. García, *Desert Immigrants: The Mexicans of El Paso, 1880–1920* (Yale University Press, 1981); Francisco E. Balderrama and Raymond Rodríguez, *Decade of Betrayal: Mexican Repatriation in the 1930s* (University of New Mexico Press, 2006); Evelyn Hu-DeHart, "Immigrants to a Developing Society: The Chinese in Northern Mexico, 1875–1932," *Journal of Arizona History* 21, no. 3 (1980); Anna Louise Fahy, "Chinese Borderland Community Development: A Case Study of El Paso, 1881–1909" (master's thesis, University of Texas at El Paso, 2001); Mel Brown, *Chinese Heart of Texas: The San Antonio Community, 1875 to 1975* (Lily on the Water, 2005); Robert Chao Romero, *The Chinese in Mexico, 1882–1940* (University of Arizona Press, 2010); J. Walter Fewkes, "The Pueblo Settlements near El Paso, Texas," *American Anthropologist* 4, no. 1 (1902), http://www.jstor.org/stable/658929; "El Paso Missions," Texas Beyond History, https://www.texasbeyondhistory.net/paso/history.html; Ricardo Quezada, "The Founding of Ysleta del Sur Pueblo and the 1681 Forced Migration from Isleta, New Mexico, to El Paso, Texas" (master's thesis, Ysleta Del Sur Pueblo, 2022).

Interviews

Alicia Martinez, my family member, interview by Jazmine Ulloa, El Paso, TX, March 7, 2021; Jorge Seyffert Terrazas, descendant of the prominent Terrazas family, interview by Jazmine Ulloa, Ciudad Chihuahua, MX, June 8, 2022; María Luisa Terrazas de Seyffert, descendant of the prominent Terrazas family, interview by Jazmine Ulloa, Ciudad Chihuahua, MX, June 9, 2022; Got Wong and Leong Wong, interview by Richard Estrada, July 28, 1978; Chew and Chew, interview, June 9, 2023; Reyes and Reyes, interview, May 12, 2023; Raúl Reyes, interviews by Jazmine Ulloa, El Paso, TX, December 16 and 29, 2020, March 4 and May 8, 2021, and January 1, 2023; Oscar Martinez Jr., interview by Jazmine Ulloa, El Paso, TX, May 12, 2023; Robert Romero, Martinez family member, interview by Jazmine Ulloa, El Paso, TX, June 11, 2022; Miguel Martinez Jr, interview originally conducted by a nephew of Raúl Reyes in 2008, recorded by Raúl Reyes on January 1, 2021; Jeffrey P. Shepherd, interview by Jazmine Ulloa, El Paso, TX, May 12, 2023; Ricardo Quezada, interview by Jazmine Ulloa, El Paso, TX, May 11, 2023; Granados, interview by Jazmine Ulloa, August 5, 2022; Miguel Jaramillo, former president of Santa Eulalia (1992–95), interview by Jazmine Ulloa, Santa Eulalia, Chihuahua, MX, June 10, 2022.

News Articles and Other Materials

Lucinda Ann Bowers, Lorena Hernandez, Bianca Lopez, and Julio Magallanes, "The Chew Legacy: The Story of Herlinda Wong Chew," El Paso Community College Library Research Guides, accessed May 9, 2025, https://epcc.libguides.com/c.php?g=754275&p=6256034; Mykah Jones, "Herlinda Wong Chew: Pioneer Businesswoman and Immigration Specialist," TSHA: Texas State Historical Association, January 21, 2020, https://www.tshaonline.org/handbook/entries/chew-herlinda-wong; Lydiette Carrión, "Apaches: Alive and Well in 21st Century Mexico," Pie de Página, February 17, 2021, https://piedepagina.mx/apaches-alive-and-well-in-20th-century-mexico/; "Rioters Made Southern Mexico Now Veritable Hotbed for the Bloody Revolution Raging in That Republic," *El Paso Morning Times*, November 23, 1910.

Chapter 5: The Year of the Hunger

The legacy of Pancho Villa—like that of the magonistas—is layered and fiercely debated. This chapter captures the search for the bandit turned revolucionario through interviews with historians on both sides of the border and the review of hundreds of cables among officers, generals, and military operatives preserved at the National Archives and Records Administration.

Books and Journals

Mel Brown, *Chinese Heart of Texas: The San Antonio Community, 1875 to 1975* (Lily on the Water, 2005); Paul J. Vanderwood and Frank N. Samponaro, *Border Fury: A Picture Postcard Record of Mexico's Revolution and U.S. War Preparedness, 1910–1917* (University of New Mexico Press, 1988); Kelly Lytle Hernández, *Migra!: A History of the U.S. Border Patrol* (University of California Press, 2010); Miguel Antonio Levario, *Militarizing the Border: When Mexicans Became the Enemy* (Texas A&M University Press, 2012); Bill Broyles and Mark Haynes, *Desert Duty: On the Line with the U.S. Border Patrol* (University of Texas Press, 2009); James Dupree, "Defining America at the Border: The Line Riders of the Mexican Border District, 1892–1924" (PhD diss., University of Oklahoma, 2019), https://shareok.org/handle/11244/319753.

Interviews

Chew and Chew, interview, June 9, 2023; James Dupree, interview by Jazmine Ulloa, El Paso, TX, June 22, 2023; Hu-DeHart, interview, January 20, 2023; Romo, interview, July 14, 2022; Martinez Jr., interview recorded by Reyes, January 1, 2021; Martinez, interview, May 12, 2023.

News Articles and Other Materials

Michael C. Meyer, "Felix Sommerfeld and the Columbus Raid of 1916," *Arizona and the West* 25, no. 3 (1983): 213–28, http://www.jstor.org/stable/40169228; Richard W. Slatta, "Timeline of the Mexican Revolution," North Carolina State University, accessed May 9, 2025, https://faculty.chass.ncsu.edu/slatta/hi216/documents/mexrevtime.htm; Bruce J. Dinges, "Henry Ossian Flipper: The First Black Graduate of West Point," TSHA: Texas State Historical Association, 1976, updated October 22, 2020, accessed May 9, 2025, https://www.tshaonline.org/handbook/entries/flipper-henry-ossian; W. Dirk Raat, "Ricardo Flores Magón: The Life and Legacy of a Revolutionary Journalist," TSHA: Texas State Historical Association, September 1, 1995, updated August 2, 2020, accessed May 9, 2025, https://www.tshaonline.org/handbook/entries/flores-magon-ricardo; "Pancho Villa Must Die," *Concordia Blade-Empire*, March 10, 1916, https://www.newspapers.com/image/93572738.

Library Materials and Archival Records

"Testimony of Col. Slocum's Wife on Columbus Raid," Hugh Lenox Scott Papers, Library of Congress; "Office of the Adjutant General Document File, Mexican Border, 2377632 (2379210–2381321)," Boxes 6807, 7645, 7646, 8128, and 8129, National Archives and Records Administration, Washington, D.C.

Chapter 6: Of Lice and Villistas

It was historians Alexandra Minna Stern and David Dorado Romo who first brought the story of Carmelita Torres to light. This chapter is largely based on interviews with them and their findings, along with a review of books, journals, and newspaper articles from the time.

Books and Journals

Mario T. García, *Desert Immigrants: The Mexicans of El Paso, 1880–1920* (Yale University Press, 1981); Kelly Lytle Hernández, *Migra!: A History of the U.S. Border Patrol* (University of California Press, 2010); Reece Jones, *White Borders: The History of Race and Immigration in the United States from Chinese Exclusion to the Border Wall* (Beacon Press, 2021); Jeffrey Marcos Garcílazo, *Traqueros: Mexican Railroad Workers in the United States, 1870–1930*, Al Filo: Mexican American Studies Series, vol. 6 (University of North Texas Press, 2012); John Raymond Mckiernan-González, *Fevered Measures: Public Health and Race at the Texas-Mexico Border, 1848–1942* (Duke University Press, August 2012); Alexandra Minna Stern, *Eugenic Nation: Faults and Frontiers of Better Breeding in Modern America* (University of California Press, 2005); Alexandra Minna Stern, "Buildings, Boundaries, and Blood: Medicalization and Nation-Building on the U.S.-Mexico Border, 1910–1930," *Hispanic American Historical Review* 79, no. 1 (February 1999): 41–81; Linda B. Hall and Don M. Coerver, "La Frontera y las Minas en la Revolución Mexicana (1910–1920)," *Historia Mexicana* 32, no. 3 (January–March 1983): 389–421; Miguel Antonio Levario, *Militarizing the Border: When Mexicans Became the Enemy* (Texas A&M University Press, 2015); Michael A. Schoeppner, *Moral Contagion: Black Atlantic Sailors, Citizenship, and Diplomacy in Antebellum America* (Cambridge University Press, 2019).

INTERVIEWS

Alexandra Minna Stern, phone interview by Jazmine Ulloa, February 15, 2021; Romo, interview, July 14, 2022; Reyes, interviews, 2020–2023; Chávez Leyva, interview, March 8, 2021.

NEWS ARTICLES AND VIDEOS

Vox, *The Dark History of "Gasoline Baths" at the Border*, video, 15 min., 2017, https://www.vox.com/2019/7/29/8934848/gasoline-baths-border-mexico-dark-history; "Bath Rioting Renewed at Santa Fe Bridge," *El Paso Morning Times*, January 30, 1917; "La cuarentena es causa de un motín en Ciudad Juárez," *El Paso Times, Edición en Español*, January 29, 1917; "Dr. U. S. Bathes 929 Mexicans! And All Survive: No Repetition of . . . ," *Chicago Daily Tribune*, January 31, 1917, p. 12; "Health of City is Endangered," *El Paso Morning Times*, January 27, 1903, p. 1; "Order to Bathe Starts Near Riot Among Juarez Women: Auburn-Haired Amazon at Santa Fe Street Bridge Leads Feminine Outbreak," *El Paso Morning Times*, January 29, 1917; "Mexican Amazons Injure 2 Soldiers in Bridge Rush," *New-York Tribune*, January 30, 1917; "Simply Adobe: Architecture Emerges from the Landscape as Naturally as Ocotillo and Agave," *Texas Highways*, August 23, 2022, https://texashighways.com/travel-news/simply-adobe-architecture/; "El Paso Border Practices Influence the Holocaust," The Texas Story Project, Bullock Museum, April 6, 2018, https://www.thestoryoftexas.com/discover/texas-story-project/el-paso-holocaust-influence.

Chapter 7: All Mexicans Must Go

BOOKS AND JOURNALS

Mel Brown, *Chinese Heart of Texas: The San Antonio Community, 1875 to 1975* (Lily on the Water, 2005); Monica Muñoz Martinez, *The Injustice Never Leaves You: Anti-Mexican Violence in Texas* (Harvard University Press, 2018); Reece Jones, *White Borders: The History of Race and Immigration in the United States from Chinese Exclusion to the Border Wall* (Beacon Press, 2021); Mae M. Ngai, *Impossible Subjects: Illegal Aliens and the Making of Modern America* (Princeton University Press, 2004); Francisco E. Balderrama and Raymond Rodríguez, *Decade of Betrayal: Mexican Repatriation in the 1930s* (University of New Mexico Press, 2006).

Interviews

Wong and Wong, interview by Estrada, July 28, 1978; Chew and Chew, interview, June 9, 2023; Dupree, interview, June 22, 2023; Hu-DeHart, interview, January 20, 2023; Reyes, interviews, 2020–2023; Martinez Jr., interview recorded by Reyes, January 1, 2021; Martinez, interview, May 12, 2023.

News Articles and Other Materials

Pedro Siller Vázquez, "Benito Juárez se refugia en Paso del Norte," Relatos e Historias en México, August 14, 2023, https://relatosehistorias.mx/nuestras-historias/benito-juarez-se-refugia-en-paso-del-norte; "Cuando Benito Juárez gobernó desde Paso del Norte," *La Verdad Juárez*, December 27, 2020, https://laverdadjuarez.com/2020/12/27/cuando-benito-juarez-goberno-desde-paso-del-norte/; Diane Bernard, "The Time a President Deported 1 Million Mexican Americans for Supposedly Stealing U.S. Jobs," *Washington Post*, August 13, 2018, https://www.washingtonpost.com/news/retropolis/wp/2018/08/13/the-time-a-president-deported-1-million-mexican-americans-for-stealing-u-s-jobs/; Jasmine Aguilera, "Why U.S. Citizens Were Deported to Mexico in the 1930s," *Time*, August 2, 2019, https://time.com/5638586/us-citizens-deportation-raids/; "Health of a City Is Endangered," *El Paso Times*, January 27, 1903, accessed April 24, 2025, https://www.newspapers.com/image/429195825/; Julia Young, "How Mexican Immigration to the U.S. Has Evolved," *Time*, March 12, 2015, https://time.com/3742067/history-mexican-immigration/. (Note: This article, in collaboration with the John W. Kluge Center at the Library of Congress, delves into the history of Mexican immigration to the United States, highlighting key periods such as the late nineteenth century, the Mexican Revolution, and the 1920s.)

Court and Archival Records

Brief for Professors Kelly Lytle Hernández, Mae Ngai, and Ingrid Eagly as Amici Curiae Supporting Respondent, *United States v. Palomar-Santiago*, no. 20-437, Supreme Court of the United States, 2021, https://www.oyez.org/cases/2020/20-437; Herlinda Wong Chew, Letters to Sturgis, August 5, 1927, to June 2, 1934, Chew Family Records; National Archives at Riverside, Record Group 85, Records of the Immigration and Naturalization Service, District 16 (Los Angeles), Calexico Substation, Series: Chinese Exclusion Act Case Files, 1893–1981 (NAID 5831059), folder titled "4407/17 Yee Wing Chew and Family," Box 8.

Chapter 8: The Search for Victoria

Books and Journals

Francisco E. Balderrama and Raymond Rodríguez, *Decade of Betrayal: Mexican Repatriation in the 1930s* (University of New Mexico Press, 2006); Anna Louise Fahy, "Chinese Borderland Community Development: A Case Study of El Paso, 1881–1909" (master's thesis, University of Texas at El Paso, 2001); Evelyn Hu-DeHart, "Immigrants to a Developing Society: The Chinese in Northern Mexico, 1875–1932," *Journal of Arizona History* 21, no. 3 (1980): 275–312, http://www.jstor.org/stable/42678263; Edward J. M. Rhoads, "The Chinese in Texas," *Southwestern Historical Quarterly* 81, no. 1 (July 1977), https://www.jstor.org/stable/30238491; Howard Campbell and Michael Williams, "Black Barrio on the Border: 'Blaxicans' of Ciudad Juárez, Mexico," *Journal of Borderlands Studies* 35, no. 1 (2020): 147–61, https://doi.org/10.1080/08865655.2018.1530130.

Government Records and Other Materials

Repatriation Certificate for Miguel Martinez, Mexican Consulate, Presidio, Texas, March 31, 1931, copy in possession of Raúl Reyes, El Paso, TX; U.S. Commissioner's Notes, 1908, RG 21, Box 4, National Archives and Records Administration, Fort Worth, TX; U.S. District Courts, Western District of Texas, El Paso Criminal Case Files, sworn statement by Yee Gong, September 11, 1912, RG 21, Box 49_1583, National Archives and Records Administration, Fort Worth, TX; Mykah Jones, "Herlinda Wong Chew: Pioneer Businesswoman and Immigration Specialist," TSHA: Texas State Historical Association, January 21, 2020, accessed May 9, 2025, https://www.tshaonline.org/handbook/entries/chew-herlinda-wong; Lucinda Ann Bowers, Lorena Hernandez, Bianca Lopez, and Julio Magallanes, "The Chew Legacy: The Story of Herlinda Wong Chew," El Paso Community College Library Research Guides, accessed May 9, 2025, https://epcc.libguides.com/c.php?g=754275&p=5406009.

PART TWO: THE BUSINESS OF DRUGS AND WAR

Chapter Nine: Homegrown Terror

See chapter 1.

NEWS ARTICLES AND VIDEOS

See chapter 1; Jolie McCullough, "El Paso Shooting Suspect Said He Ordered His AK-47 and Ammo from Overseas," *Texas Tribune*, August 28, 2019, https://www.texastribune.org/2019/08/28/el-paso-shooting-gun-romania/; "4 Years Later Remembering 23 Victims of El Paso Mass Shooting," *People*, August 3, 2023, https://people.com/crime/el-paso-mass-shooting-remembering-victims-2-year-later/; "Remembering Those We Lost on Aug. 3, 2019," *Border Report*, August 3, 2023, https://www.borderreport.com/hot-topics/el-paso-strong/remembering-those-we-lost-on-aug-3-2019/; Mónica Ortiz Uribe, "Remembering Elsa Mendoza Marquez," NPR, August 8, 2019, https://www.npr.org/2019/08/08/749303269/remembering-elsa-mendoza-marquez; "List of Victims from El Paso Shooting," KFOX14, August 5, 2019, https://kfoxtv.com/news/local/list-of-victims-from-el-paso-shooting; "Who Were the Victims of the El Paso Shooting?," *Washington Post*, August 8, 2019, https://www.washingtonpost.com/nation/2019/08/04/el-paso-shooting-victims/; "Ellos son los mexicanos fallecidos en el ataque de El Paso, Texas," Expansión Política, August 5, 2019, https://politica.expansion.mx/mexico/2019/08/05/ellos-son-los-mexicanos-fallecidos-en-el-ataque-de-el-paso-texas; Kate Taylor and Jose A. Del Real, "Who Were the Victims of the El Paso Shooting?," *New York Times*, August 4, 2019, https://www.nytimes.com/2019/08/04/us/el-paso-shooting-victims.html; Nicole Chavez, Sophie Sherry, and Christina Zdanowicz, "A Walmart Employee and a Customer Helped 140 People Escape from the El Paso Shooting," CNN, August 5, 2019, https://www.cnn.com/2019/08/05/us/el-paso-shooting-heroes/index.html; Matthew Cox, "Former Army Hawk Missile Crewman Killed in El Paso Mass Shooting," Military.com, August 6, 2019, https://www.military.com/daily-news/2019/08/06/former-army-hawk-missile-crewman-killed-el-paso-mass-shooting.html; Jamie Stengle and Astrid Galvan, "Families Struggling to Cope after Mass Shootings," AP News, August 4, 2019, https://apnews.com/article/1aa03c4a153f4f6d9881f0f11cd2c89a; Daniel Borunda and Briana Sanchez, "El Paso Walmart Shooting Victim Guillermo 'Memo' Garcia Mourned," *El Paso Times*, May 16, 2020, https://www.elpasotimes.com/story/news/local/community/2020/05/16/el-paso-walmart-shooting-victim-guillermo-memo-garcia-mourned/5188180002/; Adam Goldman, Katie Benner, and Zolan Kanno-Youngs, "How Trump's Focus on Antifa Distracted Attention from the Far-Right Threat," *New York Times*, January 30, 2021, https://www.nytimes.com/2021/01/30/us/politics/trump-right-wing-domestic-terrorism.html; Faiza Patel and Adrienne Tierney, "The Reasons Why Dylann Roof Wasn't Charged with Terrorism," Brennan Center for Justice, July 30, 2015, https://www.brennancenter.org/our-work/analysis-opinion/reasons-why-dylann-roof-wasnt-charged-terrorism; Tim Arango, Nicholas Bogel-Burroughs, and Katie Benner,

"Minutes Before El Paso Killing, Hate-Filled Manifesto Appears Online," *New York Times*, August 3, 2019, https://www.nytimes.com/2019/08/03/us/patrick-crusius-el-paso-shooter-manifesto.html; Marcy Oster, "A Year After Poway Shooting, Synagogue Remembers Victim Who 'Helped All People,'" *Times of Israel*, April 28, 2020, https://www.timesofisrael.com/1-year-after-poway-shooting-synagogue-remembers-victim-who-helped-all-people/; Simon Romero and Nicholas Bogel-Burroughs, "El Paso Shooting: Massacre That Killed 20 Being Investigated as Domestic Terrorism," *New York Times*, August 4, 2019, https://www.nytimes.com/2019/08/04/us/el-paso-shooting-updates.html.

Chapter 10: The Silence in Chuco Town

Books and Journals

Oscar J. Martínez, *Border Boom Town: Ciudad Juárez Since 1848* (University of Texas Press, 1978); Mae M. Ngai, *Impossible Subjects: Illegal Aliens and the Making of Modern America* (Princeton University Press, 2004); Aviva Chomsky, *Central America's Forgotten History: Revolution, Violence, and the Roots of Migration* (Beacon Press, 2021); Lidia G. Sandoval R. and Leticia Peña B., *Historia del cabaret y vida nocturna como transformadores de la identidad cultural en el centro de Ciudad Juárez, Chihuahua, México* (master's thesis, Benemérita Universidad Autónoma de Puebla, 2010), http://www.rniu.buap.mx/enc/pdf/xxxiii_m4_sandovalr.pdf; Drewey Wayne Gunn, *American and British Writers in Mexico, 1556–1973* (University of Texas Press, 1974); Miguel Ángel Chávez Díaz de León, "Juárez, Hemingway y Dominguín," *Hilo Directo*, January 25, 2013, http://hilodirecto.com.mx/juarez-hemingway-y-dominguin/; Howard Campbell and Michael Williams, "Black Barrio on the Border: 'Blaxicans' of Ciudad Juárez, Mexico," *Journal of Borderlands Studies* 35, no. 1 (2020): 147–61, https://doi.org/10.1080/08865655.2018.1530130.

Interviews

Howard Campbell, professor of cultural anthropology at the University of Texas at El Paso, phone interview by Jazmine Ulloa, July 27, 2022; Reyes, interviews, 2020–2023; Margie Martinez and Bertha Martinez, Reyes family members, interviews by Jazmine Ulloa, El Paso, March 4 and 8, 2021; Carmen Durán, Reyes family member, interview by Jazmine Ulloa, El Paso, TX, June 11, 2022; Letty Martinez, Reyes family member, interview by Jazmine Ulloa, El Paso, TX, June 11, 2022; Oscar Martinez Jr., interview by Jazmine Ulloa, El Paso, TX, May 12, 2023; Robert Romero, Martinez family member, interview by Jazmine Ulloa, El Paso, June 11, 2022.

News Articles and Other Materials

Trish Long, "How to Tell if Someone Is from El Chuco," *El Paso Times*, October 6, 2024, https://www.elpasotimes.com/story/news/history/2024/10/06/how-to-tell-if-someone-is-from-el-chuco-trish-long-el-paso/75513705007/; David Courtney, "The Texanist: Why Is El Paso Known as El Chuco?," *Texas Monthly*, May 2022, https://www.texasmonthly.com/being-texan/texanist-el-paso-nickname-el-chuco/; Library of Congress, "1954: Hernandez v. Texas," A Latinx Resource Guide: Civil Rights Cases and Events in the United States, accessed May 9, 2025, https://guides.loc.gov/latinx-civil-rights/hernandez-v-texas; Julia Young, "How Mexican Immigration to the U.S. Has Evolved," *Time*, March 12, 2015, https://time.com/3742067/history-mexican-immigration/; Julian Resendiz, "The Kentucky Club Stands by Its Claim as Birthplace of the Margarita," *Border Report*, June 1, 2021, https://www.borderreport.com/hot-topics/the-kentucky-club-stands-by-claim-as-birthplace-of-the-margarita/; Fred Minnick, "Cross Border Bourbon," Whisky Magazine, July 20, 2012, https://www.whiskymag.com/articles/cross-border-bourbon/; Rocío Gallegos, "Los años dorados de Ciudad Juárez," *La Verdad Juárez*, March 22, 2020, https://laverdadjuarez.com/2020/03/22/los-anos-dorados-de-ciudad-juarez/; Antonio Flores Schroeder, "Cuando Ciudad Juárez brilló por sus cabarets," Norte Digital, August 5, 2022, https://nortedigital.mx/cuando-ciudad-juarez-brillo-por-sus-cabarets/; Dave Acosta, "El Paso Music Legend Long John Hunter Dies," *El Paso Times*, January 5, 2016, https://www.elpasotimes.com/story/news/local/el-paso/2016/01/05/el-paso-music-legend-long-john-hunter-dies/78310304/; "1961: Marilyn Monroe Visits E.P., Asks Divorce in Juárez," *El Paso Times*, August 2, 2012, https://www.elpasotimes.com/story/news/history/blogs/tales-from-the-morgue/2012/08/02/1961-marilyn-monroe-visits-e-p-asks-divorce-in-juarez/31492489.

Chapter 11: American Dreamer

This and the following chapters re-create the lives of Sabino and Estela Rubio through multiple interviews with them and their daughters over the course of four years, along with a review of journals, newspaper articles, and seminal works of nonfiction on the Bracero experience.

Books and Journals

María Herrera-Sobek, *The Bracero Experience: Elitelore Versus Folklore* (UCLA Latin American Center Publications, 1979); United States Department of the Interior, National Park Service, Rio Vista Bracero Reception Center National

Historic Landmark Nomination, NPS Form 10-934 (Rev. 12-2015), OMB Control No. 1024-0276, 2019, https://home.nps.gov/subjects/nationalhistoriclandmarks/upload/2021-Fall-Rio-Vista-Bracero-Reception-Center-NHL-NOM-FINAL-508-for-LC.pdf (site discontinued); Barry C. Binder, "Los Brazos del País: Bracero Identity, 1942–1945," *Springs Graduate History Journal* 1, no. 1 (2009): 1–15, https://www.academia.edu/44796870/Los_Brazos_de_la_Pais_Bracero_Identity_1942_1945; Deborah Cohen, *Braceros: Migrant Citizens and Transnational Subjects in the Postwar United States and Mexico* (University of North Carolina Press, 2011); Kelly Lytle Hernández, "Mexican Immigration to the United States," *OAH Magazine of History* 23, no. 4 (October 2009): 25–29, https://doi.org/10.1093/maghis/23.4.25; John Archer, "The Resilience of Myth: The Politics of the American Dream," *Traditional Dwellings and Settlements Review* 25, no. 2 (2014): 7–15, https://www.scribd.com/document/793258634/25-2-TDSR-ARCHER.

Interviews

Sabino Rubio, Estela Rubio, Rubio family members, interviews by Jazmine Ulloa, Los Angeles, May 11, 2019, and April 16, 2023; Blanca Rubio, Rubio family member, interviews by Jazmine Ulloa, Sacramento, April 3, 2019, and January 2, 2021; Susan Rubio, Rubio family member, interview by Jazmine Ulloa, Sacramento, April 23, 2019; Lilly Gutierrez Reveles, El Paso, TX, interview by Fernanda Carillo, April 7, 2003, Institute of Oral History, University of Texas at El Paso; Faye Terrazas, interview by Fernanda Carrillo, 2003, "Interview no. 1571," Institute of Oral History, University of Texas at El Paso; Robert J. Shiller, Sterling Professor of Economics at Yale, phone interview by Jazmine Ulloa, July 20, 2022; Sarah Churchwell, chair of Public Understanding of the Humanities, Professorial Fellow in American Literature, Institute of English Studies, School of Advanced Study, University of London, phone interview by Jazmine Ulloa, July 25, 2022.

News Articles and Other Materials

El Paso History Alliance, "Camp Bliss: Alien Internment and POW Facility, 1942–1946," Facebook, May 5, 2025, https://www.facebook.com/elpasohistoryalliance/posts/camp-bliss-alien-internment-and-pow-facility-1942-1946camp-bliss-located-at-fort/5438741082818022; Jaime C. Rodríguez, "The Assassination," University of Texas at Austin, accessed May 9, 2025, https://www.laits.utexas.edu/jaime/jrn/cwp/pvg/assassination.html; "Mexico: The Man Who Killed Villa," *Time*, June 4, 1951, https://content.time.com/time/subscriber/article/0,33009,858085,00.html; Alberto Maldonado Garcia, "The Politics of Bracero Migration" (PhD diss., University of California, Berkeley, 2016), https://

escholarship.org/content/qt48d5q4qz/qt48d5q4qz.pdf; Jessie Kratz, "The Bracero Program: Prelude to Cesar Chavez and the Farm Worker Movement," *Pieces of History*, National Archives, September 27, 2023, https://prologue.blogs.archives.gov/2023/09/27/the-bracero-program-prelude-to-cesar-chavez-and-the-farm-worker-movement/.

Chapter 12: The Deportation Machine

Books and Journals

Aviva Chomsky, *Central America's Forgotten History: Revolution, Violence, and the Roots of Migration* (Beacon Press, 2021); Mae M. Ngai, *Impossible Subjects: Illegal Aliens and the Making of Modern America* (Princeton University Press, 2004); Adam Goodman, *The Deportation Machine: America's Long History of Expelling Immigrants* (Princeton University Press, 2020); Jia Lynn Yang, *One Mighty and Irresistible Tide: The Epic Struggle Over American Immigration, 1924–1965* (W. W. Norton & Company, 2020).

Interviews

See chapter 11.

News Articles and Other Materials

National Immigration Forum, "Legal Immigration to the United States: National Quotas & America's Immigration System," January 30, 2024, https://immigrationforum.org/article/legal-immigration-to-the-united-states-national-quotas-americas-immigration-system/; Adam Goodman, "How 1970s U.S. Immigration Policy Put Mexican Migrants at the Center of a System of Mass Expulsion," *Time*, June 23, 2020, https://time.com/5858164/voluntary-deportation-history/; Girlean McCall, "History," Texas Rice Festival, accessed May 9, 2025, https://texasricefestival.com/about/history/.

Chapter 13: Young Fronterizos

Books and Other Materials

Tony Payan, *The Three U.S.-Mexico Border Wars: Drugs, Immigration, and Homeland Security* (Praeger Security International, 2006); "The War on Drugs," History.com, updated February 7, 2020, https://www.history.com/articles

/the-war-on-drugs; Dan Baum, "Legalize It All," *Harper's*, April 2016, https://harpers.org/archive/2016/04/legalize-it-all/; Tom LoBianco, "Report: Nixon Aide Says War on Drugs Targeted Blacks, Hippies," CNN Politics, March 24, 2016, https://www.cnn.com/2016/03/23/politics/john-ehrlichman-richard-nixon-drug-war-blacks-hippie/index.html; Timothy J. Dunn, *Blockading the Border and Human Rights: The El Paso Operation That Remade Immigration Enforcement* (University of Texas Press, 2009).

INTERVIEWS

See chapter 11.

Chapter 14: Hold the Line

BOOKS AND JOURNALS

Kelly Lytle Hernández, *Migra!: A History of the U.S. Border Patrol* (University of California Press, 2010); James Dupree, "Defining America at the Border: The Line Riders of the Mexican Border District, 1892–1924" (PhD diss., University of Oklahoma, 2019), https://shareok.org/handle/11244/319753; Jonathan Blitzer, *Everyone Who Is Gone Is Here: The United States, Central America, and the Making of a Crisis* (Penguin Press, 2024); Tony Payan, *The Three U.S.-Mexico Border Wars: Drugs, Immigration, and Homeland Security* (Praeger Security International, 2006); "Pete Wilson 1994 Campaign Ad on Illegal Immigration," YouTube, uploaded February 15, 2010, by @PeteWilsonCA, https://www.youtube.com/watch?V=lLIzzs2HHgY.

INTERVIEWS

See chapter 11.

NEWS ARTICLES AND OTHER MATERIALS

U.S. Customs and Border Protection, "The Father of the U.S. Border Patrol," CBP.gov, accessed May 9, 2025, https://cbp.gov/border-security/along-us-borders/history/father-us-border-patrol; Brittny Mejia, "LA's Citizens Academy Offers a Behind-the-Scenes Look at How Police Work," *Los Angeles Times*, March 23, 2018, https://www.latimes.com/local/lanow/la-me-ln-citizens-academy-20180323-htmlstory.html; Joel Brinkley, "A Rare Success at the Border Brought Scant Official Praise," *New York Times*, September 14, 1994, https://www.nytimes.com/1994/09

/14/us/a-rare-success-at-the-border-brought-scant-official-praise.html; John Purvis, "How Has 'Operation Hold the Line' Impacted the Border, Immigration over 30 Years?," CBS4 Local, 2023, https://cbs4local.com/news/cbs4-special-reports /how-has-operation-hold-the-line-impacted-the-border-and-immigration-over -30-years-former-el-paso-texas-congressman-border-patrol-chief-silvestre-reyes -immigration-us-mexico-operation-hold-the-line-utep; Reyes Mata, "Where Are They Now? Former U.S. Rep. Silvestre Reyes," El Paso Inc., October 18, 2021, https://www.elpasoinc.com/news/local_news/where-are-they-now-former-u-s -rep-silvestre-reyes/article_b15332dc-31d6-11ec-b517-c72e399088cb.html; Justin I. Salgado, "Fortifying the U.S.-Mexico Boundary: The 1993 'Hold the Line' Experiment," Origins: Current Events in Historical Perspective, Ohio State University, June 2024, https://origins.osu.edu/read/fortifying-us-mexico -boundary-1993-hold-line-experiment; Colin Grabow, "NAFTA: 30 Years of Driving Free Trade Critics Crazy," Cato Institute, March 13, 2024, https://www .cato.org/commentary/nafta-30-years-driving-free-trade-critics-crazy; Mary Jordan, "In Mexico, Police Error or Political Execution?," *Washington Post*, February 12, 2002, https://www.washingtonpost.com/archive/politics/2002/02/12/in-mexico -police-error-or-political-execution/cc2a82bb-5a91-4950-aba3-40cbd6440cb9/; Ginger Thompson, "Wave of Women's Killings Confounds Juárez," *New York Times*, December 10, 2002, https://www.nytimes.com/2002/12/10/world/wave-of -women-s-killings-confounds-juarez.html; Jazmine Ulloa, "In Kevin McCarthy's 8-Hour Tirade, a Rambling Attempt to Show He Can Lead the Rancorous Republicans," *Boston Globe*, November 27, 2021, https://www.bostonglobe.com /2021/11/27/nation/kevin-mccarthys-8-hour-tirade-rambling-attempt-show-he -can-lead-rancorous-republicans/; Kimberly C. Brouwer, Patricia Case, Rebeca Ramos, Carlos Magis-Rodríguez, Jesús Bucardo, Thomas L. Patterson, and Steffanie A. Strathdee, "Trends in Production, Trafficking and Consumption of Methamphetamine and Cocaine in Mexico," *Substance Use & Misuse* 41, no. 5 (2006): 707–27, https://doi.org/10.1080/10826080500411478.

Chapter 15: Mexicans in Exile

Chapters on the Holguins and the Rubios like this one rely on hours-long interviews with different members of their families in El Paso and Ciudad Juárez and in Los Angeles and Sacramento, CA. I spent a day each shadowing Susan and Blanca Rubio as they debated legislation, attended fundraising and community events, and went about their everyday life. Alberto Holguin drove me around Ciudad Juárez to the Holguin business and the brothers' childhood homes.

Books and Journals

Miguel Antonio Levario, *Militarizing the Border: When Mexicans Became the Enemy* (Texas A&M University Press, 2015); Tony Cano and Ann Sochat, *Bandido: The True Story of Chico Cano, the Last Western Bandit* (Reata Publishing, 1997); Nicole Mottier, "Drug Gangs and Politics in Ciudad Juárez: 1928–1936," *Mexican Studies/Estudios Mexicanos* 25, no. 1 (Winter 2009): 19–46, https://doi.org/10.1525/msem.2009.25.1.19.

Interviews

José Alfredo Holguín, Oral History Interview, May 23, 2013, Tom & Ethel Bradley Center, California State University, Northridge, CA; Romano Holguín, interviews by Jazmine Ulloa, El Paso, TX, March 8, 2021, and May 13, 2023; Alberto Holguín, interview by Jazmine Ulloa, El Paso, TX, May 13, 2023; Luis Holguín, interview by Jazmine Ulloa, El Paso, TX, May 13, 2023.

News Articles and Other Materials

E. Eduardo Castillo, "Mexico Captures 11 Alleged Hit Men from Sinaloa Drug Cartel," Associated Press State & Local Wire, January 22, 2008; Jazmine Ulloa, "Legal Treatment May Be Worse Than Drug Cartel Plague," *San Antonio Express-News*, October 10, 2011, https://www.mysanantonio.com/sacultura/drugwar/article/Legal-treatment-may-be-worse-than-drug-cartel-2209784.php; "Mexico's Long War: Drugs, Crime, and the Cartels," *Council on Foreign Relations*, February 21, 2025; *The Guardian of Memory* (documentary), directed by Marcela Arteaga (Gefilte Films, 2019); Renata Keller, "From One Disaster to Another? Mexico's Cold War and the War on Drugs," NACLA Report on the Americas, March 22, 2016, https://nacla.org/2016-03-22-one-disaster-another-mexicos-cold-war-and-war-drugs/; InSight Crime, "Joaquín Guzmán Loera, alias 'El Chapo,'" updated October 10, 2023, https://insightcrime.org/mexico-organized-crime-news/joaquin-guzman-loera-el-chapo/; Steven Dudley, "How the Beltran Leyva, Sinaloa Cartel Feud Bloodied Mexico," InSight Crime, February 2, 2011, https://insightcrime.org/investigations/how-the-beltran-leyva-sinaloa-cartel-feud-bloodied-mexico/.

Chapter 16: Children of the Uprising

Books and Journals

Julie Hirschfeld Davis and Michael D. Shear, *Border Wars: Inside Trump's Assault on Immigration* (Simon & Schuster, 2020); Marisol Cuellar Mejia, Cesar Alesi

Perez, and Hans Johnson, "Immigrants in California," Public Policy Institute of California, January 19, 2024, https://www.ppic.org/wp-content/uploads/jtf-immigrants-in-california.pdf.

INTERVIEWS

See chapters 11 and 15.

NEWS ARTICLES AND OTHER MATERIALS

Melanie Mason and Jazmine Ulloa, "'California Versus Trump' Became an Instant Rallying Cry. But 'Resistance' Has Been More Complicated," *Los Angeles Times*, September 17, 2017, https://www.latimes.com/politics/la-pol-ca-california-trump-resistance-20170917-htmlstory.html; Andy Kroll, "The Great Exception," *California Sunday Magazine*, November 19, 2016, https://story.californiasunday.com/thegreatexception/; Jazmine Ulloa and Melanie Mason, "California's Resistance to Trump: A Political Shift," *Los Angeles Times*, November 17, 2016, https://www.latimes.com/politics/la-pol-ca-texas-california-trump-20161117-story.html; Jazmine Ulloa, "Farmworkers and Farmers Battle over Overtime Pay," *Los Angeles Times*, September 16, 2016, https://www.latimes.com/politics/la-pol-sac-farmworkers-farmers-battle-overtime-20160916-snap-htmlstory.html; Sasha von Oldershausen, "In El Paso, Demonstrators Stress Connection Between Women's Rights and Immigrants' Rights," *Texas Observer*, January 21, 2017, https://www.texasobserver.org/rights-for-women-immigrants-intersect-at-womens-march-along-texas-mexico-border/; Caitlin Dickerson, "We Need to Take Away Children," *Atlantic*, August 7, 2022, https://www.theatlantic.com/magazine/archive/2022/09/trump-administration-family-separation-policy-immigration/670604/; Caitlin Dickerson, "The Family-Separation Files," *Atlantic*, December 31, 2022, https://www.theatlantic.com/politics/archive/2022/12/the-secret-history-of-family-separation-document-collection/672146/; Ginger Thompson, "Listen to Children Who've Just Been Separated from Their Parents at the Border," ProPublica, June 18, 2018, https://www.propublica.org/article/children-separated-from-parents-border-patrol-cbp-trump-immigration-policy; Ginger Thompson, "Q&A: Ginger Thompson," C-SPAN, August 7, 2018, https://www.c-span.org/video/?449508-1/qa-ginger-thompson; "Report: U.S. Knew of Problems Family Separation Would Cause," WCNC, June 15, 2018, https://www.wcnc.com/article/news/nation-world/report-us-knew-of-problems-family-separation-would-cause/507-d21b36f5-b0f8-442c-bd35-74bd84555e5a; Reid J. Epstein, "NCLR Head: Obama 'Deporter-in-Chief,'" *Politico*, March 4, 2014, https://www.politico.com/story/2014/03/national-council-of-la-raza-janet-murguia-barack-obama-deporter-in-chief-immigration-104217.

Chapter 17: Pink and White Crosses

Interviews

See chapters 1 and 9.

News Articles and Other Materials

Uriel J. García, "El Paso Walmart Shooting Victims' Relatives Speak at Gunman's Sentencing," *Texas Tribune*, July 5, 2023, https://www.texastribune.org/2023/07/05/el-paso-walmart-shooter-sentencing/; Aaron Martinez, "Victims Receive Sense of Justice as They Confront Walmart Shooter," *El Paso Times*, July 9, 2023, https://www.elpasotimes.com/story/news/2023/07/09/victims-receive-sense-of-justice-as-they-confront-walmart-shooter/70392627007/; Erin Coulehan and Edgar Sandoval, "El Paso Walmart Shooter Sentenced to 90 Consecutive Life Terms," *New York Times*, July 5, 2023, https://www.nytimes.com/2023/07/05/us/texas-el-paso-gunman-sentencing.html; Morgan Lee and Paul J. Weber, "Gunman in El Paso Walmart Massacre Gets 90 Life Sentences," Associated Press, published in *Mercury News* (California), July 7, 2023; Melissa Luna, "Remembering Those We Lost on Aug. 3, 2019," Border Report, updated August 3, 2020, https://www.borderreport.com/news/remembering-those-we-lost-on-aug-3-2019/; "The Lives Lost in El Paso," *Washington Post*, August 8, 2019, https://www.washingtonpost.com/nation/2019/08/04/el-paso-shooting-victims/; Michael Biesecker, Reese Dunklin, and Michael Kunzelman, "El Paso Suspect Appears to Have Posted Anti-Immigrant Screed," AP News, August 4, 2019, https://apnews.com/article/immigration-shootings-us-news-ap-top-news-hispanics-df6dc60f37664833ba3b953927ef835d; Jazmine Ulloa, "Talk of an Immigrant 'Invasion' Grows in Republican Ads and Speech," *New York Times*, April 26, 2024, https://www.nytimes.com/2024/04/26/us/politics/republicans-immigration-ads-election.html; Jazmine Ulloa, "For Republicans, All Roads Lead to the U.S.-Mexico Border," *New York Times*, October 19, 2023, https://www.nytimes.com/2023/10/19/us/politics/republicans-mexico-border-israel.html; Jazmine Ulloa, "G.O.P. Concocts Fake Threat: Voter Fraud by Undocumented Immigrants," *New York Times*, April 28, 2022, https://www.nytimes.com/2022/04/28/us/politics/gop-vote-fraud-immigrants.html; Christopher Mathias, "A White Supremacist Killed Her Dad in the El Paso Shooting. Now, GOP Politicians Sound Like the Shooter," HuffPost, February 2, 2024, https://www.huffpost.com/entry/el-paso-shooting-anti-immigrant-rhetoric_n_65bbe7a2e4b0102bd2d84f24; "Horizon High School Holds Vigil for Classmate Killed in El Paso Shooting," *El Paso Times*, August 6, 2019, https://www.elpasotimes.com/picture-gallery/news/2019/08/06/horizon

-high-school-holds-vigil-classmate/1929553001/; Rosa Flores, Andi Babineau, and Ray Sanchez, "Man Who Killed 23 People in Texas Walmart Shooting Sentenced to 90 Life Terms," KOMU 8 News, updated July 7, 2023, https://www.komu.com/news/nationworld/man-who-killed-23-people-in-texas-walmart-shooting-sentenced-to-90-life-terms-by/article_50094a35-5244-5d96-873b-78efd47218dc.amp.html.

Chapter 18: Feliz Viaje

To follow the journey of Kaxh Mura'l, this chapter is largely based on interviews with friends, family members, and community leaders across the Ixil region in Guatemala, where Kaxh was born and came of age as a young activist.

Books and Journals

Marcia Esparza, Henry R. Huttenbach, and Daniel Feierstein, eds., *State Violence and Genocide in Latin America: The Cold War Years* (Routledge, 2009); Aviva Chomsky, *Central America's Forgotten History: Revolution, Violence, and the Roots of Migration* (Beacon Press, 2021); Roberto Garcia Ferreira, "The CIA and Jacobo Arbenz: History of a Disinformation Campaign," *Journal of Third World Studies* 25, no. 2 (2008): 59–81, https://www.jstor.org/stable/45194479; Giovanni Batz, *The Fourth Invasion: Decolonizing Histories, Extractivism, and Maya Resistance in Guatemala* (University of California Press, 2021); Greg Grandin, *The Last Colonial Massacre: Latin America in the Cold War*, updated edition (University of Chicago Press, 2011).

Interviews

Carlos Spector, interview by Jazmine Ulloa, El Paso, TX, May 12, 2023; Kaxh Mura'l, interview by Jazmine Ulloa, El Paso, TX, and West Florida, May 15 and 29, 2023, and March 7, 2025; La's B'oxh, interview by Jazmine Ulloa, El Paso, TX, and West Florida, May 15 and 29, 2023; Mura'l family, interview by Jazmine Ulloa, Salquil Grande, Departamento del Quiché, Guatemala, May 20, 2023; Giovanni Batz, interview by Jazmine Ulloa, Las Cruces, NM, April 14, 2021; Juan Velasco, municipal mayor of Nebaj (2024–28), interview by Jazmine Ulloa, Nebaj, Guatemala, May 19, 2023; Francisco Marroquin, interview by Jazmine Ulloa, Nebaj, Guatemala, May 19, 2023; Feliciana Herrera Ceto, first coordinating mayor of the Ixil Mayan town of Nebaj, interview by Jazmine Ulloa, Nebaj, Guatemala, April 1 and May 19, 2023; Miguel Ceto, community activist and mayor of Nebaj,

Guatemala, interview by Jazmine Ulloa, Nebaj, Guatemala, April 1 and May 19, 2023; Tobias Roberts, activist and instructor at Ixil University, interview by Jazmine Ulloa, Washington, D.C., May 21, 2023; Pamela Yates, Zoom interview by Jazmine Ulloa, May 4, 2023.

News Articles and Other Materials

Elisabeth Malkin, "Victims of Guatemala Civil War Eagerly Await Dictator's Trial," *New York Times*, March 16, 2013, https://www.nytimes.com/2013/03/17/world/americas/victims-of-guatemala-civil-war-eagerly-await-dictators-trial.html; *500 Years* (documentary), directed by Pamela Yates (Skylight Pictures, 2017); *El Buen Cristiano* (*The Good Christian*) (documentary), directed by Izabel Acevedo, (Centro de Capacitación Cinematográfica, 2016).

Chapter 19: El Paso, U.S.A.

Books

Julie Hirschfeld Davis and Michael D. Shear, *Border Wars: Inside Trump's Assault on Immigration* (Simon & Schuster, 2019).

Interviews

See chapter 18.

News Articles and Other Materials

Brandon Gray, "Beto O'Rourke Rallies in El Paso, Criticizes Trump's Immigration Policies," *El Paso Times*, March 30, 2019, https://www.elpasotimes.com/story/news/2019/03/30/beto-orourke-el-paso-rally-speech-beto-2020-donald-trump-immigration-wall/3323327002/; Simon Romero, "Migrants Are Detained Under a Bridge in El Paso. What Happened?," *New York Times*, March 29, 2019, https://www.nytimes.com/2019/03/29/us/el-paso-immigration-photo.html; Patrick Svitek, "Beto O'Rourke Running for President," *Texas Tribune*, March 13, 2019, https://www.texastribune.org/2019/03/13/beto-orourke-2020-president-announce/; Patrick Svitek and Julián Aguilar, "Beto O'Rourke Kicks Off Presidential Campaign in Texas," *Texas Tribune*, March 30, 2019, https://www.texastribune.org/2019/03/30/beto-orourke-kicks-off-presidential-campaign-in-texas/; "Donald Trump Holds a Political Rally in El Paso, Texas," Roll Call, February 11, 2019, https://rollcall.com/factbase/transcript/donald-trump-speech

-maga-rally-el-paso-february-11-2019/; "Key Findings About U.S. Immigrants," Pew Research Center, September 27, 2024, https://www.pewresearch.org/short-reads/2024/09/27/key-findings-about-us-immigrants/; Ursula Perano, "Trump Suggested Shooting Southern Border Migrants, NYT Book Excerpt Claims," Axios, October 1, 2019, https://www.axios.com/2019/10/02/trump-book-new-york-times-border-immigration; Jazmine Ulloa, "Trump's Harder Line on Immigration Appears to Resonate, Polls Show," *New York Times*, June 3, 2024, https://www.nytimes.com/2024/06/03/us/politics/trump-immigration-deportations.html; Jazmine Ulloa, Ken Bensinger, and Nick Corasaniti, "Key Takeaways from the RNC Debate on Immigration," *New York Times*, July 17, 2024, https://www.nytimes.com/2024/07/17/us/politics/rnc-immigration-trump-takeaways.html; Jazmine Ulloa, "Trump's Rhetoric on Immigration Has Deep Historical Roots," *New York Times*, November 1, 2024, https://www.nytimes.com/2024/11/01/us/politics/trump-immigration-rhetoric-history.html; Anna Flagg, "The Crime and Immigration Myth," *New York Times*, March 30, 2018, https://www.nytimes.com/interactive/2018/03/30/upshot/crime-immigration-myth.html; Annie Correal, "The Last Migrant Caravans Before Trump's Inauguration," *New York Times*, January 18, 2025, https://www.nytimes.com/card/2025/01/18/world/americas/mexico-migrants-border-trump; Ilya Somin, "Immigration Is Not Invasion," Lawfare, March 25, 2024, https://www.lawfaremedia.org/article/immigration-is-not-invasion; Caroline Linton, "Migrants Being Held Outdoors near Bridge in El Paso," *CBS News*, updated June 12, 2019, https://www.cbsnews.com/news/paso-del-norte-bridge-el-paso-texas-migrants-being-held-outdoors-customs-and-border-patrol-official-says-2019-06-11/; Michael D. Shear and Julie Hirschfeld Davis, "Trump and Allies Slash Refugee Admissions to Record Low," *New York Times*, October 1, 2019, https://www.nytimes.com/2019/10/01/us/politics/trump-border-wars.html; Susan Montoya Bryan, "Razor Wire Is Most Visible Result of $210M Deployment," *Military Times*, November 22, 2018, https://www.militarytimes.com/news/pentagon-congress/2018/11/22/razor-wire-is-most-visible-result-of-210m-deployment/; Megan K. Stack, "Why Are Republicans Sending Migrant Buses to El Paso?," *New York Times*, October 20, 2022, https://www.nytimes.com/2022/10/20/opinion/el-paso-migrant-buses-republicans.html; Simon Romero, "Migrants Moved out of Holding Pen Under El Paso Bridge," *New York Times*, March 31, 2019, https://www.nytimes.com/2019/03/31/us/el-paso-bridge-migrants.html; Global News, "Beto O'Rourke Holds Counter-Rally During Trump MAGA Event," YouTube, uploaded February 11, 2019, https://www.youtube.com/watch?v=d_nWK8ENG2Y; *Trump Holds Campaign Rally in El Paso, Texas,* PBS NewsHour, YouTube, 1:16:26, posted February 11, 2019, https://www.youtube.com/watch?v=ZYLfnqgBAvY.

Chapter 20: Oasis in the Desert

BOOKS AND JOURNALS

Vanessa Claire Johnson, "Memory, State Violence, and Revolution: Mexico's Dirty War in Ciudad Juárez" (master's thesis, University of Texas at El Paso, 2022), https://scholarworks.utep.edu/cgi/viewcontent.cgi?article=2076&context=open_etd; Sandra Cervantes, "State of Repression: The Dirty War in Guerrero, 1961–1978" (master's thesis, California State University, 2022), https://www.calstatela.edu/sites/default/files/state_of_repression_sep_pdf.pdf; International Food Policy Research Institute, *Green Revolution: Curse or Blessing*? (International Food Policy Research Institute, 2002), http://www.ifpri.org/publication/green-revolution; "The LDC Debt Crisis," in *History of the Eighties: Lessons for the Future*, vol. 1 (Federal Deposit Insurance Corporation [FDIC], 1997), https://elischolar.library.yale.edu/ypfs-documents2/476.

INTERVIEWS

See chapters 11 and 18.

NEWS ARTICLES AND OTHER MATERIALS

James M. Boughton, "The IMF and the Latin American Debt Crisis: Seven Common Criticisms," International Monetary Fund, October 10, 1994, https://www.imf.org/en/Publications/IMF-Policy-Discussion-Papers/Issues/2016/12/30/The-IMF-and-the-Latin-American-Debt-Crisis-Seven-Common-Criticisms-1853; Jocelyn Sims and Jessie Romero, "Latin American Debt Crisis of the 1980s," Federal Reserve History, accessed May 8, 2025, https://www.federalreservehistory.org/essays/latin-american-debt-crisis; Karen DeYoung, "Argentine, Chilean Repression Differ in Image, Substance," *Washington Post*, September 28, 1977, https://www.washingtonpost.com/archive/politics/1977/09/28/argentine-chilean-repression-differ-in-image-substance/ce45f01d-3ef7-4465-ad5a-df836b8a2791/; Elias E. Lopez, "Jorge Rafael Videla, Argentina Military Leader in 'Dirty War,' Dies at 87," *New York Times*, May 18, 2013, https://www.nytimes.com/2013/05/18/world/americas/jorge-rafael-videla-argentina-military-leader-in-dirty-war-dies-at-87.html; Oscar Lopez, "Mexico's Dirty War: Military Abuses under AMLO," *Guardian*, August 16, 2024, https://www.theguardian.com/world/article/2024/aug/16/mexico-dirty-war-military-abuses-amlo; David A. Sonnenfeld, "Mexico's 'Green Revolution,' 1940–1980: Towards an Environmental History," *Environmental History Review* 16, no. 4 (Winter 1992), https://www.journals.uchicago.edu/doi

/epdf/10.2307/3984948; Sarah Churchwell, "History of the American Dream," *Catalyst*, George W. Bush Presidential Center, 2024, https://www.bushcenter.org/catalyst/state-of-the-american-dream/churchwell-history-of-the-american-dream; "Eight Hundred Federal Troops Today Surrounded an Agriculture College," United Press International, May 15, 1982, https://www.upi.com/Archives/1982/05/15/Eight-hundred-federal-troops-today-surrounded-an-agriculture-college/8385390283200/.

Chapter 21: The Forgetting

News Articles and Other Materials

Jazmine Ulloa, "We've Come Back Home: Joe Biden Rebrands as the Underdog," *Boston Globe*, March 9, 2020, https://www.bostonglobe.com/2020/03/09/nation/weve-come-back-home-joe-biden-rebrands-underdog/; Jazmine Ulloa, "Coronavirus Outbreak Has Helped Trump Get the Immigration Crackdown He's Long Pursued, and Provided Him with a New Foil," *Boston Globe*, April 21, 2020, https://www.bostonglobe.com/2020/04/21/nation/coronavirus-outbreak-has-helped-trump-get-immigration-crackdown-hes-long-pursued-provided-him-with-new-foil/; Arelis R. Hernández and Nick Miroff, "Trump Administration Slows Immigration, Heightens Border Restrictions amid Coronavirus Pandemic," *Washington Post*, April 3, 2020, https://www.washingtonpost.com/national/coronavirus-trump-immigration-border/2020/04/03/23cb025a-74f9-11ea-ae50-7148009252e3_story.html; Jazmine Ulloa, "Spanish-Speaking Latino Voters Are Being Bombarded with Disinformation Ahead of the Election," *Boston Globe*, October 20, 2020, https://www.bostonglobe.com/2020/10/20/nation/spanish-speaking-latino-voters-are-being-bombarded-with-disinformation-ahead-election/; Jazmine Ulloa, "There's a Big Obstacle Looming for Coronavirus Vaccines: A Stronger Anti-Vaccine Movement," *Boston Globe*, November 28, 2020, https://www.bostonglobe.com/2020/11/28/nation/theres-big-obstacle-looming-coronavirus-vaccines-stronger-antivaccine-movement/; Jazmine Ulloa, "A GOP Bulwark on Virus in Midwest; Ohio's Governor Decisively Acts," *Boston Globe*, March 18, 2020, https://www.bostonglobe.com/2020/03/17/nation/ohio-republican-governor-has-taken-aggressive-steps-contain-coronavirus-before-becoming-an-outbreak-hotspot/; Alex Samuels, "In El Paso, an Illustration of the COVID-19 Pandemic's Stark Inequalities," *Texas Tribune*, November 21, 2020, https://www.texastribune.org/2020/11/21/el-paso-coronavirus-hispanic-texans/.

Chapter 22: The New Ellis Island

News Article

Sabrina Zuniga, "Cobra COVID la vida de aspirante al asilo," *El Diario de El Paso*, December 25, 2020, https://diario.mx/el-paso/2020/dec/25/cobra-covid-la-vida-de-aspirante-al-asilo-580189.html.

INDEX

ABOUT THE AUTHOR

Jazmine Ulloa is a national reporter for *The New York Times*. She previously reported for the *Los Angeles Times* and *The Boston Globe*, where she was part of a team that won the Toner Prize for Excellence in Political Reporting. A native of El Paso, she started out as a journalist in Texas, where she worked for newspapers in Brownsville, San Antonio, and Austin. She has made appearances on MSNBC, CNN, and CBS, as well as in Al Jazeera's documentary television program *Fault Lines*.